LAMENTATIONS

LAMENTATIONS

Issues and Interpretation

Claus Westermann

Translated by
Charles Muenchow

FORTRESS PRESS   MINNEAPOLIS

LAMENTATIONS
Issues and Interpretation

First published by Fortress Press, 1994

English translation copyright © 1994 Augsburg Fortress

Translated from *Die Klagelieder: Forschungsgeschichte und Auslegung*, published 1990 by Neukirchener Verlag des Erziehungsvereins GmbH, Neukirchen-Vluyn.

Cover design: Patricia Boman
Cover art: *Le condamné s'en est allé* by Georges Rouault, The Rosenwald Collection © 1993 National Gallery of Art, Washington

---

Library of Congress Cataloging-in-Publication data

Westermann, Claus.
  [Klagelieder. English]
  Lamentations : issues and interpretation / Claus Westermann; translated by Charles Muenchow.
    p.   cm.
  Translation of: Die Klagelieder.
  Includes bibliographical references and index.
  ISBN 0-8006-2743-1 :
  1. Bible. O.T. Lamentations—Criticism, interpretation, etc.
I. Title.
BS1535.2.W4713   1994
224'.3077—dc20
                                93-28173
                                CIP

                           1-2743
98   97   96   95   94   1   2   3   4   5   6   7   8   9   10

Contents

Preface

This study of the Book of Lamentations combines its exegetic work with attention to the critical research that has already been carried out on the book. In the course of my own work on Lamentations I have come to the conclusion that, as matters now stand in the area of Old Testament studies, this book can be properly interpreted only against the background of a survey of the research that has already been conducted on it. It seems to me that the message that the texts themselves want to convey is frequently misheard by the interpreters of Lamentations. This phenomenon in turn is rooted in certain presuppositions that have been influential in Biblical research. The influence of these presuppositions becomes apparent in the fact that not one of the previous researchers on Lamentations has pressed the question of just what a lament is. All of these previous researchers share the view that the lament simply has no theological significance. However, if one resolves to put prior assumptions aside and to take laments seriously, then one can no longer avoid exploring the question of what a lament properly is.

The necessity of viewing this question in a larger context leads the first section of our study to cast its horizon beyond the boundaries of the Old Testament itself. Here the dirge is first investigated as a secular phenomenon, and then attention is directed to the ancient lament over the city of Ur, a parallel to the Old Testament's lament over the city of Jerusalem.

C. Westermann

Translator's Comment

The editors requested that, as much as possible, this translation employ inclusive language, follow the current trend toward simpler style, and use the NRSV. The fact that all German nouns carry clear gender distinctions complicates the goal of gender-neutral translation, while Dr Westermann's good academic German is not always compatible with contemporary stylistic trends in English. This translation tries to strike a fair balance between editorial desiderata and faithfulness to its original text. Dr Westermann characteristically relies upon his own translations of Biblical texts, and in order to reflect his understanding of the material it has only rarely been possible to use the wording of NRSV.

Because of this book's importance as a scholarly commentary, special care has been directed toward accurate presentation of detail. This has included the correction of a number of minor errors that appeared in the first edition of the German original. It is sincerely hoped that this translation will be of service to both the communities which Dr Westermann addresses: the academy and the church.

Charles Muenchow

Selected Literature on the Book of Lamentations[1]

Commentaries

1850-1920: Otto Thenius, *Die Klaglieder* [*sic*] (KeH 16; 1855); Max [Richard Hermann] Löhr, *Die Klagelieder des Jeremia* (HKAT VI/2; 1893); *ibid.*, *Die Klagelieder des Jeremias* [*sic*] (HKAT III/ 2,2; ²1906); *ibid.*, *Die Klagelieder* (HSAT[K]; 1923); Karl Budde, "Die Klagelieder," in *Die fünf Megillot* (KHC XVII; 1898); Arthur S. Peake, *Jeremiah* [*and Lamentations*] (CeB; 1911).

1921-1960: Wilhelm Rudolph, *Die Klagelieder* (KAT XVII/3; 1939, ²1962); Max Haller, "Die Klagelieder," in *Die fünf Megilloth* [*sic*] (HAT I/18; 1940) 91-113; Friedrich Nötscher, *Die Klagelieder* (Echter Bibel: Das Alte Testament, II/2; 1947, ²1962); Hermann Wiesmann, *Die Klagelieder* (1954); Hans-Joachim Kraus, *Klagelieder* (*Threni*) (BK[AT] XX; 1956, ⁴1983); Theophile J. Meek, *The Book of Lamentations* (IB VI; 1956) 1-38; Claus Westermann, *Jeremia und Klagelieder* (Stuttgarter Bibelhefte; 1956); Artur Weiser, *Klagelieder* (ATD XVI/2; 1958); Edouard Paul Dhorme, "Les Lamentations," in *La Bible, L'Ancien Testament II* (Edition de la Pléjadel; 1959).

1961-1985: E. Cothenet, "Lamentations," in *Dictionnaire Catholicisme hier, aujourdhui, demain* (1967) VI:1725-32; Otto Plöger, "Die Klagelieder," in *Die fünf Megilloth* (HAT I/18; ²1969) 127-64; Delbert R. Hillers, *Lamentations* (AB 7A; 1972); Otto Kaiser, *Klagelieder* (ATD XVI/2; ³1982); S. Paul Re'emi,

---

[1] The abbreviations here used are conventional in the academic study of the Bible. Specific identification of sources can be found in Brevard S. Childs, *Introduction to the Old Testament as Scripture* (1979), 19-24 [*Trans.*].

"The Theology of Hope: A Commentary on Lamentations," in
God's People in Crisis (International Theological Commentary;
1984) 73-134; Hans Joachim Boecker, *Klagelieder* (ZBK.AT
XXI; 1985).

Monographs and Essays
1880-1920: Karl Budde, "Das hebräische Klagelied," *ZAW* 2
(1882) 1-52; Max [Richard Hermann] Löhr, "Der
Sprachgebrauch des Buches der Klagelieder," *ZAW* 14 (1894)
31-50; *ibid.*, "Sind Thr. IV und V makkabäisch?" *ZAW* 14 (1894)
51-59; *ibid.*, "Threni III und die jeremianische Autorschaft des
Buches der Klagelieder," *ZAW* 24 (1904) 1-16; Hermann Gunkel,
"Klagelieder Jeremiae," in *RGG* ([2]1929) III:1049-52.

1921-1950: Hedwig Jahnow, *Das hebräische Leichenlied im Rahmen
der Völkerdichtung* (BZAW 36; 1923); Theodore H. Robinson,
"Notes on the Text of Lamentations," *ZAW* 51 (1933) 255-59;
Maria Cramer, *Die Totenklage bei den Kopten* (Akademie der
Wissenschaften in Wien. Philosophisch-historische Klasse.
Sitzungsberichte, 219. Bd.2; 1941); Enno Littmann, *Abessinische
Klagelieder: alte Weisen in neuer Gewandung* (1949).

1951-1970: Norman K. Gottwald, *Studies in the Book of Lamentations*
(SBT I/14; 1954, [2]1962); Samuel N. Kramer, "Lamentation
over the Destruction of Ur," in *ANET* [= *Ancient Near Eastern
Texts Relating to the Old Testament*, ed. J. B. Pritchard ([2]1955)]
455-63; Enno Janssen, *Juda in der Exilszeit* (FRLANT 69; 1956);
Hans-Joachim Kraus, "Klagelieder Jeremiä," in *RGG* ([3]1959),
III:1627-29; Giorgio Buccellati, "Gli Israeliti di Palestina al
tempo dell'esilio," *Bibbia e oriente* 2 (1960) 199-209; Bertil
Albrektson, *Studies in the Text and Theology of the Book of
Lamentations* (Studia Theologica Lundensia, 21; 1963); Samuel
T. Lachs, "The Date of Lamentations V," *JQR* N.S. 57 (1966/67)
46-56; J. A. Emerton, "The Meaning of *'abnê qōdeš* in
Lamentations 4:1," *ZAW* 79 (1967) 233-36; Thomas F. McDaniel,
"The Alleged Sumerian Influence upon Lamentations," *VT* 18
(1968) 198-209 (with additional bibliography on Sumero-
Akkadian laments over cities); Gilbert Brunet, *Les lamentations
contre Jérémie. Réinterprétation des quatre premières lamentations*

(Bibliothèque de L'École des Hautes Études, Section des Sciences Religieuses, LXXV; 1968); Peter R. Ackroyd, *Exile and Restoration: A Study of Hebrew Thought of the Sixth Century B.C.* (1968).

1971-1985: William F. Lanahan, "The Speaking Voice in the Book of Lamentations," *JBL* 93 (1974) 41-49; Robert Gordis, "The Conclusion of the Book of Lamentations [5:22]," *JBL* 93 (1974) 289-93; Siegfried Bergler, "Threni 5--nur ein alphabetisierendes Lied? Versuch einer Deutung," *VT* 27 (1977) 304-20; Rainer Albertz, *Persönliche Frömmigkeit und offizielle Religion: Religionsinterner Pluralismus in Israel und Babylon* (Calwer Theologische Monographien A/9; 1978) 58-73; Brevard S. Childs, *Introduction to the Old Testament as Scripture* (1979) 590-97; Renate Brandscheidt, *Gotteszorn und Menschenleid: die Gerichtsklage des leidenden Gerechten in Klgl 3* (Trierer Theologische Studien 41; 1983); Bo Johnson, "Form and Message in Lamentations," *ZAW* 97 (1985) 58-73.

On the text: James A. Kelso, *Die Klagelieder: Der masoretische Text und die Versionen* (1901); Theodore H. Robinson, "Notes on the Text of Lamentations," *ZAW* 51 (1933) 255-59; *ibid.*, "Once More on the Text of Lamentations," *ZAW* 52 (1934) 309-10; G. R. Driver, "Hebrew Notes on 'Song of Songs' and 'Lamentations'," in *Festschrift Alfred Bertholet zum 80. Geburtstag*, ed. Walter Baumgartner *et al.* (1950) 134-46; Thomas F. McDaniel, "Philological Studies in Lamentations. I-II," *Bibl* 49 (1968) 27-53 and 199-220; Hans Gottlieb, *A Study of the Text of Lamentations*, trans. John Sturdy (Acta Jutlandica 48: Theology series 12; 1978).

On the meter: Karl Budde, "Das hebräische Klagelied," *ZAW* 2 (1882) 1-52; Joachim Begrich, "Zur hebräischen Metrik," *ThR* 4 (1932) 67-89 (a comprehensive review); Friedrich Horst, "Die Kennzeichen der hebräischen Poesie," *ThR*, 21 (1953) 97-121 (a comprehensive review); Sigmund Mowinckel, "Zur hebräischen Metrik. II," *StTh* 7 (1953) 54-85; Theodore H. Robinson, "Hebrew Poetic Form," in *Congress Volume. International Organization for the Study of the Old Testament. 1953*

(SVT 1; Leiden, 1953) 128-49; G. Wallis, "Akrostichon," in *BHH*
(1963) I:62.

Introductions

R. H Pfeiffer (1941); A. Robert / A. Feuillet (1957); E. Sellin
/ L. Rost (1959); A. Bentzen (1959); G. W. Anderson (1959);
O. Eissfeldt (1964); E. Osswald, in *BHH* (1964) II:960-61; O.
Kaiser (1969; [5]1984); W. H. Schmidt (1979); R. Rendtorff
(1983).

Literature Especially Pertaining to Chapter One

C. H. Bergengruen, "Gedanken für H. Jahnow," in *1879-1979:
Elisabethschule Marburg* (Marburg, 1979); Walter Beyerlin, ed.,
Near Eastern Religious Texts Relating to the Old Testament (OTL;
1978) [= *Religionsgeschichtliches Textbuch zum Alten Testament*
(ATD Ergänzungsband 1; 1975)]; Hedwig Jahnow, *Das hebräische
Leichenlied* (BZAW 36; 1923); Samuel Noah Kramer,
"Lamentation over the Destruction of Ur," in *ANET* ([2]1955)
455-63; Thomas F. McDaniel, "The Alleged Sumerian Influence
upon Lamentations," *VT* 18 (1968) 198-209.

Literature Especially Pertaining to Chapters Two and Three

Peter R. Ackroyd, *Exile and Restoration* (1968); Christoph Barth,
*Die Errettung vom Tode in den individuellen Klage- und Dankliedern
des Alten Testaments* (1947); Hermann Gunkel / Joachim Begrich,
Einleitung in die Psalmen (1933); Willi Schrottoff, *"zkr,"* in
Theologisches Handwörterbuch zum Alten Testament, eds. Ernst
Jenni and Claus Westermann (1971) I:507-18; Claus
Westermann, "Gebet im Alten Testament," in *RGG* ([3]1958)
III:1213-17; *ibid.*, "Das Hoffen im Alten Testament: Eine Begriffs-
untersuchung," in *Forschung am Alten Testament: Gesammelte
Studien I* (ThB 24; 1964) 219-64; *ibid.*, "Die Rolle der Klage in
der Theologie des Alten Testaments," in *Forschung am Alten
Testament: Gesammelte Studien II* (ThB 55; 1974) 259-68; *ibid.*,
Praise and Lament in the Psalms, trans. Keith R. Crim and Richard
K. Soulen (1981) [= *Lob und Klage in den Psalmen* (1977)]; *ibid.*,
The Living Psalms, trans. J. R. Porter (1989) [= *Ausgewählte
Psalmen* (1984)]; *ibid.*, "Boten des Zorns," in *Forschung am Alten
Testament: Gesammelte Studien III* (ThB 73; 1984) 96-109; *ibid.*,

The Parables of Jesus in the Light of the Old Testament, trans. and ed. by Friedemann W. Golka and Alastair H. B. Logan (1990) [= *Vergleiche und Gleichnisse im Alten und Neuen Testament* (1984)]; *ibid., Prophetic Oracles of Salvation in the Old Testament* (1991) [= *Prophetische Heilsworte im Alten Testament* (FRLANT 145; 1987)]; Walter Zimmerli, *Ezekiel: A Commentary on the Book of the Prophet Ezekiel,* trans. Ronald E. Clements, ed. Frank Moore Cross, Jr. and Klaus Baltzer, with the assistance of Jay Greenspoon (Hermeneia; 1979 -) [= *Ezechiel* (BK[AT] XIII/1-2; 1969)].

Chapter One

The Dirge and a Lament over the Death of a City

Re: Hedwig Jahnow, *Das hebräische Leichenlied im Rahmen der Völkerdichtung*

Jahnow sets the laments from the Book of Lamentations in the broad context of dirges as attested in folk literature. As a traditional genre of such literature (chapter III), the dirge is closely associated with mourning practices (chapters I and II). Many examples of dirges are attested in the traditional poetry of the world's peoples. In contrast, only a few remnants of "Hebraic funeral poetry" are still extant (chapter V).

In the Old Testament only two dirges have been preserved as they would actually have been spoken:

> Then the king intoned a dirge for Abner:
> "Must Abner die as a fool dies?
> Your hands were not bound,
> Your feet were not fettered.
> As one falls because of scoundrels, you have fallen."
> And all the people wept over him again.
>
> (2 Sam 3:33-34)

> The people whom you trusted have led you astray
> and have overcome you;
> now your feet are stuck in the mire,
> they leave you in the lurch!
>
> (Jer 38:22)

1

Although similar, 2 Sam 1:19-27 and Jer 9:16-21 are in fact artistic imitations of genuine dirges.

What we know of dirges in ancient Israel is based almost entirely on inference from their secondary usage in the Old Testament (chapter VI). Among the texts in question a distinction must be drawn between short texts, which closely resemble the actual dirge, and longer texts, which deviate more extensively from the original pattern. The relevant short texts are Amos 5:2, Jer 9:9 [9:10 Eng.], Isa 1:21-23 and Ezek 26:17-18. All of these are prophetic announcements of judgment clothed in the language of a dirge.

> Fallen, no more to rise, is maiden Israel;
> thrown to the ground, no one raises her up!
>
> (Amos 5:2)

> Take up weeping for the mountains, a song of lament for
>   the meadows!
> For they are laid waste, no one any longer passes through!
>
> (Jer 9:10a)

> How you have been destroyed...O celebrated city!
> Now the islands tremble...
>
> (Ezek 26:17-18; cf. also Jer 9:16-21)

Motifs encountered in all of these short texts include the following: an announcement that a death has occurred, a summons to mourn, a thematic statement of finality, a contrast motif, a reference to the impact of the demise upon immediate bystanders, and some description of the general state of distress. Common to the five short texts cited [by Jahnow] is the fact that an announcement of judgment against Israel is cast in the language of a dirge. Since we are here dealing with texts of the eighth and seventh centuries [BCE], it is probable that they are based upon actual dirges. These texts predominantly contain only a single motif each—though occasionally somewhat expanded. Genuine dirges must originally have been quite short.

A group of six popular sayings in the Book of Ezekiel, each of which is expressly designated a *qināh* ["dirge"], forms the core of the elaborated texts (chapter VII). The designation *qinah* appears as early as 2:10, in the commissioning of the prophet. Already here, however, it is clear that *qinah* is being used in a derivative sense. Actually, the prophet is being instructed to announce judgment upon both his own people and foreigners. So in fact we do not have here a call to voice a dirge over a deceased individual. Rather, the announcement of the community's destruction is designated a dirge *by way of analogy*. Calling the announcement a dirge has the effect of anticipating the destruction; it is regarded as though it had already happened. Thus one really cannot say—as Jahnow nonetheless does—that the genre of the dirge is to be found in these texts, albeit at a stage of its dissolution.

Nowhere else in the Old Testament does the word *qinah* occur so frequently as it does here, in these sayings in the Book of Ezekiel. In 2:10 we find, "...written on it [viz., the scroll] were words of lamentation [*qinîm*] and mourning and woe." In 19:1 we read, "as for you, raise up a lamentation [*qinah*] for the princes of Israel." For additional occurrences, see 19:14, 26:17, 27:2, 28:12, 32:2, 32:16.

It is understandable how most exegetes follow Jahnow in ascribing these texts to the genre of the *qinah*. Even Walter Zimmerli, in his commentary on the Book of Ezekiel, ascribes 26:17-18, 27:3-16, 28:12-19 and 32:2-16 to this genre. However, the function of all these texts is clearly that of announcing judgment. Under the impact of such a function, the texts indirectly come to resemble dirges. Functionally, the texts help to generate conditions appropriate for a dirge. By and large, however, even in the most detailed of these texts from Ezekiel only one motif genuinely characteristic of the dirge is employed, namely a contrast between the former and the present state of affairs. The contrast motif was especially well suited to dramatic and colorful depiction of the destruction of a city (as in the case of the magnificent "ship" Tyre). As the elaborations progress, however, other analogies come to the fore: tree, grapevine, lion, crocodile—in addition to the magnificent ship. The net effect of all these analogies is that the similarity to the dirge recedes into the background. In truth, such texts are no longer dirges. Any attempt still to discern in them the structure of a dirge must surely be in vain! On the contrary, it is precisely in these elaborated texts that one can see how the standard motifs of the dirge are now occurring in isolation. Consider, for example, the following:

> Although your mother was quite a lioness, still... (her cubs were captured)...!
>
> (Ezek 19:1-9)

> (Like a grapevine, your mother was torn out by the roots!)
>
> (Ezek 19:10-14)

Cf. also Ezek 27: Tyre as a magnificent ship is contrasted with its ignoble destruction; the reaction of those who witness this destruction is also described.

In Ezek 28:11-15 the magnificent, divinely favored city is toppled; in the immediately following verses some reactions to this event are mentioned (cf. also 32:2-16).

Isa 14:4-21, the depiction of the king of Babylon's descent into Sheol, is a popular saying of the same sort as the above texts from the Book of Ezekiel. However, this Isaianic text is not called a dirge. Rather, it is described as a "taunt" (v 3). Of the motifs characteristic of the dirge it makes use of only the contrast motif, in v 12. Isa 23:1-14, the announcement of the destruction of Sidon, belongs in the same category. This latter oracle more closely resembles the dirge, since it contains several of the characteristic dirge motifs. Playing a dominant role is the summons to mourn, which runs as a *leitmotif* throughout the whole poem: "Wail, O ships of Tarshish, for your fortress is destroyed...! (v 1a; cf. vv 4, 6, 10, 14). Closely allied to this element is the proclamation of the destruction (equivalent to the announcement of death). As is the case in Lamentations, so also here the city is personified as a woman ("...O abused daughter Sidon!" [v 12]). Following the proclamation of destruction is the contrast motif, comparing the former state of affairs with the current one (vv 6-9). In vv 7 and 8 one also finds the feature of amazed questions that one frequently encounters elsewhere as well, such as in Lam 2:15c. As so often, so also here the wrath of Yahweh is identified as the cause of the destruction. Even inanimate objects are summoned to lament, as also in Lam 1:4a-b.

Of the texts considered above, only Isa 23:1-14 resembles at all closely chapters one, two, and four of Lamentations. However, Isa 23:1-14 is prophetic announcement, spoken in advance of the actual collapse of the city. Chapters one, two, and four of Lamentations, on the other hand, are laments spoken subsequent to the overthrow of the city. Consequently, one finds the communal lament sharing motifs from the dirge only in chapters one, two, and four of Lamentations. The texts considered immediately above do not exhibit a comparable sharing of motifs.

Because Jahnow thought she could discern the genre of the dirge in all the texts just mentioned, she assumed that chapters one, two, and four of Lamentations were a "modification of the dirge" (118), a "reshaping of a profane genre into religious verse" under "the influence of the popular psalms of lamentation" (170), "most clearly by means of such elements as the summoning of Yahweh, the lamenting over the distress, the plea for Yahweh to take notice, the confession of guilt." Jahnow did not realize that, with this list of features as she enumerated them on her pp. 170-71, she actually sketched out the structure of the communal lament as a distinct genre. That is, she did not simply list isolated motifs; rather, she described a coherent whole. Had she added to her list the motif of the petition directed against enemies, she would have generated a full description of the communal lament. Moreover, this genre is best described precisely in the sequence of motifs that she gave! From this point it is only a short step to the recognition that, in fact, it is the structure of the communal lament which underlies Lam 1, 2, and 4. Only subsequently did the distinctive motifs of the dirge come to be attached to the structure of this particular type of lament. The impetus for the latter development is easily recognizable. Under the circumstances prevailing at the time, the survivors were led to experience the destruction of their city as its death.

Summary: The Dirge

The Texts

I.   Dirge on the occasion of the death of an individual: 2 Sam
     3:33-34 and Jer 38:22 (both contain only one motif), and
     poetic reshaping of the same in 2 Sam 1:19-27 and Jer 9:16-21.

II. Dirge used in a derivative fashion:
     A. Functioning as a lament: Lam 1, 2 and 4 (associated
         with the communal lament)
     B. Functioning as a prophetic announcement of judgment:

         1. Short sayings: Amos 5:2, Jer 9:9 [9:10 Eng.], 9:16-
             21 [9:17-22 Eng.], Isa 1:21-23; Ezek 26:17-18.
         2. Expanded texts:
             a) Popular sayings containing the contrast motif:
                 Ezek 27:2-36, 28:11-19, 32:12-16, Isa 14:4-21; the
                 same directed against Israel: Ezek 19:1-9, 10-14.
             b) Isa 23:1-14 : a popular saying containing several
                 motifs from the dirge and resembling the
                 laments in Lamentations.

On the basis of these texts, one can conclude that the Old
Testament does not exhibit a distinct "dirge" genre. (A genre
is a structured literary form characterized by a fixed sequence
of motifs.) Neither does the Old Testament provide us with
enough material to reconstruct such a genre for ancient Israel.
However, the texts clearly do establish the existence of dirges
in ancient Israel. These dirges contained distinct and recurrent
motifs which arose out of the specific features of the burial
ceremony. The several dirges which have been preserved, as
well as the passages containing elements derived from the
dirge, as a rule contain in each case only one or two of their
characteristic motifs—most commonly, the contrast motif.
The few texts which do contain a series of motifs (1 Sam 1:19-
27, Isa 21, Jer 9:16,21 [17,22 Eng.]) convey the impression of
having been poetically reshaped (so also Jahnow). The motifs
characteristic of the dirge, motifs which at one time were
associated with particular features of the burial ceremony or
stages in the public performance of the dirge, are as follows:

An opening cry of ah!, alas!, or the equivalent; a mournful cry as such (sometimes with direct address of the deceased); a summons to mourn (sometimes even addressed to inanimate objects); a proclamation that a death has occurred (sometimes with reference to the mode of death); a comparing of the former with the present state of affairs (the contrast motif), including a eulogizing of the deceased; a description of the mourner's pain or of the general state of misery; reference to the effect all this is having on the bystanders; questions expressing bewilderment at what has happened.

One tends to find the following elements in combination:

A mournful cry with an address of the deceased ("Alas, my brother!"); a mournful cry with a proclamation of the death (as is still found in the Easter hymn "Ach, grosse Not! Gott selbst ist tot!" ["Ah, what a disaster! Death has seized our Master!"]); a mournful cry followed by the contrast motif; a summons to mourn joined with a proclamation of the death; a mournful cry along with both the contrast motif and reference to the reaction of the bystanders; the contrast motif along with praise of the departed as a hero.

Unlike the prophetic texts, chapters one, two, and four of Lamentations do not have the function of announcing an impending disaster. Rather, these chapters presuppose that "death" has already occurred. In terms of their function, then, they resemble the original dirge. They are the only texts, therefore, in which motifs from the dirge could have become associated with the communal lament.

The significance of Jahnow's investigation lies, on the one hand, in the way she collected and employed extra-Biblical texts illustrating the traditional dirge and, on the other hand, how she established the significance of the dirge and its associated motifs for interpretation of the Old Testament. However, her thesis that chapters one, two and four of Lamentations are modified dirges cannot be maintained. In terms of their structure, these chapters are communal laments—laments which have borrowed motifs from the dirge.[1]

The Distinctiveness of the Dirge

The dirge was originally performed by the family and within the confines of the family. The death of a family member was bewailed in a fashion similar to that reflected in Gen 23. Aspects of its familial character were preserved in the later development of the dirge. Witness, for example, the prototype of the wailing mother: Rachel mourns for her children (Jer 31:15; cf. Lam 1:18ff, 2:20ff). Women in particular were called upon to perform the dirge; they could even join together to form a guild of mourners (Jer 9:16-21 [17-22 Eng.]). However, the dirge directly voiced by relatives of the deceased is older than the guild-dirge, as is shown by the ancient cries "Alas, my brother!" (1 Kgs 13:30) and "Alas, my sister!" (Jer 22:18). The same pattern is reflected in non-Israelite dirges. One frequently encounters the phenomenon of a mother bewailing her only son. In the oral tradition lying behind the Old Testament many dirges were composed by women; women were also the ones who preserved them and passed them on (cf. again Jer 9:16-21 [17-22 Eng.]).

After a nomadic group settles down, it follows as a matter of course that the place of residence gets taken up as a feature of the funeral ceremony. The mourning rites begin at the deceased's dwelling, continue along the route to the place of burial, and are concluded at the grave site. The dirges are always tied in with the other mourning rites. They occur as brief, rhythmic utterances. The mournful cry itself can be either an inarticulate shriek or a lucid cry of agony. In an animistic setting such a cry had apotropaic significance. In some texts the mournful cry itself is still clearly separated from the actual dirge (e.g., in Ezek 27:29-31, on which cf. Jahnow,

---

[1] For information regarding Hedwig Jahnow herself I would direct the reader's attention to note 20 on page 298 of the Otto Kaiser commentary, which contains the following comment: "...on her life and death cf. Charlotte Bergengruen née Hensel, 'Gedanken für H. Jahnow, geb. 21.3.1897, und gestorben in Theresienstadt,' in *1879-1979 Elisabeth-Schule Marburg*, ed. H. J. Schmelz and K. Prätorius (Marburg, 1979) 96ff." May those who read these words join me in honoring her memory!

40ff.). Dirges originated as oral literature and were passed on as such. Only at a later stage did they become a form of literary expression (cf. 2 Sam 1:17-27 alongside 3:33-34). Even then, however, the oral tradition persisted alongside the literary.

Dirge Motifs in Lam 1-5

Lam 1: Motifs characteristic of the dirge crop up several times in the first six verses. At the very outset one encounters a mournful cry (the same element opens chapters two and four), which is closely tied in with a contrast motif in vv 1a-c and 6a-c and with a description of misery in vv 2a and 4c. The latter element is expanded by the comment in v 2b that "not one is left to console her" and by the elaboration, in v 4a-b, that "the roads to Zion mourn...." The section comprised of the first six verses, then, is largely molded by the dirge. In vv 7-22, on the other hand, motifs characteristic of the dirge virtually disappear. In v 8c one finds a brief description of agony, while a summons to mourn has been inserted in two places: in v 12 and again in v 18.

Lam 2: The dirge plays even less of a role in this chapter. Following the opening mournful cry, the traditional feature of a complaint directed to God has been transformed into a description of suffering (by a transposition from the second-person to the third-person form of address). The same sort of transposition has occurred with the normally first-person-plural form of lamentation found in vv 8b-13, the particular motifs of which properly belong to the plaintive lament [*Leidklage*]. In vv 1b, 2c and 3a one finds the contrast motif (an overthrowing), while in v 8c there follows the element of describing the misery ("he caused to mourn both rampart and wall"). In v 10 the mourning by the survivors of the catastrophe is described as though it were a mourning for some deceased person (they "sit silently on the ground"); here the plaintive lament becomes indistinguishable from the dirge. Also worthy of mention here is the motif of incomparable suffering in v 11a-b (and also perhaps in v 13), as also those of the clapping and hissing of the passers-by in v 15a-b and the bewildered question in v 15c. In the summons to mourn and to beseech Yahweh, in v 18, the plaintive lament has become entwined with the dirge.

Lam 4: The mournful cry at the outset introduces a description of misery which stretches over the first ten verses and which is largely determined by the contrast motif comparing current with former conditions: gold that has lost its luster, precious stones cast into heaps, the children of Zion once valued as gold but now worthless as clay pots (cf. also vv 3, 5, 7, 8, 14, 15). Additional motifs characteristic of the dirge are not to be found in this chapter.

Lam 5: Chapter five is a communal lament. There is good reason, however, why this text stands where it does rather than in the Book of Psalms. The whole weight of this chapter lies on the lengthy first-person-plural lament in vv 2-18, a lament which has been transformed into a description of misery and which describes the aftermath of the catastrophe of 587—a fact which brings this text into close connection with chapters one and two of Lamentations. Just notice, for example, the wording of v 3 ("We have become orphans, fatherless; our mothers became like widows"). The description of misery in v 17 has a similar function.

Lam 3: In vv 42-51 of chapter three one finds a fragment of a communal lament, stretching from the confession of guilt (v 42) to the intimated plea for God's favor (v 50, transposed so as to read after v 51). The description of misery in vv 48, 49 and 51 is a motif from the dirge, as is the expression "terror and pit became our lot" in v 47 (a fixed expression, as is shown by the remarkably similar wording in, for example, Isa 24:17 and Jer 48:43).

Were one to see the five chapters of Lamentations laid out in two separate columns defined by the respective motifs of the genre of the lament of a suffer and those of the dirge, it would immediately become apparent that the dirge plays a relatively minor role in these five chapters. Even more than that, one would see that the motifs from the dirge occur in no recognizable array in these chapters; there is no regular sequence to the several motifs which occur more than once. These two facts alone make it certain that the plaintive lament, in its form as a communal lament, is determinative for the structure of these texts. The dirge has exerted a decidedly secondary influence here (*contra* Jahnow, Gunkel, and the many exegetes who have followed them).

Nonetheless, it must be admitted that the juxtaposition of motifs from the communal lament, on the one hand, and the dirge on the other, gives the impression of having been carried out deliberately. Under the immediate impact of the catastrophe of 587 the collapse of Jerusalem was described in such a way that motifs from the dirge enriched the communal lament. This was because the collapse of the city was experienced as its death.

Re: Samuel N. Kramer, The Sumerian "Lamentation over the Destruction of Ur"

This lament over the city of Ur, stemming from sometime in the first half of the second millennium BCE, is a parallel—albeit distant—to the Book of Lamentations and therefore must also be considered in conjunction with its interpretation. Even apart from this connection, however, the Lamentation over the Destruction of Ur is an artistically crafted song which conveys, in powerful and moving fashion, the reality of the destruction of a Mesopotamian city around the beginning of the second millennium. Since this particular form of poetry is alien to us, and since even after repeated reading its internal relationships are difficult to recognize, I will initially break down the 436 lines of the poem into abridged units and offer a few explanatory comments.[2]

The complete poem is comprised of eleven songs of differing lengths.

lines 1-38 (First Song [Prologue]): the gods have abandoned their temple
lines 39-72 (Second Song): summons to lament over the city of Ur
    69-72: the city is bewailed by those who have witnessed its destruction

---

[2] See, in addition to Kramer's translation in *ANET* (pp. 455-63), the abridged version of the text as given on pp. 116-18 of *NERT* (*Near Eastern Religious Texts Relating to the Old Testament*, ed. W. Beyerlin.) [Dr. Westermann's (German) citations generally reflect the rendering of the Sumerian text as given in *ANET*, but occasionally they are closer to the rendering of *NERT*. Which of the two (English) versions most closely resembles Dr. Westermann's reading of the Sumerian text will be indicated in parenthesis immediately following the citation—*Trans.*]

lines **73-133** (Third Song): Ningal's efforts to save the city
   73-102: Ningal's intercessory plea before Nanna (twice)
   103-21: Ningal seeks, in vain, to effect the city's deliverance
   122-33: proclamation of the city's demise (several times)
lines **134-69** (Fourth Song): Anu and Enlil maintain their
   resolve to destroy the city
lines **171-204** (Fifth Song): destruction of the city;
   Enlil calls down the storm
lines **205-50** (Sixth Song): the aftermath of the storm;
   Ningal leaves the city
lines **251-328** (Seventh Song): Ningal's lament over Ur
lines **330-84** (Eighth Song): supplication to Ningal for
   restoration
lines **388-96** (Ninth and Tenth Songs): the storms have
   caused the city to be inundated
lines **419-35** (Eleventh Song): plea for restoration, sacrifice,
   praise of the god

The structure of the whole is best understood by starting from its center, the fifth and sixth songs. These two songs offer a dual account of the city's destruction. The fifth song depicts the catastrophe as a storm called forth by Enlil. The sixth song focuses on the aftermath of Enlil's storm. In the fifth song the storm appears as a natural catastrophe, a tumult of the elements; lightning, gloom, and earthquake accompany the storm. The sixth song expresses the storm's aftermath in its full brutality; the storm has demolished the city (these lines form the transition), which now lies in ruins. Survivors are groaning, corpses litter the city's outskirts, dead bodies lie in the gates and on the streets, unburied and exposed. Within the city famine is rampant. Families are decimated, with little ones having been torn from the laps of their mothers and elderly folk having been burned along with their houses. Mother is separated from daughter, father from son. Women and children are abandoned, personal belongings are scattered everywhere. The temple is destroyed, the warehouses are reduced to ashes. Interspersed are cries of woe, frequently repeated. "Alas for my city!" "Alas for my house!" "The people groan."

Preceding the central section, which describes the ruin of the city and which comprises the fifth and sixth songs, is an introductory section which obviously leads up to it. The first song is a prologue. It sets the destruction of the city of Ur in the broader context of the activities of the gods. It does this because the destruction of a city entails the destruction of its temples, and that in turn is visualized as the gods' losing their places of residence. Thus the prologue announces, in a litany of identically worded clauses, that the gods of Sumer have abandoned their temples, have given up their places of residence. This imagery depicts the religious dimension of the city's ruin.

The third and fourth songs also depict the religious aspect of the city's ruin. Ningal, the patron goddess of Ur, intercedes for her city and tries everything she can to avert its destruction. Repeatedly she pleads that it be spared. She carries her plea to Enlil and finally even to Anu, the highest god of all. She is unsuccessful. Anu and Enlil remain firm in their resolve to destroy the city. These efforts by Ur's patron goddess to preserve her city are extensive; they are described in part of the second song as well as being the center of attention in songs three and four. All of this speaks to the underlying conviction that the city's fate is determined by the outcome of controversies among the gods.

The section comprising the third and fourth songs (lines 73-169) is preceded, in the second song (lines 39-72), by the actual introduction to the lament. This introduction consists of a summons to raise a lament over Ur; the city is to be bewailed by those who have witnessed its destruction (lines 39-62 and 65-72). Both the summons to lament and the theme of the witnesses' participation are, in terms of their origin, motifs from the dirge. Thus, just as in Lamentations (chapters one, two, and four), so also here we find a mixing of genres: motifs from the dirge are joined to the plaintive lament.

Following the central section (fifth and sixth songs) there occurs, in the seventh song, the lament of Ningal over her city of Ur. There are two distinct aspects to Ningal's lament. First of all, the religious aspect is continued as the story is told from the perspective of the gods. Ningal was defeated in her efforts to preserve her city. Her city was decimated, and she was unable to prevent its destruction. Now she takes up a lament over the ruins. "In her stable, in her sheepfold the lady utters bitter words: 'The city has been destroyed by the storm!'" (ANET 251-52a [slightly emended to reflect author's reading—*Trans.*]). She laments over the implication of that for herself. "Woe is me—in my city, which has perished, I am no longer the queen!" (NERT 286). "Woe is me, where shall I sit me down, where shall I stand up?" (ANET 294). "Woe is me, I am one who has been exiled from the city, I am one who has found no rest..." (ANET 306-08). "O my house of Sin in Ur, bitter is thy destruction" (ANET 327).

Another aspect besides the religious one appears, however. Ningal, the patron goddess of the city, personally takes up the lament over her city; she performs the lament over Ur in much the same fashion as does Lady Zion, in whom the city of Jerusalem is personified, in Lam 1, 2 and 4. So the Sumerian lament continues as the goddess Ningal herself expresses the horror of the city's conquest and the ensuing misery. She bewails the decimation of the city by pickaxe and fire (lines 258-60), making reference to the destruction both outside and within the city walls (lines 261-64). She goes on to mention how the waterways have become clogged with silt, how no grain grows in the city's fields, how there is no fruit in the vineyards, how all personal possessions have been lost. Moreover, "my daughters and sons ...have been carried off," and there are no field workers or shepherds to be found anywhere. The goddess graphically expresses her agony over the scene: she tears her hair, she beats on her breast, she cries aloud. "Woe is me, I am one whose house is a stable torn down, I am one whose cows have been dispersed" (ANET 304). Emphatically she adds, "In the debris of my destroyed house I lay me down alongside thee as a fallen ox, from thy destroyed wall I stand not up!" (ANET 319-20 [slightly emended to reflect author's reading—*Trans.*]).

In the eighth song (lines 330-84) Ningal's lament over Ur (viz., the seventh song) is taken up by the city itself and continued in the form of a supplication, addressed to Ningal by the surviving inhabitants, to the effect that the goddess might once again show favor to her city. "Make thy heart like water!" runs the refrain in lines 331-38. With a motif borrowed from the petitionary prayer, the lament shifts focus to the area of cultic celebration. "In...thy house of feasts, they celebrate not the feasts" (ANET 355); "thy song has been transformed into weeping...thy music has been turned into lamentation!" (ANET 359-60). In lines 373-74 an accusatory tone intrudes: "O my queen, verily thou art one who has departed from the house; thou art one who has departed from the city. How long, pray, wilt thou stand aside in the city like an enemy?" (ANET). Then follow the elements of a plea to return ("...like an ox to thy stable, like a sheep to thy fold" [ANET 378]) and a wish for restoration: ("May Anu, the king of the gods, utter...'tis enough!'" [ANET 381]. See also ll. 423-24: "O Nanna [consort of Ningal—*Trans.*]! May thy city which has been returned to its place, step forth gloriously before thee!...may it proceed before thee!").

In the closing section of the composition (lines 419-35), the devotion of the city's inhabitants is reaffirmed ("The humble who have taken thy path...before thee is their cry" [ANET 419-20]). Offerings are presented to the gods and forgiveness of sins is sought. Then, corresponding to the vow of praise at the end of the Biblical psalms of lament, the Sumerian lament concludes "O Nanna, thy city which has been returned to its place exalts thee" (ANET 435).

The material which falls between the eighth and the eleventh songs (the ninth and tenth songs, lines 387-414) belongs—at least in terms of its content—back at the beginning of the whole composition. Here "father Nanna" is implored that he might constrain "the great storm" from breaking in upon the city: "...let not that storm establish itself near thy city!" (ANET 406); "like the great gate of night may the door be closed on it!" (ANET 411).

This great poetic lament clearly contains elements of the dirge. The summons to mourn stands at the beginning (lines 39-64), followed by reference to the participation of the bystanders (lines 65-72) and the formal proclamation of the destruction (viz., the death), the latter motif being joined to a cry of woe (lines 65-66, 122-33, and repeated several more times thereafter). Moreover, there is explicit reference to the mourning-like behavior of Ningal (lines 299-301). Expressions of mournful agony are repeated throughout the poem: "the people groan"; "bitter is thy destruction." In the given context such expressions make very good sense!

The composition as a whole, however, is not a dirge. Rather, it is clearly and unmistakably a plaintive lament—one corresponding to the so-called communal lament in the Old Testament. This genre begins with an element of address. Starting with line 211 of the Sumerian composition, where human beings begin to speak, the element of addressing a deity occurs frequently. The characteristic tripartite division of the lament can also be recognized here. The Sumerian composition is overwhelmingly a first-person-plural lament, with Ningal being included in the "we" who do the speaking. In lines 373-77 one finds a trace of the element of an accusation against deity: the goddess has abandoned her city. The element of lament about an enemy has been consciously transformed in this instance; in the place of the enemy one finds "the great storm" which Anu sends against the city. The human enemies who actually carried out the destruction are mentioned only once, and then very briefly: "the Subarians and the Elamites" (line 244).

Again as is the case with the Biblical lament-psalms, here also the element of petition follows the lament proper. The petition is cast in various forms, with intercessory prayer receiving a special emphasis. Also characteristic of the lament genre is the way the element of petition is separated into a plea for a change of heart (lines 378-80) and a plea for restoration (lines 381-84). The conclusion also resembles the Biblical psalms, specifically in the offering of sacrifices and the praise of the deity—in the sense of a vow to render praise—at the end.

Moreover, the starkly religious aspect permeating the whole composition unmistakably shows that the lamentation over Ur corresponds, not to the dirge, but to the plaintive lament. As a parallel to the laments in the Book of Lamentations, then, the Lamentation over the Destruction of Ur further confirms that the former are not dirges to which individual motifs of the communal lament have been attached. Rather, in their very essence they are communal laments. When transposed into the same sort of context as the Lamentation over the Destruction of Ur, they likewise have attracted to themselves various motifs original to the dirge.

Alongside this formal correspondence in structural features is the general similarity in atmosphere between the lamentation over Ur and the laments in the Book of Lamentations. This feature of similar atmosphere is due to the common, underlying experience of the destruction of a city—an experience perceived as affecting the city itself as well as its inhabitants. In each case the city is personified; to each city is ascribed something like a human consciousness. Thus direct address of the city is possible: "O city of a great name—now you are destroyed for me, city of high walls—your land has perished!" (NERT 65-66). And the city is itself able to lament: "His [viz., Nanna's] city which has been destroyed—bitter is its lament, his Ur which has been destroyed—bitter is its lament!" (NERT 75-76).

Also notice the way the city's inhabitants are portrayed. The various groups of the city's populace are all mentioned, because they have all been affected by the destruction. It is noteworthy how the very same groups of people are singled out in both the lament over Ur and the laments over Jerusalem. Families are torn apart and destroyed, scattered as their houses are demolished. Families include the elderly, who perish in the burning ruins, men and women in general, fathers and mothers in particular, youths, children, and infants. All these categories of people are mentioned together because the collapse of the city has a similar effect upon them all.

All sorts of property was being kept in the city, including everyone's household belongings. Now all of that is destroyed or carried off. In the process, the city's culture is likewise demolished. Furthermore the roads and the canals, the market-places, the gates, the fields, the vineyards and the gardens—all have been laid waste. Civil order collapses. There are no longer any magistrates, any municipal assemblies, any effective laws. The city has lost its leadership.

The temples are destroyed along with the houses. The activities of the cult are brought to an abrupt end. There can no longer be any celebrations; festivals have come to an end; singing has ceased. "Thy song has been turned into weeping...thy music... into lamentation" (ANET 359-60; cf. Lam 5:15).

The same process takes place in both cases. The destruction of the respective cities results in the same sort of suffering on the part of the defenseless inhabitants. It is precisely this which makes the lamentation of the survivors so similar in both cases. The congruity of the underlying experience even reaches into the domain of relationship with deity. That is shown by a comparison focusing on the motif of the plea for a change of heart on the part of the deity (lines 369-84). "Ur seeks you [viz., Ningal] like a child lost in the streets, your house stretches out its hand toward you—like a man who has lost everything" (NERT 370-71). To be sure, these lines have no direct parallel in the Book of Lamentations, but they could just as well stand there as in the Sumerian poem.

It is regrettable that this astonishing parallel, the Lamentation over the Destruction of Ur, has received so little attention—indeed, almost none—in the interpretation of the Book of Lamentations. Despite significant differences, it cannot be denied that we are here dealing with a genuine parallel; in quite a number of places an almost exact correspondence can be established. It is not the particulars, however, which are decisive in establishing the parallel. Decisive, rather, is the fact that in both the lament over Ur and in Lamentations the destruction of a city is described from the point of view of the conquered who have lived through the catastrophe. In each case the lament of the distressed—the cry of those who experienced the horror—so powerfully gripped those who wrote down these words that they took pains to preserve them and pass them on to subsequent generations. It is precisely the respect being shown for the perspective of those directly affected by the catastrophe that gives such power to both the lament over Ur and the laments over Zion. To appreciate this power, all one need do is contrast such lamentation of a dying city with the "official" mode of writing history, a mode for which the suffering of the conquered has no—or, at best, very little—significance.

Re: Thomas F. McDaniel, "The Alleged Sumerian Influence upon Lamentations"

On the basis of a comparison between the relevant Sumerian texts and the Hebrew text of the Book of Lamentations,

McDaniel seeks to show that the dependence of Lamentations on the various Sumerian laments over destroyed cities—a dependence taken for granted by a number of scholars— cannot be confirmed.[3] In order to establish his thesis, McDaniel sets out fourteen citations from Lamentations, compares them with corresponding Sumerian passages (mostly taken from the "Lamentation over the Destruction of Ur"), and inquires after a possible dependence of the Hebrew statements upon the Sumerian. He arrives at the conclusion that no direct literary dependence is demonstrable, nor is such even likely. Although in several cases a limited similarity does exist, in each such case the similarity either amounts to a single word, without extending to its meaning, or else closer parallels can be found within the Old Testament itself. (In several cases there are also Ugaritic parallels.)

McDaniel's conclusion is that no path of transmission, by means of which the Sumerian text from the beginning of the second millennium could have come down to the poet of Lamentations in sixth-century Judah, is discernible. Nor, indeed, is such a path of transmission even likely. The same improbability holds with regard to Judeans' becoming acquainted with the Sumerian text during their exile in Babylon. In sum, the thesis of a literary dependence of Lamentations on the various Sumerian laments over destroyed cities cannot be maintained.

McDaniel's conclusion is correct, in so far as it goes. A literary dependence of Lamentations on the Sumerian texts has not heretofore been established, nor is such a dependence likely to be established in the future. However, with this conclusion not all has yet been said regarding the relationship of the respective texts to one another. This holds true even

[3] In addition to the "Lamentation over the Destruction of Ur," McDaniel cites the following works: C. J. Gadd, "The Second Lamentation for Ur," in *Hebrew and Semitic Studies Presented to Godfrey Rolles Driver*, ed. D. W. Thomas and W. D. McHardy (London, 1963), 59-71; A. Falkenstein, "Ibbisin Klage," in *Sumerische und akkadische Hymnen und Gebete*, ed. A. Falkenstein and W. von Soden (Zurich and Stuttgart, 1953), 189-92; S. N. Kramer, "The Lamentation over the Destruction of Nippur," in *Sumerian Literary Texts from Nippur in the Museum of the Ancient Orient at Istanbul* (AASOR 23; 1944) 33-36; *ibid.*, "Die Klage um die Zerstörung von Akkade," in *Sumerische Hymnen und Gebete*, 187-89.

when one keeps in view their temporal and spatial distance from each other. At the beginning of his article, McDaniel emphasizes that a series of similarities or correspondences in the respective texts really has no bearing on the question of literary dependence. It has none because the experiences of people involved in the overthrow of a city are everywhere the same, or at least similar. "Poets...would likely refer to the hunger, famine, pestilence, the social disintegration during the siege...the spoils...the loss of valuables...the captivity...the destruction of the city walls and temple..." (p. 200). Reference to none of these features attests to literary dependence. Rather, correspondence between features goes back to similarity of experiences. McDaniel especially argues this point over against H.-J. Kraus. (See the latter's remarks on pp. 9-10 of his commentary on the Book of Lamentations.) The same line of argument holds true when encountering references to weeping, to lamentation, to cries of woe, and so forth. In all of this, as well, McDaniel is certainly correct.

There remains, however, the simple fact that these texts closely resemble one another. This much holds true even when the possibility of a literary dependence of the younger upon those much older, and far removed in point of origin, has been eliminated. One is still led to ask how this similarity can be explained.

In ancient Sumer, as in Israel, the dismay felt by those who managed to survive the destruction of a city was so intense that their lamentation was molded into artistic form and came to be written down. These are the core features held in common by the two bodies of literature in question. It both places the laments themselves—the lamentation as such—took on such elevated and positive significance that they were preserved for future generations.

There is an additional feature in common. The destruction of one's city was perceived as an event not only of political but also, and concurrently, of religious import. Therefore in ancient Sumer the lamentation was directed to the gods just as, in ancient Israel, it was directed to God. Even though the nature of the relationship to the divine as brought to expression in the respective laments shows fundamental differences, this much remains the same: the divine plays a role both in the destruction of the city itself and in the people's reaction to that destruction. Thus the lament is directed toward the divine realm.

There is also a common feature in the way the destroyed city is understood. The suffering of Ningal, the patron goddess who is not able to avert the destruction of her city, corresponds quite clearly to the personification of the city in Israel (the city = Zion = a suffering woman). Lines 319-20 express most emphatically how Ningal participates in the suffering over the destruction of her city: "In the debris of my destroyed house I lay me down alongside thee as a fallen ox, from thy destroyed wall I stand not up!" Ningal suffers along with her destroyed city—a state of affairs closely resembling the suffering of the personified mother Zion with regard to her own city.

Common to both is also a very noteworthy feature in the way the populace affected by the destruction of the city is depicted. This feature has to do with the explicit categorization of the various groups within the populace as a whole, in terms of how they have been variously affected by the catastrophe. The same thing happens in the Sumerian lament as happens in the Biblical Book of Lamentations, with an evident focus on the defenseless and helpless nature of the sufferers. Mentioned explicitly are the elderly trapped in burning houses, mothers and their children, and the fact that the strong as well as the weak perish with hunger. Certainly all of these details could have been expressed in a few summarizing clauses. However, those who wrote down these laments in both Sumer and Jerusalem were concerned to let the pathos of the distinctive groups within the populace as a whole find appropriate expression, for precisely such a feature belongs to the essence of the lament. In the same vein, both there and here the tearing apart of families is explicitly and elaborately described. Children are said to have been snatched from the bosoms of their mothers—a notable feature held in common by the two blocks of literature.

Finally one must note a similarity of a linguistic, or more precisely of a form-critical, sort. To be sure, this is a similarity which does not catch the eye when the comparison focuses only on isolated clauses. From a form-critical point of view, both the

Sumerian texts and the texts from the Old Testament stand within the broader context of the history of the lament as such. In both cases the texts belong to the category of the communal lament, even though they comprise a distinct group within that overall category. When the texts are viewed in terms of their genre affiliation, a number of characteristic structural relationships can be recognized (see above, pp. 6-8). Especially important is the fact that several motifs of the dirge have been joined to the plaintive lament (in its communal form) just as much in Lamentations as in the Lamentation over the Destruction of Ur—a fact which McDaniel also notes, although only in passing.

How is one to explain such structural similarity in texts so far removed from one another, both temporally and spatially? What is one to make of such relatedness? Unfortunately, these are questions which heretofore have hardly been noticed or deemed worthy of investigation. However, they are certainly questions worthy of closer examination.

In conclusion, I would like to advance one more conjecture. Such a structural—and at the same time substantive—affinity between texts which lie temporally and spatially so far removed from one another occurs elsewhere in the Old Testament only with regard to the episodes relating to the primordial history, in Genesis 1-11. To this one must add the parallels to the narrative of a great deluge as found throughout the world. It is just possible that the initial experiences with destruction of great cities—which indeed constituted small "worlds" in their own right—in several cultural areas left such a deep impression upon those affected that these episodes of destruction were elevated to the rank of primordial human experiences. Alongside the experience of a natural catastrophe which effectively destroys a "world" was set the experience of the destruction of a great city through human instruments of power—through the overpowering army of a conqueror. Thus, as by a great deluge all living things are annihilated, so also much the same happens when a city is overthrown. It was something new in the chronicles of human experience when, at a number of places across the globe, a level of material culture was attained such that an armed horde became capable of leveling a whole city to the dust. The experience of such a destruction also coined distinctive forms of expression, forms which could appear in quite different settings. This supposition receives some support when it is seen that the basic comparison employed in the "Lamentation over the Destruction of Ur," namely the city's destruction by the "great storm" which the high god Anu commands to break out against it, contains an allusion to that archetypal natural catastrophe of primordial times.

Chapter Two

History of Interpretation

Interpretation of Lamentations around the Turn of the Century
Karl Budde

In the introduction to his commentary on Lamentations, Budde deals with the location of the book in the canon, its name, its form, and its contents. With regard to form, he decides that it is a dirge over the personified city of Jerusalem subsequent to its destruction in 587 BCE. Chapter three deviates from the other chapters in that here the speaker of the song bewails his own fate. Chapter five is not a song of lament at all, but rather a prayer. Then follows a detailed examination of the question of Jeremianic authorship, concluding that Jeremiah could not have been this work's author. With this conclusion, the view that all the songs in the book had the same author also falls apart. The alternative, which is more likely, is that they had different authors. The core of the book is comprised of chapters two and four, which probably stem from the same writer, an eyewitness to the events depicted. Chapter three lacks authenticity throughout. It presupposes that the other four chapters have already been drawn together into a collection; it thus forms the keystone for the book in the form it came to assume in a later time, perhaps in the third century BCE. "We are here dealing with a thoroughly secondary piece of work, one which can hardly be dated too late." The "I" in 3:1 must refer to an individual; only in vv 40-47 of the third chapter does the fate of the people as a whole become the theme. Some later hand put in the figure of an individual spokesperson—probably intending Jeremiah—in order to create a (supplemental) high point for the book and give it unified shape.

The individual songs ("chapters") are each introduced by a brief determination of their particular form and content. In its treatment of the individual verses, the commentary consists mainly of remarks on the state of the text and the meaning of individual words or phrases. Included is the identification of a number of parallel texts. These parallels are collected predominantly from the Old Testament, occasionally from the New Testament, but never from the religious literature of the broader Biblical milieu. The commentary sets its material in no broader contexts—neither theological, nor literary, nor any other kind. No questions are asked regarding theological or religious significance. The commentary's emphasis lies uniformly on detailed philological explication of the text. Such an approach does have the advantage of avoiding the importation of religious or theological concepts not appropriate to the text at hand. In contrast to most of the more recent commentators, Budde has correctly recognized the peculiarity of chapter three and its late origin.

Max Löhr

Löhr wrote his first commentary on Lamentations in 1893. As the very title of that commentary (*Die Klagelieder des Jeremia*) shows, the book was ascribed to Jeremiah. Two essays which Löhr published in 1894 are actually addenda to this commentary. In the first of these essays, "Der Sprachgebrauch des Buches der Klagelieder" ["The Linguistic Usage of the Book of Lamentations"], Löhr examined the issue of the "authenticity" of the laments ascribed to Jeremiah by investigating their linguistic usage. By "linguistic usage" Löhr here really means only vocabulary, or the occurrence of specific words. Because whole clauses or fixed forms of expression were not included in the comparisons, his conclusions are clouded by a high degree of uncertainty. This is especially the case where he tries to determine literary dependency—and thereby time of origin— on the basis of the occurrence of particular words in other writings.

In his second essay, "Sind Thr. IV und V makkabäisch?" ["Are Lam 4 and 5 Maccabean?"], Löhr rejects S. A. Fries' hypothesis that the first three chapters of Lamentations are a

cohesive text stemming from Jeremiah, while chapters four
and five possibly stem from the Maccabean era. Löhr rejects
this hypothesis on the grounds that it is based only on a
comparison of isolated sentences.

Löhr published a third important essay in 1904: "Threni III
und die jeremianische Autorschaft des Buches der Klagelieder"
["Lamentations 3 and the Jeremianic Authorship of the Book
of Lamentations"]. Here he lays groundwork for the second
edition of his commentary, published in 1906, with a thorough
study of the third chapter of Lamentations. He begins by
surveying the literature important to the lively discussion of
whether the speaker in this text is to be understood in a
collective or an individual sense:

> B. Stade (1887): Lam 3 deals almost exclusively with the
> suffering of a individual, specifically with that of Jeremiah.
> R. Smend (1888): Lam 3 is a communal song, the "I" who
> here speaks is the community as a whole.
> M. Löhr (1893): Löhr agrees with Smend.
> K. Budde (1898): Lam 3 is the song of an individual [against
> Smend].
> E. Kautzsch (1902): Kautzsch contests Budde's
> interpretation.
> G. Beer (1902): Lam 3 is a communal song.

Löhr, who had earlier defended the collective interpretation,
now maintains that the difficulties here emerging can be
eliminated through a detailed investigation of chapter three.
In carrying out such an investigation, he starts from the fact
that, in vv 48-51, an individual clearly stands out from the
community as speaker—the feature which leads him to reverse
his earlier stance. Two originally separate psalms are to be
found in vv 1-24 and 52-66. The composer of chapter three
apparently took these existing psalms and added the intervening
section (vv 25-51). This middle section comes directly from the
hand of the composer. The chapter as a whole is an artfully
constructed poem serving what Löhr suspects was the
composer's intent, namely that of having the prophet Jeremiah
come forward and, by means of reference to the fate which he

himself experienced, address a sort of penitential sermon to the people. The section which the composer himself produced, vv 25-51, is notable for its sense of religious individualism and perspective of universalism, the latter coming to expression through use of the late divine epithet "the Most High." The composer used the acrostic pattern to structure the overall composition. Chapter three is the most recent of the songs in Lamentations; its time of origin is similar to that established by Budde.

The continuing significance of Löhr's study lies, first of all, in the recognition that chapter three is a composition whose various sections arose in different ways and are to be evaluated somewhat independently, secondly in that this chapter is the most recent of the songs in Lamentations (following Budde) and, finally, in that the beginning and the concluding sections—originally two independent psalms—were not originally in acrostic form but only subsequently had this feature imposed upon them by the composer.

Löhr incorporated his revised understanding in the second edition of his commentary, published in 1906 (in the series *Handkommentar zum Alten Testament*). In 1923 he produced one more study on Lamentations, the brief "Die Klagelieder" [in *Die Heilige Schrift des Alten Testaments*, 4th. ed., edited by Alfred Bertholet]. In this last study he regarded chapters one, two, and four as literary—rather than folk—poetry exhibiting a theologico-political character, specifically in that the poet here emphasizes the guilt of Israel's prophets. "The thoughts and sentiments of the poet are presented in lyric form." The fifth song is an communal prayer. The third song is the product of a scribe and is intended to give the whole collection a midpoint (as also Budde). "This song allows the prophet Jeremiah to step forth and address the people in the form of a penitential sermon." This understanding was subsequently taken up by Rudolph, but with significant modification. For Rudolph, the third chapter was from the outset—that is, already by the single (so Rudolph) author responsible for all five songs—conceptualized as the midpoint of the whole book. Löhr, on the contrary, had chapter three come into being only long after the other four chapters had already appeared.

One difficulty with Löhr's understanding is that, while he clearly backs off from the assumption of actual Jeremianic authorship, he still assumes that the middle section—although stemming directly from the composer—nonetheless is a sort of penitential sermon, a device by which the composer can make it appear as though the prophet Jeremiah is speaking. (Budde holds a similar view). To be sure, Löhr correctly recognizes that the language and the ideas of this penitential sermon belong to a late era; he knows, in other words, that Jeremiah himself could not have spoken in this fashion. Nonetheless, he claims to see reflections of Jeremiah in all the sections of chapter three. This leaves a muddied picture. Perhaps the tradition of Jeremianic authorship continues to work unconsciously on Löhr.

1920-1960
Hermann Gunkel

Through his designation of its genres—a designation resting upon the investigations of Jahnow—Gunkel has exerted a decisive influence upon the interpretation of the Book of Lamentations that has stretched right up to the present time. Referring to Jahnow's work, Gunkel designated Lam 1, 2, and 4 as dirges. "Chapters one, two, and four belong to the genre of the communalized [*politisches*] dirge; here the dirge has attracted several motifs characteristic of the communal lament and thereby acquired content significant to a wider audience." Through this process of joining motifs from the communal lament to the dirge, the originally profane genre has been transformed into religious poetry. The fifth poem is a pure communal lament. Lam 3 is of mixed genre, but it starts out as a lament of an individual. With vv 21-39 all sorts of consoling thoughts and insights from Israel's wisdom tradition get attached to the petitionary portion of the lament, while vv 42-47 move into the language of the communal lament. Vv 48-51, on the other hand, glide over into the genre of the lament of an individual once again. In vv 52-58 "the individual recalls how Yahweh rescued him when in deadly peril." Vv 59-66 form the conclusion, a prayer for the destruction of the speaker's enemies. The chapter as a whole is to be seen as stemming from a literary era in which the boundaries separating the various traditional genres were being blurred. This particular song does not unify the whole book and give it a sense of flow (contra Budde); rather, the chapter stands on its own. It is understandable how Old Testament research could not rest content with this actually quite vague interpretation of chapter three.

Wilhelm Rudolph

Rudolph takes the view that chapter one of Lamentations was written under the impact of the first deportation, in 597 BCE, while the remaining chapters were composed after 587 BCE. Since it is Rudolph's opinion that all the songs in Lamentations come from the same hand, however, this breakdown is not particularly significant. All of the songs have been composed in response to the catastrophe by someone who was an eyewitness. Chapters one, two, and four imitate the style of the dirge, but the poet varies the genres in that chapter five is a communal lament and chapter three a composition of mixed genre. Even in chapter one the pattern of the dirge is soon abandoned. The train of thought is not strictly logical. The poet deals with a single theme; the songs preserve thematic rubrics. When the theme gets interrupted, the poet later comes back to it. Interestingly enough, Rudolph more than once claims to be in agreement with the Gunkel-Begrich *Einleitung in die Psalmen* while making no explicit use of its findings.

According to Rudolph, the overall intent of Lamentations is "to lead the people to a proper understanding of the ways of Yahweh and thereby also to a proper form of behavior." One of his comments on Lam 1:12-16 has quite a different ring to it, however: "Now must Zion herself cry out, expressing what lies on her heart." For Rudolph, however, the phenomenon of lamenting as such has no real significance. As he puts it, "Likewise in chapter four the poet does not remain bogged down in mere yammering." Lamentation is "mere yammering"; it is not a legitimate form of expression in its own right. In the same vein, Rudolph admonishes that one should not endlessly engage in mere lamentation.

With regard to Lam 3, Rudolph explicitly sets his views apart from other interpretations of this chapter. Above all, he contests the following explanations: (a) the collective interpretation, (b) the "I" as representing the community, (c) that an individual is speaking of his personal experience, and (d) that the composition has a liturgical character. Actually, according to Rudolph, chapter three attaches to chapter two. The individual who begins to speak in 3:1 is supposed to be Jeremiah. The composer of chapter three puts his own words into the mouth of this "Jeremiah," and the prophet demands confession in the place of grumbling (similarly Löhr). The composer clothes in the generalized truth expressed in vv 25-27 what Jeremiah supposedly learned from personal experience. Rudolph reads vv 42-47 as a penitential psalm.

For Rudolph, the theological significance of Lamentations lies in the way these songs are intended to elicit the proper understanding of the desperate situation centered around the destruction of 587 BCE. Yahweh himself ordained that it be so; it was Israel's well-deserved punishment. However, the example set by Jeremiah in chapter three makes clear that the grace of Yahweh has not come to an end. There is no reason to despair, for the promise of Yahweh stands sure. The only remaining way out of the desperate situation, however, consists in turning back to Yahweh.

When it comes to the exegesis of chapter three—especially its middle section—Rudolph's work is at its most thorough, for here the fervor of the Book of Lamentations reaches its crescendo. For Rudolph this happens as a matter of course, since for him the composer of chapter three is identical with the composer of the other songs (differing here from Löhr). He sees no essential difference, either in form or content, between the middle section of chapter three and the other chapters. For Rudolph (as also later for Kaiser), what is theologically essential is expressed in the form of a timeless, universal teaching. Thus to him it is irrelevant that the terrible events of 587 BCE are not mentioned at all in chapter three.

A important step in the history of the interpretation of Lamentations lies between Löhr and Rudolph. When Löhr (similarly Budde) speaks of chapter three as the midpoint of Lamentations, he has in mind some composer of the middle section of that chapter—some "scribe" whom he assigns to the fourth or third century—who took it upon himself to create a focal point for the already extant collection comprised of chapters one, two, four and five. For Rudolph, however, chapter three stems from the same person responsible for the other chapters, which is to say from an eyewitness to the events of 587 BCE. Rudolph does not even mention the alternate interpretation of Löhr, nor does he enter into the arguments for a late dating of chapter three. Subsequent research has gone even further along the tack taken by Rudolph.

Max Haller

In the matter of designating genres, Haller follows Gunkel and Jahnow. However, this plays only a small role in his interpretive work. He does not pursue the relationship between the communal lament and the dirge; he is satisfied (as is Eissfeldt) simply to establish the fact of a mixing of genres. Haller finds no discrete life-setting [*Sitz im Leben*] for the individual songs. As a whole, the collection was put together for use on memorial days. Neither does Haller speak to the issue of the structure of the laments; he concentrates only on the individual motifs. He thinks the whole composition could be a dirge, but then again the dirge could constitute only a portion of the whole. In any case, he regards 2:20-22 as a small dirge.

Haller corrects and emends the Masoretic Text in a number of places, often for reasons of meter. His changes in the text do not always seem necessary. Following Gunkel, Haller sees the theological significance of Lamentations to lie in its repeated transition from dirge to religious poetry. As he several times puts it, the poet thereby ascends to "a higher plane." In 4:11-16, for example, "The poet ascends to a higher plane of vision." The religious significance of the composition is primarily confined to the third song, however. The middle section of chapter three "is religiously the most significant part of the whole book of Lamentations." Here patient suffering finds hope. The penitential motif of vv 39-41 belongs to this most significant material. Throughout the composer has in mind the image of Jeremiah, out of whose fortunes he would like to generate consolation for his people. One can best understand chapter three as commentary upon the first and second songs.

Friedrich Nötscher

After a short introduction to the composition as a whole, Nötscher's commentary proceeds to give specific introductions to each of the chapters and offers explanatory verse-by-verse comments. The several songs are at the same time provided with superscriptions: chapter one—misfortune and guilt; chapter two—the punishing God; chapter three—suffering, and overcoming suffering; chapter four—the terrible sacrifice; chapter five—a lamenting prayer. The whole is a collection of five plaintive religious poems having as their subject the same national catastrophe. No unified plan underlies the collection; each song is intelligible in itself and could stand on its own. Even within the individual songs there is no real flow of thought; "first one, then another thought comes to the fore."

The poet employs the form of the profane, communalized dirge in chapters one, two, and four (here following Jahnow and Gunkel); chapter five is partly modeled on the communal lament. All the songs have the same composer, and all arose after 587 BCE. The individual songs were organized on the basis of leading ideas. Nötscher's exegetic work hardly goes beyond brief explanations and remarks about the subject matter.

Nötscher answers the question of how chapter three relates to the other songs by attempting to understand this chapter on the basis of what is said in the other songs—this despite what he said in his introduction. "In all probability the poet regards himself as one with his people, looks upon his own suffering as tied up with the national affliction, and so feels himself called to speak in the name of the people as a whole." Several interpreters have followed Nötscher on this point.

Norman K. Gottwald

All the poems stem from the time after 587 BCE, and all were composed by the same individual (with the possible exception of the fifth song). The poems were written down and recited independently of one another. Gunkel and Jahnow were right to investigate the Book of Lamentations as a colection of songs fitting in with those to be found in the Book of Psalms. However, the songs in Lamentations do not all belong to one type. The reason why the poet drew upon dirges is that he wrote while in the midst of a scene of death and surrounded by burial sites. After these introductory remarks, however, Gottwald does not pursue correlations with the Psalms or connections with the dirge. He sets the questioning of the meaning of the catastrophe over against the Deuteronomic doctrine of retribution. Why, it was asked, did the people have to suffer all of this so soon after a reform? This process of questioning in turn led to a crisis of faith. The tension which resulted is the key to the theology of the Book of Lamentations. The rest of the study concentrates on developing this theological, or spiritual, aspect of the event. It does so by juxtaposing a "theology of judgment" with a "theology of hope."

In the "theology of judgment," emphasis falls upon the theme of fulfilling the pronouncement of judgment as significant for continuity in the action of Yahweh. The "theology of hope" shows up in the strikingly many prayers which appear in the laments. What is important about these prayers is that they endeavor to prompt God to act anew. Apart from these prayers, the "theology of hope" is rooted entirely in chapter three. Remembrance of God's covenant loyalty renews hope. For hope to be realized, however, return to God is necessary. This means repentance and a "submissive spirit." With regard to filling in the details of such hope, however, Gottwald himself remarks that "...it has remained indefinite at best" because 3:13-33 so lacks specificity.

Bertil Albrektson

Albrektson takes Gottwald's study as his starting point and objects that nothing is said of the Josianic reform in any of the songs of Lamentations. To be sure, if the songs emphasize that the collapse of Israel was God's punishment upon her for her guilt, then that is thoroughly congruent with the Deuteronomic doctrine of retribution. Albrektson maintains, however, that the theology of Lamentations is actually determined by another sort of tension, namely that due to the Zion tradition, a tradition presupposed more than once in Lamentations. Allied with this tradition is belief in the inviolability of Zion. In the wake of 587 BCE this belief stands in sharp contrast to experienced reality. The real background to the theology of Lamentations is tension generated by contrast between belief and reality.

While one can agree with Albrektson's arguments as far as they go, it is remarkable how he nowhere addresses the fact that the Book of Lamentations deals with laments. This fact he simply lets pass by. He is only interested in theological concepts and their reciprocal relationships.

Theophile J. Meek

Meek's commentary on Lamentations occupies only a short section of the volume which contains it. As Meek sees it, songs one through five (perhaps one through four) are the work of a single poet. Meek confirms by detailed argument that Jeremiah cannot be the author of this material. However, there are many points of contact between Lamentations and the Psalms. The songs of Lamentations were recited in a cultic setting and eventually, because of their use in the cult, were brought together into a collection. It is possible that the author of chapter three wanted to play the role of a Jeremiah; in 3:40-47 he identifies himself with his people.

The book was written in order to clarify the meaning of God's strict dealings with his people; it means to draw a lesson from the past. The songs exhibit deep sadness, but they also radiate hope—especially song three.

Hans-Joachim Kraus

The five songs arose soon after the catastrophe of 587 BCE. Chapter three is, in effect, the oldest commentary upon the other four songs (so also Eissfeldt). Either cult prophets or priests composed the songs. Kraus rejects Gunkel's designation "communalized dirge"; rather, these songs are "laments over the demolished sanctuary," analogous to the lament over Ur. Like the latter, they were composed for solemn cultic memorials and were performed liturgically. The acrostic structure of the first song is perhaps a secondary feature (but then the same would have to hold for the second and fourth songs as well!). Kraus finds a meaningful flow of thought, or intelligible structure, only in the fifth song. Twice he offers an explicit schema for the structure of the third song, but his schemas do not fully agree with one another. For Kraus, chapter three is "the true high point of Lamentations." The meaning of the chapter is to be found in vv 1-33 and 52-66 (personal songs of lamentation). These verses mean to show the community the way to overcome its distress and to help it find a new sense of reliance upon Yahweh. They present a paradigm for preaching to and teaching the community. However, Kraus then asks "whether the whole chapter does not stand at a certain distance from public worship" and whether "Lam 3 is not a secondary composition based upon discourses and songs derived from public worship."

The theological significance of Lamentations (discussed by Kraus in an appendix in the second edition of his commentary) lies in the fact that the catastrophe was God's punishment and that the people of God recognize their guilt and do penance. In chapters one, two, four and five any explicit message of salvation is lacking; there are only a few prayers. In chapter three, however, a way to overcome the disaster is shown. The good news is here to be found in the way the lament of the individual becomes a message of salvation. There is still room for hope. So one could truly call chapter three the heart of Lamentations. The phenomenon of the lament as such has no significance for Kraus; for him the laments only point in the direction of the majesty of divine judgment.

Artur Weiser

In his interpretation of Lamentations, Weiser also places heavy emphasis on chapter three. His work on this one chapter takes up more room than his work on all the other four put together. According to Weiser, Lam 3 is "something other" than the rest of the chapters. Nonetheless, it is by the same author, and it deals with the same national catastrophe. The apparent divergence among the individual forms and genres is counteracted by a common "pastoral trait." At the nucleus stands the faithful urgency of someone deeply affected by the fate of the people. The "I am one who..." of 3:1 presupposes an audience; the speaker's words are meant for a community. In chapter three the poet speaks directly and draws upon personal experience. The poet speaks with the same authority that the singers of the Psalms possessed. The confession of this individual has paradigmatic significance for the community as a whole. "The poet willingly assumes the pastoral leadership of the community."

The theological significance of Lamentations lies in its endeavor to open up a pathway along which the people can move through a dangerous crisis of faith and return to their God. Since the calamity was a divine punishment, the poet issues a call to self-examination and to repentance. The poet's aim is to remove the barriers that are blocking access to the gracious God.

The synopsis of the religious significance of Lamentations which Weiser offers at the beginning of his commentary draws almost exclusively on chapter three. One consequence of such an approach is that Weiser consistently underestimates the value of laments. For him, the laments are an acknowledgement of the judgment of God, or else they are an expression of a deep religious need. Weiser repeatedly emphasizes "...the danger that accompanies persistent lamentation"—in these and in similar words. Only once in the whole commentary, in a remark directed to 5:16, does he say what a lament really is: "The lament is a natural expression of a suffering human being."

It is noteworthy how Weiser, in his interpretive work on Lamentations, makes considerable use of the language of a Protestant theology of Christian community. Terms such as faith, confession, spiritual care, caring concern, and "pastoral leadership of the community" abound; Israel itself is characteristically designated a "community." "The poet wants to lead the community out of lament and into a new communion with God."

Edouard Dhorme

In the French Bible *Edition de la Pléjade* Dhorme contributes the introduction (148-51) as well as the translation and footnotes (1478-1502) for the Book of Lamentations. In the introduction he treats the issues of the work's form, its *Sitz im Leben*, its author, and its time of origin; he also offers a brief survey of the contents of the five songs. The *leitmotif* of all the songs is the catastrophe of 587 BCE. Dhorme calls attention to the distinctiveness of chapter three and of chapter five (a prayer) over against chapters one, two, and four. Chapter three has a markedly individual character, and it resounds with echoes of the Psalms, Job, and Deutero-Isaiah. "The contrast between this strongly individualized psalm and the elegies over the ruin of the nation...leads us to attribute it to an author other than that of chapters one, two, and four." Given the nature of the references to a communal catastrophe in vv 48 and 51, it is most likely that chapter three was inserted into an earlier collection consisting of chapters one, two, and four. Chapter five also deviates from the style of the communal lament; it is a prayer stemming from yet another author. The Book of Lamentations thus encompasses the work of three different authors. The earliest was the one to compose chapters one, two, and four— chapters whose common origin strikes Dhorme as indisputable. The next author was the one responsible for chapter three. Chapter five stems from the last of the three authors. This final song was perhaps added only in order to bring the total number in the collection to five, in imitation of the Pentateuch. The whole collection arose between 587 and 538 BCE.

Dhorme has a high estimation of the beauty and the poetic power of these songs. In his opinion it is remarkable that their acrostic style does not seriously impinge upon their artistic merits.

Dhorme follows his introduction with a close and careful translation of all five songs, complete with footnotes on all the verses (1478-1502). In his notes Dhorme continuously draws attention to the difference in manner of expression between Hebrew and French (in most cases the differences hold also with reference to German [and English!]), and he offers an equivalent translation. He draws attention to literary and stylistic fine points such as alliteration, and to various allusions, associations and wordplays. In several places he deems important the shift from third person to second person. He is very cautious about suggesting emendations to the Hebrew text; he suggests only a few, and then only such as have already been proposed by other exegetes.

Dhorme points out many parallels with passages elsewhere

in the Old Testament (even a few in the New Testament), as well as noting all the parallels within the several songs themselves. However, he draws hardly any parallels with extra-Biblical literature. One looks in vain for any mention of the lament over Ur or the obvious parallels to motifs of the dirge—a serious defect. The treatment contains no section explicitly dealing with the theological significance of Lamentations.

1961-1985
Robert Gordis

Careful philological work on the text is the hallmark of this investigation. Gordis ignores the close relationship of Lamentations with Psalms; the various genres of the psalms, their characteristic motifs and type of language—all this he doesn't even mention. When it comes to interpretation of chapter three, Gordis takes as his starting point its fundamental difference from chapters one, two, and four. However, he explains the arrangement of its sentences and sections on the basis of grammatic relationships and the development of ideas. This makes the alteration between singular and plural the main problem that Gordis must treat. He finds the solution to this difficulty in the notion of "corporate personality" (H. W. Robinson), which Gordis calls "fluid personality." This concept is then supposedly the key to the understanding of chapter three, which one could call a Joban lament. "Individual and nation are blended together." However, the notion of "fluid personality" is really of no aid in the intepretation of Lamentations. In many places the exegete must still go on to ask whether, in the case at hand, the reference is to a single individual or to the people as a whole. Gordis himself confirms this when, with reference to 3:40ff, he maintains, "From his own misery the poet imperceptibly passes over to the tragic condition of his people."

Gilbert Brunet

In his *Les lamentations contre Jérémie* Brunet starts out from the observation that the remark in Lam 4:12 ("The kings of the earth did not believe...that foe [*ṣar*] or enemy [*'ōyēb*] could enter the gates of Jerusalem") refers to both external and internal enemies. He regards the internal enemy as the pro-Babylonian party subsequent to the events of 597 BCE, a party to which Jeremiah also belonged. Correspondingly, Lamentations is to some extent a document reflecting a civil conflict; it is a work of the nationalistic party in this conflict. The author of Lamentations is an opponent of Jeremiah, perhaps the chief priest Seraiah. The work has been preserved because it was in effect usurped by the opposition, in that Jeremiah came to be seen as its author.

For a number of reasons this interpretation of Lamentations cannot be maintained (e.g., on 4:12 cf. 1:5 and 2:4,17). One must agree, however, with the conclusion that one indisputable purpose of Lamentations is simply to portray the people's dismay as brought about by the collapse of their city. These laments are a cry; their greatest significance lies precisely in this fact. "It is they that have put pain in the Bible."

E. Cothenet

Cothenet's article is divided into several sections, dealing in turn with Lamentation's place in the canon and its use in liturgy, the contents of the five songs (briefly summarized), their literary genre and style, the matter of authorship and time of origin, and the theological significance of the material.

The texts are to be assigned to different genres. One finds motifs taken from the dirge, but the songs bear a closer resemblance to communal laments than to dirges since, in the songs, God is often addressed and prayed to directly. The songs rank high as poetry. They all stem from the same author who, however, could not have been Jeremiah. In some cases, especially in chapter three, one must suppose literary dependency; the dependency of 2:14 on Ezek 13:10 is certain. In a number of places the author adopts images and expressions characteristic of the psalms of lament. In terms of overall style, Lamentations reads like an anthology (so also Kaiser). The songs arose between 587 and 538 BCE.

Cothenet sees the theological significance of Lamentations as growing out of the people's shocked dismay at, above all, the destruction of the temple despite all earlier assurances of its inviolability. In the face of this reaction the author places heavy emphasis upon the misdeeds of Israel, of its prophets, and of its priests. It is these misdeeds that have called down the angry judgment of God. The enemies were only the instruments of the divine judgment, even though recompense will in turn fall upon them for their own wickedness.

In spite of everything, the people need not despair. Yahweh's rule remains unshaken, and Yahweh's anger does not endure for ever. The goodness of Yahweh will be renewed (3:31-32). To enjoy the divine goodness once again, it is necessary to confess sins, to turn to Yahweh, and in quiet confidence to await the restoration of divine favor (3:25-26).

Despite its typically Jewish character, Lamentations is of religious value for Christians as well. One must simply read the text in the light of the full history of salvation.

Otto Plöger

This philologically precise commentary tends to be very cautious when it comes to making judgments about disputed matters. It does not take issue with other interpreters; it maintains a noncommital stance where dissent might arise. "Any comprehensive interpretation is largely dependent upon the personal inclination and experience of the interpreter."

While it was earlier customary to think of Lamentations as a compilation of separate songs (e.g., E. Sellin), in more recent studies the attempt to see connections between the chapters dominates. In keeping with this tendency, Plöger thinks it possible that all five songs had one and the same author. In terms of their genre, the songs are composite in nature. Plöger follows earlier interpreters in seeing the dirge as providing the structural framework for chapters one, two, and four. (However, Plöger does not specify just what the nature of this framework is.) In chapter three the underlying genres are treated with considerable freedom. Plöger has reservations about Kraus' cultic interpretation of Lamentations, although he takes it as certain that this material was handed down in cultic circles.

No overarching flow of thought can be seen in the songs. Plöger attempts to establish a structure for the songs through their changes in speaker, especially in the case of chapter one.

By and large, however, he rests content with discussing the contents on a verse-by-verse basis.

Likewise for Plöger the genre of the lament as such has no independent significance. "In a song of lament the feature of lamenting, regardless of how extensive it may be, has no importance in its own right" (161-2). Or again: "It is not the describing of calamity, but rather the pleading for reversal of fortunes, that provides the occasion for the song of lament" (125). But then one must ask, why are these texts designated songs of **lament**?

Accoording to Plöger, the intent of the book as a whole is "to instill a disposition, amidst a crisis of faith, that can lead to a transformation." The author hopes to show Israel a way to overcome its suffering. The emphasis in chapter three falls on the confession of sin, in vv 40-42. The poet is motivated by a pastoral intent. Wrapping up his study, Plöger emphasizes that everything so painstakingly arrived at in chapters two through five was already presupposed in chapter one (p. 164). Chapter one could therefore be a synopsis of that which was more broadly developed in chapters two through four and in chapter five.

Brevard S. Childs

After a brief but valuable survey of previous research (pp. 591-93), Childs reiterates the general consensus that Lamentations arose as a reaction to the events of the year 587 BCE. Chapter three stands apart from the others in that it transforms these events into the personal fate of an individual, one who represents the people as a whole. The theological significance of Lamentations is primarily to be discerned in this third chapter. The "canonical shape" of Lamentations comes to the fore in the way chapter three captures the events of 587 BCE in cultic language and in a cultic context. Chapter three is written in the language of faith because here petitionary prayer has supplanted the dirge. However, Childs is incorrect when he says that the prayer in chapter three, cast in the traditional cultic language of Israel, has taken over the place occupied by the dirge in chapters one, two, and four. Even in chapters one, two, and four the element of prayer predominates, with only a few features of the dirge added on, and chapter five is a communal lament like those found in the Book of Psalms. It is difficult to understand how Childs can maintain that only in chapter three, but not in the other chapters, "the language of faith" (which is to say, cultic language) predominates. The communal laments in the other chapters likewise contain such features as invocation of God, plea for God's gracious intervention and, associated with the latter, confession of sins. Is it then the case that only the lament of an individual, and not also the communal lament, is "Israel's true form of supplication"?

Moreover, the third song by no means contains only liturgical or supplicatory language. On the contrary, of the five songs in Lamentations chapter three is the only one that abandons Psalm-like language (in its middle section, in vv 26-41) and takes up instead the language of wisdom and admonition. Given the way the author of chapter three has deviated from the unambiguously liturgical sections of the psalms whose style he is imitating, the notion of a deliberate transformation of historical into liturgical language is highly unlikely.

Delbert R. Hillers

In the matter of determining the genre, Hillers follows Jahnow and Gunkel. However, he is also of the opinion that only modest help for interpreting Lamentations is to be gained from form-critical study. These poems may well have been used on occasions of public mourning, starting as early as only shortly after the fall of Jerusalem. To be sure, no logical progression of thought is displayed in the songs. However, they do exhibit a clear psychological progression, best seen in the way the language advances from the detachment of third-person speech to the intimacy of first-person speech. This arrangement yields a sense of development. These lamentations primarily help the survivors express their nearly unspeakable horror and dread. The Book of Lamentations is, above all, simply an account of the terrors that swept over Jerusalem, terrors which entailed the loss of all the precious symbols that formerly mediated Israel's sense of trust and confidence in God. Lamentations expresses a pain that could still be mediated through these same words even centuries after the events themselves had transpired. Yet the book also contains an element of confession; it sets the terrible events under the prophetic announcement of judgment and does not deny the part played by the transgression of the people.

In the middle of the book, in chapter three, a deliberately unnamed person who has suffered under the wrath of God speaks while using the genre of the personal lament. This person, an archetypal sufferer (an "Everyman"), succeeds in gaining the confidence that God's goodness has not come to an end. Through this individual the poet is opening for the people a way to the future. This is the climax of the book; it is the focal point of the whole. When suffering comes, a human being should simply accept it, being submissive before God. This leads to the call for repentance. Starting with v 42 the connections are less obvious. Despite the disparate elements to be found there, Hillers maintains that the section comprised of vv 42-66 is a collective prayer.

The interpretation of Hillers is one of the few in which the lament, as lament, is taken seriously. Moreover, in the way he deflects attention away from the notion of a progression of thought—a feature which in any case is not to be found—and directs it instead to the progression from third-person speech to first-person speech, he has observed something essential for a proper understanding of the psalms of lament.

When it comes to interpreting the concluding section of chapter three, however, Hillers appears to become unsure of himself; he advances only conjectures.

Rainer Albertz

In his *Persönliche Frömmigkeit und offizielle Religion,* Albertz lays out the structure of Lam 3 and then directs attention to its middle section, vv 21-39 (pp. 183-85). The new perspective which Albertz brings to the material is the way he sees chapter three as illustrating how "the personal lament assumes a function of strengthening the whole people's faith" in God (p. 183). By this, individual piety becomes significant for the community's normative religion. Lam 3 is an individual's account of having been rescued by Yahweh. This account has undergone considerable secondary expansion. The middle section, vv 34-

39, is new material which breaks out of the boundaries set by the traditional genre; in these verses the rescued individual challenges the reproaches which the people have been casting against God. Albertz accounts for the mixing together of such different genre elements by saying that cultic procedures are being reflected here. In effect what happened is that, on the occasion of a public ceremony of lamentation, various individuals testified to their own experiences of having been rescued by Yahweh. Through their own avowals of confidence in Yahweh, they hoped to encourage the group as a whole, to help it find a renewed sense of direction. The gist of these individuals' avowal of confidence, uttered in v 24, is expanded and generalized in the following verses; their experiences of rescue are transformed into a general teaching. This teaching in turn serves to provide backing for the counsel to maintain "an attitude of submission" (referring specifically to v 27). The speaker in these verses intends to say something like this: As long as we maintain hope in situations of personal exigency we can also trust that Yahweh will rescue our people when the group is in dire straits. As long as such hope can be maintained, there is reason to continue voicing the communal lament.

It can be questioned whether the attitude of hope really is the same as that of submission. When Albertz concludes by saying there is reason to continue voicing the communal lament as long as one maintains hope in situations of personal exigency, that statement hardly accords with the challenge in v 39: "Of what do human beings complain? Let us all master our own sins!"[1] Albertz himself expresses a reservation in his note 137: "...the experience of helpless individuals does not hold true for groups with political power."

Otto Kaiser

Characteristic of Kaiser's interpretation is the way he understands the Book of Lamentations strictly as literature. He refers to the songs as reiterative poems, or as anthological poetry (as, earlier, Cothenet—for criticism of which see H. J. Boecker), and he views them wholly from literary perspectives.

---

[1] Cf. my entry "Gebet II. im AT" in *RGG* (³1958) III:1213-17.

His perspective comes to the fore already in his late dating of
the material. (According to Kaiser, the second song came into
being around the middle of the fifth century, the first song
sometime during the latter half of the fifth century, the fourth
song around the end of the fifth century, and the third song
sometime in the fourth century.) Kaiser quite deliberately
separates the origin of these songs from the catastrophe of 587
BCE. In his opinion they convey no accounts by eyewitnesses;
they are simply not a direct reaction to that terrible event.
Rather, the first four songs are spiritual poetry. Only the fifth
song is a traditional communal lament—although Kaiser
accounts for the origin of this song in literary-critical terms as
well, seeing it as a later outgrowth of an earlier kernel.

The Psalms, and the genres of the Psalms, bear no real
significance for Kaiser in his exegetic work on Lamentations.
This holds true even with regard to Lamentations' singular way
of blending elements from the plaintive lament and the dirge.
He likewise explains the relationship of the songs to one
another in literary terms. Chapter one is dependent upon
chapter two and, in fact, intends to correct it. Again, "...the
fourth song draws out the consequences of the first three."
Because chapter four is not a prayer, its continuation through
chapter five is necessary—although according to Kaiser chapter
five is not a prayer either, but rather a spiritual poem. Literary
dependency plays a considerable role. Very different sorts of
texts can be designated "lament." The whole of chapter five is
lament, as are vv 1-20 of chapter four and vv 20-22 of chapter
two. In the same vein, vv 9c and 11c of chapter one are two
"mini-laments." Kaiser designates 1:1-11 an "account of
suffering," [*Leidbericht*], which reads very much like an alternate
designation for "lament." Kaiser's alternate designation can be
explained by the fact that he regards these verses as an imitation
of a lament rather than a genuine one.

Chapter three presents an individual who, in a situation of
extreme peril, almost fell victim to despair. However, through
reflection upon the fundamentals of Israelite faith this individual
found renewed confidence in the divine succor. Out of this
experience the same individual summons the people not to
doubt the power of Yahweh. The speaker's own experience

assumes paradigmatic significance. The voice of the speaker is that of someone who survived the catastrophe of 587 BCE. However, since Kaiser would not have the third song appear until sometime in the fourth century, this can only mean that the poet is speaking in the guise of a survivor of those times. Consequently Kaiser repeatedly emphasizes how the poet appears in the guise of an eyewitness. Against this view, H. J. Boecker and others have rightly objected that the deeply moving pathos of those who speak in the laments in chapters one through five (excluding chapter three) would be difficult to account for if one assumes such a temporal distance from the precipitating events. The impression which most interpreters have received, namely that it is eyewitnesses speaking in the laments, has not been refuted by Kaiser.

Renate Brandscheidt

This study tries to find new criteria for determining the form and assessing the distinctiveness of the five songs. Particular emphasis falls on the third song, since the understanding of this song shapes the overall understanding of the Book of Lamentations. Brandscheidt characterizes chapter three as a "judicious lament of a righteous sufferer." It is a composition which incorporates elements from different genres. A single speaker makes use of the old genres and in the process creates a new form whose content both instructs and encourages (so also Plöger). It starts out in the autobiographical style of a Psalm 73. The section comprising vv 25-33 reflects upon the conduct of a human being in suffering, while vv 34-39 transmit insights from the wisdom tradition. Since sin is the ultimate cause of suffering, in v 39 human beings are prohibited from lamenting—those who survive to lament are still sinners. The lament directed toward God in vv 1-20 of chapter three exhibits behavior unfitting for the truly pious. On the other hand, the proper way to act is demonstrated in the call to confession in vv 40-41. Next comes an exegesis of chapters one, two, four, and five—material which Brandscheidt characterizes as "plaintive realization of divine judgment." The form-critical features do not suffice for determination of a specific genre here. Brandscheidt concludes that the occasion for the third song is the same as that for the book as a whole. The structure underlying both blocks of material is the same: lament—account—instruction—account—lament (p. 213). Only at the very end, in the summary to her investigation, does Brandscheidt emphasize that the Book of Lamentations is an interpretation of the events of 587 BCE from a Deuteronomic point of view. (Earlier on, in her exegetic work, she had made no mention of this.) Chapter three blends with the other songs of lament to form a literary (?) unity, not only of a redaction-critical but also of a form-critical (?) sort. From this it follows for Brandscheidt that the condemnation of lamenting in 3:39 ("a stance unbecoming for the truly pious") must apply to all five songs. In the conclusion to her study, the author once again underlines her negative assessement of lamentation. "Before the lament can be accorded a favorable response, one thing must be very clear to the people: Yahweh has ordained the punishment on account of the people's sin." Only "...when they have the proper attitude over against God are the people not prohibited from lamenting" (p. 212).

From this point of view, the lament has ceased to be simply a basic human reaction to acute suffering. Now lamenting is allowed only when one has the proper attitude!

S. Paul Re'emi

In his introduction Re'emi takes up the matter of the name of the book and its place in the canon. The canonicity of Lamentations was never contested. With regard to form, or type, it is a *qināh* (lament, dirge), a composition for the purpose of mourning the dead or responding to a communal tragedy. To be sure, a number of other formal components also appear, in chapter three especially elements of the personal lament. Altogether there are five self-standing songs, all of which except the fifth have been handed down in acrostic form: four songs of lament (chapters 1-4) and one prayer (chapter 5) of high literary merit. The songs were meant to be read in the context of cultic ceremonies of lamentation. Initially they served as a way for the remnant which survived the catastrophe to express their sadness and their pain.

As far as author and time and place of origin are concerned, Re'emi holds that Lamentations was produced in Judah—

probably in the vicinity of Jerusalem—in close temporal proximity to the catastrophe of 587 BCE. Chapter one was perhaps composed shortly after the deportation of 597 BCE (so also Rudolph). Despite its personalized point of view, chapter three was presumably produced at the same time as chapters one, two, and four. In any case all five songs arose between 597 (however, more likely 587) and 538 BCE. Jeremiah cannot be the author; in the light of 4:17-20 the author was quite likely a member of the royal court. The author was neither a prophet nor a priest; the author wrote out of personal experience. The first four songs stem from the same writer, while the fifth song was later added as a prayer. (On p. 128, however, Re'emi suggests that the author of chapters four and five was one and the same person.)

With regard to determination of genre, in his introduction Re'emi calls chapters one through four laments, while chapter five he calls a prayer. (Later on he also once refers to chapter five as a communal lament). There is a difficulty here in that no clear distinction is drawn between the dirge and the plaintive lament, which in turn blurs the distinction between the communal lament and the lament of an individual. In the introduction *qināh* is taken to mean either dirge or lament, referring either to mourning for the dead or to situations of public distress. In the Old Testament, however, *qināh* designates only the dirge, never a communal lament such as, e.g., Ps 80. To be sure, the lamenting cry and the motif of contrast are appropriately identified as characteristic elements of the dirge. In the same vein, crossovers from the lament to the genre of petitionary prayer are correctly recognized. For example, Re'emi notes how the acknowledgement of sin goes beyond the boundaries of the dirge in 1:5, and he remarks that "Where God is addressed directly [as in 1:9c and 11c] the dirge passes over into being a prayer" (see also 4:6, 19). Yet Re'emi assigns the songs as a whole to the category of the *qināh* (so, for example, chapter four "is composed in the style of a dirge"), while at the same time he states, with regard to chapter two, that the song has nothing to do "with a secular dirge" because it speaks of the actions of God. There remains a lack of clarity here, a defect which crops up again and again.

When it comes to evaluating the theological significance of Lamentations, the commentary of Re'emi exhibits a considerable difference when compared to most of the others. Here no devaluation of the lament, either direct or indirect, can be traced. The lament is acknowledged as having its own theological importance—a fact repeatedly recognized throughout the commentary.

According to Re'emi, Lamentations primarily arose out of the need felt by the oppressed remnant to give expression to their pain and their sadness. The intrinsic function of the songs is lamentation. Here Zion unfolds before Yahweh the horror of the situation and, with it all laid out, turns directly to God. In this way the description of what has been experienced is transformed into a prayer (commenting specifically on 1:20). In several places Re'emi speaks, either directly or indirectly, of an accusation or a reproach directed against God; behind the "O Lord, look at my affliction" of 1:9c (cf. also v 11c) stands "a silent reproach of the Almighty." He senses the same silent reproach against God behind the clauses which describe the terrible fate of the children (2:11-13). What have these children done that they must suffer so terribly?

Throughout the whole commentary runs the question which the songs of lament bring to expression in one way or another: How could God have allowed this to happen? An accusation against God also resonates through these laments (so, e.g. at 1:5,18-22; 2:2-9; 3:12; 4:16). The poet seems tormented by the question of how God could have so treated the people of God (4:12,16). The deeper reason for the crisis of faith lies in the fact that the people of God never thought it possible that such a calamity could happen. This went against the promises of God—promises which must certainly be eternally valid.

Re'emi holds that, in 1:16, the dismayed poet acknowledges the "terrible justice of God" and yet, in 5:20-22, presses the question of why. The people's dismay is too deep for words (1:16). Even the poet can offer no satisfactory explanation (2:18-20); his mind is tormented by doubt (5:22). In this "Why?" directed toward God one catches an echo of extreme dread such as that which comes to expression in Psalm 22— words uttered by Jesus on the cross. At this point Re'emi recalls the Holocaust and the agonizing question which arises out of it, namely whether God is still attentive.

In all of this the genuine theological significance of the lament is recognized. This runs contrary to all the attempts to devalue or to interpret away the feature of lament in the Book of Lamentations.

Re'emi's interpretation of chapter three, on the other hand, is not convincing. To be sure, he recognizes the difference between chapter three and the other chapters, with regard to form and content. However, he follows (explicitly) the interpretation of Weiser (see above, pp. 35-36) to the effect that these differences are transcended by a common pastoral tendency running through the material. Re'emi also follows Weiser in the way he sees the poet blending his identity with the people. To Re'emi it is evident that chapter three speaks of the fate and the experience of a single individual while at the same time dealing with the condition of the people as a whole. It is not correct, however, to say that the poet who so identifies himself with his people is also functioning over against them in some sort of official capacity. "The poet speaks to the people of his own deliverance" (referring to vv 52-61) and thereby consoles them. According to Re'emi, however, the poet is also admonishing the people to confess their sins and return to Yahweh. But this line of interpretation is impossible. The poet either identifies himself with his people or else he is fulfilling a task that has been laid upon him. One who is admonishing and instructing his people is thereby standing over against them; such a person cannot at the same time be merging his identity with the people. Failing to observe this distinction leads to some sharp contradictions. In his treatment of the opening verses of chapter three Re'emi says, "It is evident that the author is speaking of the experience of an individual." (Much the same is said with reference to 3:52-54.) But Re'emi continues by saying the poet is speaking of the suffering of his people on the occasion of the enemy's attack. The logic of this analogy would lead him to equate the individual's experience of deliverance with the people's experience of liberation. However, what the respective parties have experienced is thoroughly different, as can be shown quite clearly by the parallels which the author draws out of the Psalms.

It is even more difficult to understand how Re'emi can say, when dealing with 3:39-41, that v 39 is the proper response to the issue raised by a lament. Does he not recognize how it is typical of laments passionately to summon the hearers to lamentation (cf. 2:18-19), but that vv 39-41 abjure lamentation, instead summoning the hearers to engage in self-examination and to return to Yahweh? Re'emi's confusion is patent when he says, "Lamenting is of no help until they return to God."

In conclusion: In his interpretation of chapter three Re'emi again takes up the endeavor, already earlier attempted, to solve the chapter's difficulties through the thesis that the poet identifies himself with the people. When he does this, however, he only succeeds in demonstrating, more clearly than was recognized formerly, the dubious quality of such an endeavor. On the plus side, Re'emi's commentary makes an important and promising contribution in the way it takes seriously the lament precisely as a lament.

H. J. Boecker

It is advisable, at least initially, to view the five songs as independent entities. Quite likely the third song arose at a considerably later time than the others. The authors of the various songs were not members of any specific professional guild. "They were people who wrote their laments under the impact of the terrible events." (Boecker thereby rejects Kaiser's late dating.) The fifth song is a communal lament, while the other songs are of mixed genre. Since the work of Jahnow it has been widely acknowledged that motifs characteristic of the dirge have been taken up in the first, second, and fourth songs. The third song comprises an entity in its own right. Their acrostic form tells us that these songs did not originate in the cult, but they soon came to be used in ceremonies of lamentation amidst the ruins of the temple.

As do others, Boecker seeks to discern some sort of intrinsic arrangement of the material through variations in the speaker. As he himself comes to realize, however, little success is to be gained by such an approach. This much is shown when, for example, Boecker emphasizes that Zion is the central figure in both halves of chapter one but then goes on to consider how one could also designate Yahweh as the central figure. The same holds true when Boecker says the clause in 2:17—to the effect that everything was planned and ordained by Yahweh— is the central idea of the second song but then cannot go on to show how this idea is there developed. The reason for the latter is simple: laments have no central ideas. It is also striking how Boecker characterizes 2:11 ("my eyes are spent with weeping") as a "self-manifestation of the poet" which interrupts the flow of thought. As did Brandscheidt, Boecker finds 4:21-22 problematic; he does not see that these clauses correspond to an established concluding motif familiar from the the psalms of lament.

Chapter three he recognizes as a distinctive unit with a very complicated structure. In Boecker's opinion, the supposition that chapter three is a compilation of formerly independent texts cannot be maintained because its acrostic form testifies to its fundamental unity. He does not consider that this acrostic form might be secondary (a thesis advanced—it will be recalled—already by Löhr). 3:25-39 presents a progressive train of thought which serves to help the hearers assimilate the disaster as one sent by God to instruct and to admonish. The speaker is someone whose personal suffering has become interwoven with that of the people. The third song also belongs in the context of the events of 587 BCE. The same speaker holds forth in all the verses of the song. Here Boecker runs into difficulties, however, since he must in the final analysis fall back on bald assertions. How can it be said that it is throughout one and the same speaker when this person, in vv 49-50, issues a summons not to give up lamenting until God once again turns with favor toward the people but, in v 39, admonishes the people to give up lamenting? In what way can the speaker then serve as an example?

With regard to the theological significance of Lamentations, Boecker starts from the fact that a description of the calamity constitutes a decisive feature in all the songs. "All five songs reflect the impact of the terrible disaster....The poets who composed Lamentations have faced up to the reality of the misery....Distress and misery ought to be vocalized, indeed they need to be cried aloud!" The terrible event is understood as

God's judgment, and God's judgment was in turn a response to Israel's guilt. As far as anticipation of future renewal goes, the songs are rather reserved. However, mixed in with the laments one does find prayers.

In sentences such as these the fact that Lamentations consists of **laments** is taken seriously. No attempt is made to devalue their significance. However, also for Boecker chapter three serves as the focal point of the five chapters. Chapter three seeks to assimilate the catastrophe within a theological framework. Its main theme is that hope is possible if grounded upon the divine faithfulness. "The one speaking this prayer invites the community to follow along on a path leading out of the current state of distress and toward a better state of affairs confidently expected in the future."

Now, however, if what Boecker says at the beginning is accurate ("It is most likely that chapter three arose considerably later [than the other four]."), it is important to proceed carefully here. This means that chapter three was addressed to a situation which was no longer identical to the situation presupposed by the other four chapters. Moreover, this means that the section in the middle of chapter three which instructs and admonishes the addressees to adopt an attitude of silent submission—the admonishment to leave off lamenting, to engage in self-examination, and to return to Yahweh—applies to a significantly later period of time.

Bo Johnson

According to Johnson all five chapters in the Book of Lamentations come from the same author. To be sure, this author employed different styles in the various sections of the book. Still, Lamentations is an unbroken literary work. It answers a question which the text itself raises; it offers a solution to a problem which the text itself brings up. Johnson neither takes up the fact that the book deals with laments nor enters into discussion about the difference between the dirge and the plaintive lament.

Johnson thinks that the individual songs are arranged purely in terms of a conceptual pattern. He holds that the first four songs consist of a "fact half," a central point, and an "interpretation half." However, this view rests on very weak footing. Johnson regards chapter three as the middle of the whole Book of Lamentations, and he places particular emphasis on the central section of this chapter. Here he finds the definitive answer to the question posed by the Book of Lamentations. That this central section deviates sharply from its surrounding material, in both form and content, presents no difficulties for Johnson. Quite at the end of his study Johnson raises the question of whether chapter five might not be the oldest section of the book. However, certain difficulties arise because of the arrangement of the material in this chapter: "The verses are added to each other with not very much coherence...." Most interpreters prior to Johnson had designated chapter five a communal lament, a genre whose defining traits are clearly recognizable here. An intepretation of Lamentations such as Johnson's—one along purely conceptual lines and which ignores the preceding history of interpretation—is hardly able to uncover the meaning and the intent of this book.

Summary
Time of Composition
The *terminus a quo* for the origin of the Book of Lamentations is firm. These songs must have arisen after the destruction of Jerusalem in 587 BCE; they clearly come "from the era after the fall of Jerusalem" (Gunkel). There is also widespread agreement regarding the *terminus ad quem*. Most interpreters hold that Lamentations arose before 538 BCE, when the exiles began to return; only a few deviate from this point of view. (Here one must ask, however, whether it is possible to be even more precise about the *terminus ad quem*, specifically whether it can be pushed back to 550 BCE).

There is also a fairly broad consensus placing the origin of Lamentations quite soon after the event of 587 BCE, since the direct impact of that calamity can still be felt in these songs. According to Gunkel, the material is "...not all that far removed from 587." The majority of intepreters say the same, or much the same; most introductory works likewise take this stance. Not a few go even farther and assume that the authors of the songs were eyewitnesses to the calamity. Some assume a different time of origin for each song (thus Löhr, Sellin / Rost, Kaiser). Where this stance prevails, some assign the earliest point of origin to songs two and four or to songs four and five (Löhr, Haller), or even to songs one, four and five (Feuillet). In the same vein, others say that songs one and three are later (Eissfeldt, G. W. Anderson), while others assign pride of place in this category to song five (Gunkel, Weiser, Dhorme, Re'emi). With regard to chapter three, a majority pleads for a late—or even a very late—time of origin (Budde [who speaks of this chapter as a "secondary piece of work"], Löhr, Sellin / Rost, Haller, Meek, Boecker).

Several interpreters identify as the time of origin for the Book of Lamentations the broad stretch between 587 and 538 BCE; however, they do so tentatively and without finding solid reasons for such a dating (Meek, Feuillet, Eissfeldt, Rendtorff, Schmidt). Rudolph assumes that chapter one arose shortly after 597 BCE; so far only Weiser has agreed with this. In the nineteenth century interpreters occasionally advocated a late dating for all the songs; more recently only Kaiser has defended this point of view. (According to Kaiser, the earliest of the songs arose around 450 BCE and the most recent during the course of the 300's. [In a personal correspondence, Kaiser informs me that he has now abandoned his hypothesis of a late dating for Lamentations; see his article in the new EKL.) Boecker attacks such late dating. Still, Lachs sets the fifth song in the Maccabean period.

Place of Composition

It is almost unanimously accepted that the songs originated in Jerusalem. A few interpreters would not want to exclude the possibility of an origin within the community of the Babylonian exiles.

What can be concluded, with regard to time of composition, on the basis of this broad consensus regarding place of composition? The most important feature is that the *terminus a quo* stands firm. There is no serious challenge to the view that the songs represent a reaction to the disaster of 587 BCE. That the *terminus a quo* for the origin of a biblical book can be so firmly established is something of a rarity. The reigning certainty regarding this point has, as one of its consequences, the fact that differences of opinion with regard to the other interpretive issues lose some of their significance. Whether or not several of the songs were composed at some temporal remove from 587 BCE and the time when the other songs were composed is not all that important, at least not as long as the reference of the texts in question to the precipitating event remains assured. A dating of all five songs in their proper chronological sequence is something that can never be determined with any degree of certainty—a fact which was already emphasized by Gunkel. Also, those researchers who cautiously accept the Edict of Cyrus (538 BCE) as the *terminus ad quem* are to be seen as in the right. However, it must be noted that this *terminus ad quem* merely serves as a temporal boundary; the songs bear a positive relationship only to their *terminus a quo.* To be sure, not all researchers accept that the authors of the songs were eyewitnesses to the events of which they speak. On the other hand, no convincing argument has yet been advanced that these songs could not have come from eyewitnesses.

The scholarly certainty regarding the *terminus a quo* has yet another consequence. If it is really the case—as so many interpreters accept—that the songs arose under the impact of the destruction of Jerusalem, then the assumption of a late time of origin (as, formerly, Kaiser) becomes highly unlikely. Would an author more than a hundred years after the event really write as though he had actually been present at it? That the thesis of a late time of origin for Lamentations will still find much of a following is simply too much to assume. Let it be mentioned here only one more time that Lachs assigns to the fifth song a date in the Maccabean era. Since he bases his hypothesis solely on a consideration of isolated sentences, however, his hypothesis is unsatisfactorily grounded.

Author(s)

There are three possibilities for the authorship of this material: Lamentations has a single author, Lamentations has several authors, or it is impossible to determine how many authors Lamentations has. These three points of view are defended in approximately equal measure. Those interpreters who are open to the possibility of either single or multiple authorship (Weiser, Hillers, Kraus, Schmidt) have obviously taken for granted that the texts themselves do not yield sufficient information to make a determination about authorship. Gunkel grounds his decision for multiple authorship thus: "Each poem has something distinctive about it." (Arguing in similar fashion are Meek, Pfeiffer, Eissfeldt, Robert / Feuillet, Sellin / Rost ["only one author is an impossibility"], Haller, Osswald, Boecker—as well as, among earlier interpreters, Budde and Löhr.) Re'emi accepts a single author for chapters one through four, but he posits another (later) author for chapter five. Dhorme repeatedly speaks of three authors: the one responsible for chapters one, two, and four, the one who produced chapter three, and the one who composed chapter five. Several interpreters suppose that the authors belonged to definite guilds or professional circles. Thus Kraus refers to circles of official cultic prophets or the Jerusalemite priesthood, Kaiser speaks of Levitic temple singers, Smend talks about prophetic circles, and Osswald makes reference to a firmly fixed cultic tradition. Boecker turns against this point of view by suggesting that the authors were not members of any particular profession but instead were just people who had been deeply influenced by the terrible calamity. (In the opinion of Re'emi, they were members of the royal court.) Already Gunkel stressed how the poems give voice to the mood of ordinary laypersons who bore the brunt of the disaster (so also Re'emi). In keeping with this is the fact that the songs speak the language of ordinary discourse, not that of any specialized group, school or profession. This much can be seen even in the sorts of analogies used in the songs.

Several interpreters defend the view—more or less emphatically—that all the songs have the same author (Nötscher, Rudolph, Weiser, Plöger, Gottwald, Brandscheidt, Johnson and Cothenet). These are the same people who defend the literary unity of chapters one through five (esp. Brandscheidt). One gets the impression, however, that this thesis grows not so much out of the texts themselves as out of these individuals' interpretation of the texts.

Out of the preceding discussion concerning the authorship

of Lamentations one can see, once again, that the traditional view of Jeremianic authorship has for all intents and purposes been abandoned. In modern times this traditional view has been emphatically defended by Wiesemann in several publications, but his views have found no support. Even Rudolph's assumption of an indirect Jeremianic authorship has not been taken up by anyone else. In addition to the difficulties already mentioned, the position which advocates the same author for all five songs suffers from the lack of its defenders' ability to point out semantic traits that could support their position. This especially holds true with regard to 3:26-41. So the assumption of multiple authorship remains the more probable.

Composite or Unified Work?

As Plöger confirms, the prevailing tendency in critical scholarship until recently was to start with the assumption that the Book of Lamentations is a collection of originally independent texts that were joined at some later date (thus Gunkel, Löhr, and most of the introductions). At the present stage of scholarship, however, there is a tendency to investigate the connections between the chapters. Plöger does this himself, and the same tendency is exhibited in the work of Kaiser and Brandscheidt. Of course, where one assumes a single author and views chapter three as the midpoint of the book as a whole (as is done especially by Brandscheidt and Johnson), then it follows as a matter of course that Lamentations is to be understood as a coherent work divided into five chapters. Conversely, it also follows as a matter of course that the thesis of origination at different times leads to the view of Lamentations as a composite work.

Regardless of stance on this question, unanimity prevails in regarding Lamentations as a work of high literary or poetic merit (e.g., Dhorme, Cothenet, and Re'emi).

Determination of Genre and Form-Critical Characteristics

With regard to determining genre and form-critical characteristics, the basic works remain those of Gunkel (esp. his *Einleitung in die Psalmen*, co-authored by Joachim Begrich).

With particular reference to the Book of Lamentations, special attention must also be paid to Jahnow's investigation of the dirge (see above, pp. 1-11), as well as to Gunkel's entry "Klagelieder Jeremiae" in the second edition of *Die Religion in Geschichte und Gegenwart.* To date the history of interpretation of Lamentations has exhibited no extensive controversy, but neither has there been any critical testing of the theses advanced in the above-named works. For example, when Hillers says that the determination of the genre must proceed on the basis of the work done by Gunkel and Jahnow, until now no one has thought to contest such a view. To be sure, several interpreters do not expect very much to come of a determination of the genre and the form-critical characteristics (as, e.g., Hillers himself). In other cases it is maintained that the information necessary for a determination of genre is insufficient in the case of Lamentations (so, e.g., Brandscheidt). Frequently a study will begin by noting the similarity of Lamentations to the Psalms and the genres of the latter, but then this insight goes on to play no role in the actual exegesis. An example of this occurs when Brandscheidt says, "The rationale for the striking juxtaposition of a consoling word to Zion right next to a threat against Edom (in Lam 4:21-22) cannot be explained." In saying this she overlooks the fact that the dual wish (or the petition developed along a positive as well as a negative pole) is a fixed element at the end of the psalms of lament. However, there are other studies in which the Psalms and their characteristic genres are never even mentioned (so, e.g., Gordis and Johnson).

In the matter of determining genre, unanimity of opinion holds sway at one point; all interpreters designate chapter five a communal lament. Even though a few employ other terms to designate this chapter, they nonetheless all agree in their estimation of its character (cf. Smend: "Only chapter five offers a clear example of a distict genre"). This wide-ranging agreement rests upon the *Einleitung* of Gunkel / Begrich, which treats Lam 5 as a communal lament. Not one of the interpreters we have noted has yet challenged the prevailing unanimity by noting that, at one very important point, chapter five deviates from the pattern of the communal lament. It is because of the deviation at this very point that Lam 5 has been handed down, not as one of the communal lament psalms, but rather in the collection which comprises the Book of Lamentations. (See our exegetic work on Lam 5, in chapter four).

Wide-ranging unanimity of opinion also exists with regard to the designation of chapters one, two, and four as dirges. (Gunkel actually here used the expression "communalized [*politisches*] dirge.") I count fifteen interpreters who agree with this designation. Smend sees in the dirge the basic form-critical element of the songs in the Book of Lamentations; Plöger sees the dirge as providing the underlying structure for this material. Eissfeldt's attempt to determine the structure of chapter one is noteworthy. In keeping with the prevailing opinion, he designates this song a dirge. However, he then says the following concerning vv 9 and 11: "Already in 9c and 11c the style of the dirge is abandoned." He then proceeds to argue that, in fact, this song cannot really be a dirge. Eissfeldt's attempt to determine the structure of chapter one comes very close to recognizing that, in fact, we are here dealing with a psalm of lament. I have already shown, in my discussion of Jahnow and Gunkel (see above, pp. 28-29), that the unanimity of opinion regarding the genre of chapter one rests on shaky ground. In fact, Jahnow has not demonstrated the existence of a structured dirge, complete with fixed sequence of motifs, corresponding to the structures evident in Psalms. The designation of Lamentations one, two, and four as dirges stands in need of correction.

Several interpreters are more cautious. According to Schmidt and Boecker, motifs from the dirge have been taken up in chapters one, two, and four. (This much is correct.) Other interpreters (Hillers, Kaiser, Brandscheidt) designate these same chapters "mixed forms." (Cothenet emphasizes that they more closely resemble communal laments than dirges.)

All but completely lacking is serious consideration of why, in the whole of the Old Testament, it is only in these three chapters that the plaintive lament is brought into association with the dirge. What does this association signify? (Dhorme does not even mention the dirge.) Only Gottwald—if I read him correctly—has thought about this matter. At any rate, he suggests that the dirge has become associated with songs of lamentation because the author of this material wrote while surrounded by scenes of death and burial. Here it is recognized that the uniqueness of the situation led to the combining of the dirge with the plaintive lament. Boecker also makes at least passing reference to this reason for the association. Some interpreters note a transition from lamentation to prayer, either through the change from a third-person to a second-person mode of speech or through a direct addressing of God (so, e.g., Re'emi).

Life-setting

Since the time of Gunkel it has been the practice also to raise the question of the "life-setting" (*Sitz im Leben*) of the Biblical material. Of course, interpreters who view Lamentations in purely literary terms find this question irrelevant. In fact, however, there is no other book in the Old Testament whose contents force the question of the life-setting more strongly than Lamentations. The question whether these laments are genuine or artificial simply intrudes of its own accord. If they are artificial, then they have no setting in the public life of the community; they are the outgrowth of the writer's own imagination. If they are genuine, on the other hand, then they have as their life-setting some public proceeding which characteristically took place at a specific locale and at a particular time, some proceeding which involved giving vocal expression to suffering. It would have been a proceeding which made room for suffering to be expressed and heard (so Re'emi). Of course, many interpreters think that the voices of eyewitnesses are to be heard in Lamentations. However, they tend not to draw from that observation the really important conclusion, namely that these laments are an outgrowth of oral tradition. In other words, behind these laments stand oral proceedings in which the dread events that were witnessed are preserved in memory and passed on by word of mouth. It is difficult to understand how, in the wake of the efforts of Gunkel, Jahnow, and the Scandinavian school [which placed a heavy emphasis on the role of oral tradition in the development of the Biblical material—*Trans.*], none of the interpreters of the Book of Lamentations has paused to consider whether an earlier stage of oral transmission might not also lie behind the present composition. The problem with which we are dealing comes to the fore particularly in the way many interpreters discuss the origin of Lamentations. If they take up the question of the life-setting at all, they tend to say that, while these laments may not actually have been composed for cultic purposes, they were nonetheless employed in the cult as soon as they appeared in written form. Almost none of the interpreters of Lamentations has taken seriously the notion that these laments might actually have been spoken by the shocked survivors as they mourned the catastrophe of 587 BCE—or, moreover, that these same laments might then have been preserved by those survivors and passed on to the wider circles of their acquaintances and descendants. What all of this would amount to is the existence of a genuine oral tradition for these laments. Apparently, such a possibility has struck most interpreters as too strange to contemplate. The conviction that a book must first be written before its material can be employed in cultic ceremonies of lamentation seems to have been so strongly entrenched as to block awareness of other possibilities. One must also assume that the oral tradition lying behind these laments continued long after a few of them were written down and, indeed, that it continued even after the several steps in the task of putting them together to form a collection had been carried out.

In any case, that some sort of oral proceeding was a constitutive feature of the life-setting of these laments in the Book of Lamentations is firmly anchored in the Biblical tradition itself. Most Biblical exegetes concur in seeing the rites mentioned in Zech 7 and 8 as referring to ceremonies commemorating the day on which Jerusalem was destroyed. These passages indicate that the laments of the Book of Lamentations early on formed a part of the liturgy for the Ninth of *Ab* within Jewish cultic tradition—a practice which has been continued in the Office of Holy Week in the Roman Catholic church. On the basis of these passages Sellin / Rost correctly conclude the following: "Perhaps with the exception of the third, from early on the individual songs were employed in memorial services on the anniversary of the destruction of Jerusalem." Re'emi agrees, and in a similar vein Bentzen says, "It is very probable that the poems have been composed for use at such mourning services. They seem to come fresh from the impression of the catastrophe." All the interpreters assume that the laments in the Book of Lamentations, once written down, were employed in memorial services commemorating the day Jerusalem was destroyed. The custom of reading these laments on the day commemorating the destruction of Jerusalem continues right up to the present time in the context of Jewish worship. However, the use of these laments is hardly restricted to this one day. To cite the comments of Professor D. D. Vetter (Bochum) in a letter he sent to me, "The significance of this collection of laments far exceeds their annual recitation. As frequent references in the Talmud and the existence of their own midrash (*Echa Rabbati*) show, the laments of the Book of Lamentations have been an object of continual study on the part of pious Jews. In similar fashion we see on every day of fasting proclaimed in response to a crisis, from the Middle Ages right up until recent times (and especially during times of persecution and banishment), a form of cultic lamentation shaped by the Book of Lamentations."

Two interpreters in particular have asked how the use of these laments in cultic contexts relates to their acrostic form. However, they have come to somewhat differing conclusions. Boecker writes, "Their acrostic form tells us that these laments did not originate directly out of cultic proceedings, but rather that—once written down—they quickly came to be used in a cultic setting." Kraus, on the other hand, states, "It is possible that Lam 1, in its acrostic form, is already a secondary development of the original lament as employed in the cult." The issue of the acrostic form deserves fuller discussion. Here it is only important to note that the acrostic form is not an original feature of the lament. If one takes as the starting point the earlier phase of oral transmission, then it follows *eo ipso* that the acrostic form is a secondary development.

Structure and Arrangement

The importance of structure, or of inner arrangement of material, is recognized and appreciated by almost all exegetes. They are also united, however, in recognizing that it is very difficult—apart from chapter five—to discern a structure or to perceive an arrangement of the material in the Book of Lamentations. No unified train of thought can be found here; the songs exhibit no unambiguous flow of ideas. Observations to this effect occur frequently in the writings of the interpreters of Lamentations. Löhr wrote already in 1906, "The author advances his few ideas without any clear development." This often-encountered observation actually betrays the expectation that there ought to be some clear train of thought appropriate to these songs—that it would be some sort of defect if such were in fact missing. However, the question is not asked whether Lamentations might have some sort of structure quite different from a train of thought, something other than a structure based on a flow of ideas. If this question were asked, the way to answer it would lie close at hand: The sequence of clauses and sections in Lamentations must correspond to that exhibited by the Psalms. (This is obviously the case with regard to chapter five.) However, until now no interpreter has attempted a precise structural comparison between Lamentations and the Psalms. As has been widely noted, only Lam 5 offers no difficulties in the matter of structure; its arrangement is easily recognizable because it is free from the necessity of beginning each new sentence with the next letter of the Hebrew alphabet. (Only Johnson argues to the contrary here.)

The difficulties regarding structure thus hold for only chapters one through four. To be sure, the presence of such difficulties is not always admitted. This becomes clear in the case of contrasting evaluations of the same text, and also in the case of inconsistencies in the work of the same author. The question whether a consistent train of thought was ever intended by the author of the songs in the first place is left hanging. The whole issue is simply evaded by the many interpreters who substitute comments about the content, on a verse-by-verse basis, in place of attention to the difficult issue of structure. Even interpretive headings placed over the whole text, or over parts of the text, cannot be too closely phrased; they must be more or less stereotypically worded. (This is easily seen by comparing the superscriptions generated by various interpreters.) Most common is the attempt to divide the text according to different speakers; change of speaker is supposed to serve as the basic criterion for arranging the material. However, there is frequent change of speaker only in the first song; in the others the speaker changes only rarely or not at all. Moreover, this criterion really does not work even in the case of the first song because here one speaker is interrupted by another—a feature which, as several interpreters note, has a disruptive effect. Even apart from this effect, however, it is highly questionable whether the change of speaker is meant to have any structural function at all (see the excursus on pp. 138-40).

The unresolved difficulty of explaining the sequence of the parts in these songs is particularly obvious in a number of comments made by the interpreters of Lamentations. Where they seek to explain a dubious connection between sentences, they generate comments such as the following: "In v 17 the speaker demands to be heard"; "In vv 18-22 Zion once again begins to speak"; "Zion, who herself enters into the discourse" (a remark found no less than six times!) or "Zion interrupts the speaker"; "Zion confesses"; "...those directly affected are themselves given an opportunity to lament"; "The cry sounds forth the theme"; "The petition is directed to Yahweh in hymnic form"; "The thoughts of the poet alternate from...to..."; "Now the poet slides into the roll of an eyewitness"; "Before the lament can be voiced one thing must be clear to the people"; "The singer now once again takes up the theme of..."; "From there the singer goes over to..."; and "in this context the poet recalls...."

To this must be added the evident perplexity in the area of terminology. The various forms of speech on display in Lamentations are identified in downright arbitrary fashion. The very same author designates the text as a whole a "song of lamentation" [*Klagelied*] but then goes on to say, "The actual lament begins only in v 20" or "[chapter] 3 is a personal lament, ending in a prayer." Often the element of petition, a characteristic form-critical feature of a psalm of lament, is independently identified as a "prayer"—and then so complete and independent a psalm as chapter five is identified in the same way. One and the same sentence is characterized now as a lament, now as a prayer. A clause is designated a "mini-lament" [*Kleinklage*], then shortly thereafter an "impulsive sigh" or a "miniscule psalm of lament." A thorough follow-up on just what a lament is, or just what a prayer is, nowhere occurs in the work of these interpreters.

Finally, some interpreters abandon the customary form-critical terminology and generate interpretive scenarios which have only a remote relationship to the texts. They then attempt to force the texts to fit into those scenarios. Examples of this occur when Brandscheidt maintains that the precipitating occasion for the third song is the same as that of the other four (her pp. 225-31), or when Johnson divides the first four songs into "fact halves," central points, and "interpretation halves."

This overview adequately suffices to show that the discussion of the structure, or the internal arrangement, of the Book of Lamentations must be built upon a new foundation.

Lam 3 in Relationship to Lam 1, 2, 4, and 5

Most interpreters draw attention to the singular nature of chapter three within the five chapters of Lamentations. For example, Boecker says, "Chapter three forms a singular whole," and Dhorme comments that chapter three must have a different author than chapters one, two, and four. However, the singular nature of chapter three is explained and evaluated in very different fashion. With the evaluation of chapter three, it is important to note that a radical shift has taken place. In fact, this shift is the most important one in the whole history of research upon the Book of Lamentations. Back when the criteria for interpreting Lamentations were primarily literary-critical in nature—one might just as well say, before Gunkel—Lam 3 was overwhelmingly viewed in negative terms. Budde judged chapter three a "derived work of totally secondary quality"; Stade's estimate of the chapter was similar. Gunkel himself adopted the judgment of Budde: "Chapter three quite clearly shows signs of being a derived work." In his *Introduction*, Pfeiffer calls chapter three "the most artificial." Similarly, Meek points out that the third song lacks originality, and Löhr sees in it "the mark of a scribe." Correspondingly, chapter three is regarded by many interpreters of this period as the latest segment of Lamentations (see above, pp. 54-55). Then a very significant shift of a full one-hundred-eighty degrees took place, a shift already intimated in a remark by Löhr. Löhr viewed chapter three as the latest text in the collection, but he also supposed that the author of chapter three was at the same time the final redactor of the collection as a whole. It was the intent of this author/redactor that chapter three serve as the midpoint of the collection.

For Haller the religious significance of Lamentations lies particularly in chapter three. That this chapter forms the center—the core or the pivot—of the Book of Lamentations is also the opinion of Rudolph, Nötscher, Weiser, Kraus, Hillers, Plöger, Gottwald, Childs, Boecker, and Johnson. Boecker calls it "...the central song of Lamentations." Brandscheidt goes the farthest when she maintains that the overall understanding of Lamentations depends upon one's understanding of chapter three. Such wide agreement regarding the central, indispensable significance of chapter three is little short of amazing. In fact, I have yet to come across a clearly contrasting opinion. Only Gunkel's point of view shows a marked deviation from the norm: "The chapter does not give unity and focus to the whole book; rather, it stands apart and is to be judged on its own."

Evaluation of Lam 3 as a Literary Composition

By most interpreters chapter three is designated a "song" or a "poem." In other words, it is regarded from the outset as a unified composition, even though such an evaluation is made without argument (e.g., "The unity of the song presupposes..." [Kaiser]). Such an evaluation lies close at hand because of the acrostic form, which in this song is especially pronounced (emphasized in particular by Boecker). On the other hand, there are a few interpreters who regard chapter three as a composite work. Thus Brandscheidt writes, "Lam 3 is a composite work which combines elements of various genres." O. Plöger describes Lam 3 as a "synthetic unity." Brandscheidt agrees with Plöger on this point: "Plöger is correct; here a single speaker makes use of the old genres and, through them, creates a new form that has an instructive and inspiring impact."

However, this characterization is imprecise in that, while it holds true for the expansion in vv 26-41, it does not suit the whole text, 3:1-66. Along this same line, it is a very risky venture when Weiser, Rudolph, Plöger, Brandscheidt and others suppose that 3:1-66 was composed by the same author who wrote the other songs. The differences in speech are simply too great.

It seems this much is sensed where reservations are voiced regarding the internal unity of chapter three, and the homogeneity between chapter three and the other chapters. Weiser feels that chapter three differs somewhat from the other songs, although he conjectures that the divergent parts are held together by the strength of a common spiritual tendency (thus also Re'emi), while Kaiser maintains that "The song as a whole is a primer with didactic-paradigmatic intent." However, all of these attempts to establish the unity of chapter three actually apply only to parts of its sixty-six verses. A thesis advanced during the earlier phase of research to the effect that chapter three "arose through a process of combining several precursors" (Gunkel) is rejected by several exegetes (Gunkel himself, Boecker, Kraus [by implication]). Gunkel accounts for chapter three by explaining that it arose in a late period, stylistically speaking, when the boundaries separating the various genres had become blurred. Kraus fluctuates in his explanation and asks "whether the whole chapter did not come into existence at a certain remove from the events depicted, as a secondary composition crafted out of songs and cultic utterances." Similarly, Rendtorff observes that "It almost has the effect of being an independent liturgy." Eissfeldt leaves open the possibility that the juxtaposition of chapter three with the others might at least represent the earliest instance of commentary upon those songs. The net effect of all these remarks is a demonstration that the explanations so far offered with regard to the composition of chapter three, in distinction to the other songs, do not yet suffice.

Individual and Community in Lam 3

All recent attempts to determine the internal arrangement of chapter three start with the assumption that the song is a unified literary composition, a song or a poem whose conceptual arrangement necessarily becomes an object of inquiry. None of these attempts fully concurs with the others. A particular difficulty facing these attempts arises with trying to associate what is said by an individual with what is said by a community. Especially in cases where chapter three is seen as the core of the whole collection, interpreters must concern themselves with the fact that here Jerusalem's lament over the catastrophe of 587 BCE recedes completely into the background. Chapter three is fully stamped by an individualizing character; it both begins and ends in the form of a personal lament—as is generally admitted. This problem crops up in different ways, as a comparison of the attempted solutions of Löhr and Hillers shows. As long as Jeremiah was regarded as being the author of Lamentations there was no problem; it was the prophet himself who was speaking in chapter three. It was for this reason that the affirmation of Jeremianic authorship persisted for so long and continued to have an influence in the assumption of an indirect form of Jeremianic authorship (Löhr, Pfeiffer, Meek, Rudolph). Obviously, the reasons for arguing against Jeremianic authorship speak also against the attempts to associate the prophet indirectly with Lam 3. The explanation of Budde and Stade to the effect that a single individual is speaking throughout the whole chapter, and that the chapter therefore deals only with personal issues, has generally been given up. This is so especially because such an explanation does not adequately deal with the complex situation in chapter three—something recognized already by Löhr. For a long time now a number of interpreters have taken the "I" of 3:1 in a collective sense; the discussion concerning this stance is clarified in Löhr's summarizing remarks. This particular interpretation must be abandoned because many verses—such as v 27—only make good sense when they are read as referring to a single individual, and also because the "I" must on several occassions clearly be distinguished from the people as a whole. The same objection applies to the thesis that some representative of the community is meant by the "I" of this chapter (Keil, Ewald, Oettli, Ricciotti, Rinaldi).

The notion of a "corporate personality" seems to offer a new solution to this problem, for often in the Old Testament a whole community's experiences are presented as though they had happened to an individual. Anderson advances this sort of explanation; Gordis does the same, though he speaks instead of a "fluid personality" ("individual and nation are blended together"). More recently, this approach has been adopted by Re'emi. However, the notion of a "corporate personality" really does not help to explain chapter three, because in Lam 3 one encounters in close juxtaposition clauses which can only be referring to either an individual or to a community.

Because all these explanatory attempts fail, interpreters have taken the stance that one must simply rest content with the fact that individual and community stand juxtaposed in Lam 3, even though this state of affairs cannot adequately be accounted for. Rendtorff explains, "The precise nature of the sufferer here remains a mystery." Hillers refers to "a typical sufferer, an Everyman." According to Eissfeldt, "A suffering figure is presupposed as well known." Brandscheidt adds, "In the opinion of most interpreters the poet himself laments in chapter three (so also Weiser, Rudolph, Kraus, Boecker, etc.) and, to be sure, in the language and with the authority of a Psalmist" (likewise Weiser).

From this state of affairs several interpreters come to a conclusion that seems necessary to them even though it is not grounded in the text. Thus Kaiser writes, "We have to suppose that some connection exists between the suffering of the individual and that of the people." This connection is supposed to be the fact that both have a common enemy. As formulated by Boecker, "The suffering of the speaker is tightly intertwined with that of the people"—again, they have the same enemy. Nötscher emphasizes that "The poet regards himself as one with his people, he regards his own suffering as part of the national affliction" (so also Re'emi). Another explanation carries the preceding one a step further; it is also no more than a hypothesis. This "Everyman," the unknown sufferer whose passion is so tightly intertwined with that of his people, is described as a teacher or a consoler or an admonisher, as one who delivers a penitential sermon to the people. He feels himself called to speak in the name of the people (Nötscher); he draws upon his own personal experiences in order to have a pastoral effect upon the people (Weiser). Indeed, many interpreters speak here of a paradigmatic significance and a pastoral intent (including Plöger, Hillers, Boecker, and Re'emi). All these explanations presuppose the unity of 3:1-66, as though that were something given without question. For example, Kaiser takes it as self-evident that "The song (i.e., chapter three) as a whole is a primer with didactic-paradigmatic intent, directed to how suffering Israel can overcome its distress." Kraus characterizes the whole chapter as "paradigmatic proclamation and instruction of the community." However, this is not the case. At most it can apply only to the middle section of the chapter (the part prepared for by the "I" of 3:1 [so Weiser]), but not to all of 3:1-66.

These two hypotheses—the hypothesis that the suffering of "Everyman" is bound up with that of the people, and the hypothesis that the whole text (3:1-66) is parenesis and instruction—not only both lack foundation in the text, but they also conceal the one feature decisive for an adequate explanation of Lam 3. This particular text, if heard on its own terms, deals unambiguously with the catastrophe of the year 587 BCE in not a single one of its clauses. Not only is there missing any reference to the hardship which the people had to bear on the occasion of this catastrophe, but also one does not find here the feature typical of chapters one, two, and four, namely the combining of the dirge with the plaintive lament. One gets the impression that the interpreters of chapter three have simply failed to perceive how far removed are its clauses, with their edificatory or pastoral language, from the bloody reality of the event of which the other songs speak. Can one really say this chapter is the culmination of the lamentation which takes place in the other songs?

In other words, the affirmation that "in chapter three the issue is the same national catastrophe that is being dealt with in chapters one, two, four, and five" (Weiser, similarly already Eissfeldt) must be examined anew. There have already been some indications of a defection from the *communis opinio.* The earlier assumption that chapter three was constructed out of several pre-existent works is still occasionally mentioned, even though generally rejected. Gunkel emphasizes that chapter three stands on its own, that it does not presuppose the other chapters and does not intend to give unity and focus to the book as a whole. Anderson considers the possibility that, "on account of its individual character, it is possible that chapter three does not refer to 587 at all...." Hillers concedes that chapter three bears little relationship to 587 BCE; Plöger holds out for such a relationship only in the case of vv 45-48; Boecker makes the same claim for vv 34-36 and 43-48. For Rudolph, only an indirect connection exists between chapter three and the events of 587 BCE.

However, none of this has yet led to a change in the understanding of Lam 3. In my opinion, the desired change can only be brought about in so far as the insights of an earlier phase in the history of the interpretation of Lamentations are taken up anew: on the one hand, the insight that Lam 3 was put together from components of divergent origin (Löhr, Budde) and, on the other hand, that the language of this chapter's middle section—with regard to both content and form— points to a late origin, suggesting that this material arose long after chapters one, two, four, and five.

Closer Determination of the Middle Section of Lam 3

The middle section of Lam 3 is divided and arranged by the interpreters in various ways. However, even Gunkel's analysis of the structure of this section is not convincing. Most interpreters use similar categories to designate its contents: consoling insights of various sorts, ideas drawn from Israel's wisdom tradition, didactic or parenetic expressions similar to wisdom teachings (Weiser, Kraus, Brandscheidt, Boecker). Some place emphasis on the text's themes of reflection upon the change of fortune and confession of sins, others upon the theme of pious submission (Gottwald, Hillers, Kaiser, Albertz). Brandscheidt emphasizes the disavowal of lamentation on the part of guilty individuals.

As this summary indicates, most of the interpreters agree that this middle section is of didactic-parenetic nature and has, at least in part, a sapiental character. They see its intent as an admonishment toward proper behavior and its goal as a call to confession of sins and a return to God. On the other hand, most attempts to determine more precisely the internal relationship of the various parts of this middle section fail. The same goes for the analysis of its language and its origin, as well as the relationship of this section to the other parts of chapter three, and beyond that to the other laments in the book as a whole. (For particulars, see the following excursus.)

Excursus: Conceptual Structure and Order of Events

In most of the interpretive efforts the arrangement of the text is understood to be primarily conceptual in nature. Nearly all the authors we have surveyed inquire after the conceptual ordering of the individual songs of lament—i.e., after the train of thought, or the progression of ideas. Beyond that, they inquire after the conceptual relationships existing among the five songs, or the five chapters of the book. The talk is steadily of themes, of leading ideas, of problems and their solutions, of questions and their answers.

> Löhr: It is the thoughts and sentiments of the poet that are here expressed.
>
> Nötscher: The individual songs are arranged according to their main ideas.
>
> Boecker: Main ideas are stated and then developed in a flow of thought; an intellectual process is at work.
>
> Gordis: The poems exhibit a flow of thought.
>
> Johnson: A purely conceptual arrangement is present.
>
> Rudolph: The flow of ideas is not strictly logical. The poet treats a certain theme; when the theme is interrupted, the poet later comes back to pick up that theme again.
>
> Nötscher: The individual songs exhibit no strictly controlled flow of ideas; now one theme comes to the fore, now another. No unified plan underlies the collection.
>
> Kraus: An intelligible flow of ideas, or a systematic structure, occurs only in chapter five.
>
> Plöger: The songs do not allow for recognition of a purposeful arrangement of ideas.
>
> Haller: The songs exhibit no logical progression of ideas.
>
> Johnson: Lamentations is an answer to a question, a solution to a problem or a resolution of a conflict; there is "not very much coherence."

Kaiser: The fourth song draws consequences from the first
   three songs.
Plöger: The first chapter is a synopsis of chapters two
   through five.

These are but illustrations. Now, if the principle of
arrangement for these songs of lamentation was primarily
conceptual in nature, that would mean that they had been
planned as a whole, had been thought out, had in effect grown
out of the mind of an author. However, songs of lamentation
are misunderstood when they are seen in this way. A conceptual
structure shapes a speech, an essay, a treatise, an investigation,
a commentary, an academic lecture, a presentation, a letter. It
does not do so with a lament. To be sure, the ideas of an author
play a role in the genesis of a song of lamentation, at the time
of its composition when he writes it out. However, this does not
make the song of lamentation an intellectual work. Although
one can find specific associations between ideas within the
songs of lamentation, associations which grow out of an author's
powers of reflection, nevertheless the overall ordering of the
material is not primarily determined by intellectual
considerations. Rather, the arrangement is governed by a
course of events—as also happens with psalms. Songs of
lamentation are prayers. They are reaction to something that
has happened. In the lament the one who suffers appeals to the
one who brought about the suffering. In the complaint against
God something happens between the appellant and the One to
whom the appeal is directed. Since psalms are prayers, where
something in fact transpires between the human being and
God (or between God and the human being), they are primarily
shaped by a sequence of events. It is the underlying sequence
of events which gives structure to psalms, in their various
genres. The phenomenon of psalmic structure (of an
articulation of parts within psalms) means that a psalm is to be
understood as a whole, the various motifs of a psalm as aspects
of a totality—as sentences which acquire their meaning in
relationship to that totality. Conversely, the phenomenon of
psalmic structure does not refer to thoughts arranged in
sequence, thoughts organized along the lines of conceptual

logic. The components of psalms are, instead, stages in a sequence of events.

In the work which, more than any other, established the form-critical method of investigation (Gunkel / Begrich, *Einleitung in die Psalmen* [1933]), too little attention was paid to this particular feature. The history of the phenomenon of prayer determines that, in the Book of Lamentations just as much as in the Book of Psalms, we are dealing primarily with sequences of events.[2] The history of prayer in the Old Testament unfolds in three phases; there is, in effect, a three-fold history of calling upon God. In the earliest phase, only short expressions where employed when calling upon God. We find such prayers embedded in narratives. (The earliest lament-prayers are identified above, on p. *1*.) Here the prayer constitutes but one aspect of the event as it unfolds in the narrative (e.g., the lament of Cain [Gen 4:13b-14] or the lament of Samson [Judg 15:18]). Here the prayers are stages in the overall flow of events described in the narrative. These narratives, in turn, are not interrupted by the insertion of a prayer (although we might be inclined to see it this way). On the contrary, without the prayer they would have been seen as incomplete. At this early stage, each prayer intrinsically belongs to its encompassing event, whether it is a lament, a supplication, a petition, a cry of praise, or a vow to render praise.

In the second phase in the development of prayer in the Old Testament, the various motifs which earlier had stood alone as prayers in their own right were brought together to form a psalm. This process is tied to the history of worship in ancient Israel. Nonetheless, even the psalms are shaped by a sequence of events. This can be seen in the way the avowal of trust follows upon the lament proper (with the *wāw adversitivum* falling between), which then leads to the petition, and finally to the vow to render praise. This sequence of events is shown quite clearly in the narrativized psalm of praise (psalm of thankgiving) with its retrospection upon the state of distress: I cried out—God heard—God rescued me. To be sure, themes of a conceptual

---

[2] Cf. my entry "Gebet II. in AT" in *RGG* ([3]1958) III: 1213-17.

nature embellish this basic structure in the Psalms, such as reflections upon the mighty acts of God (as in Pss 8 or 139). Basically, however, both the Psalms and Lamentations are shaped by their connections to events. Something *happens* in them. Therefore, one ought first to inquire about the underlying sequence of events.

Matters changed only in the third phase, the phase of the extensive prose prayers such as one finds in Ezr 9 or Neh 9. Only at this stage is a conceptual arrangement of the material dominant, although between the second and the third phases one can locate transitional forms.

The Theological Significance of Lamentations in Prior Research

In most interpretive efforts a dual answer has been given to the question of the theological intent of Lamentations: (a) either these laments offer some sort of explanation, or (b) they point to a way out of a crisis.

> Nötscher: The poet pursues a religious aim; he wants to make clear that the calamity is seen as an instance of divine judgment.
>
> Meek: These texts arose not only to commemorate the fall of Jerusalem but also to explain the meaning implicit in this as an act of Yahweh. The goal of the text is that Israel should draw the proper conclusion from the event.
>
> Rudolph: The intent is to lead the people to a proper understanding of the ways of Yahweh and thereby also to show them the right way to act.
>
> Weiser: The Book of Lamentations aims to help the people find their way back to God in the midst of a serious crisis of faith. The poet summons the people to self-reflection and to repentance.
>
> Plöger: Addressed to a situation of religious uncertainty, the book seeks to resolve doubts and open a way for the people to come to a new understanding.
>
> Hillers: Lamentations tries to make clear the hidden meaning of the catastrophe.
>
> Boecker: The book aims to open a channel through which Israel can assimilate the disaster theologically, namely by seeing it as a divine judgment.

Schmidt: In the form of prayer, Lamentations seeks to interpret the situation as one brought about by human guilt.

The level of agreement among almost all the interpreters is astounding. One gets the impression that the question about the intent of the Book of Lamentations finds a clear and unambiguous answer in its texts. There are only a few interpreters who offer quite a different answer to the question about the intent of Lamentations.

Hillers: The Book of Lamentations is, first and foremost, an account of the terror and the dreadful happenings which befell Jerusalem. Above all, these laments offered a means by which expression could be given to the distress and the agony accompanying the event— reactions which, through these laments, have echoed down through the centuries (so also Re'emi, and in much the same wording.)

Brunet: The laments in the Book of Lamentations are an outcry of a devastated people; "it is they that have put pain in the Bible."

Boecker: "All five songs have arisen under the terrible impact of the catastrophe of 587...The depiction of calamity is a decisive aspect of each song...The poets of Lamentations have withstood the reality of misery...Distress and agony should not only be expressed, it should be shouted!"

Rendtorff (who at least says this by implication): Lamentations gives evidence of being a reaction to the catastrophe of 587.

If one now considers the answer of the majority to the question about the intent of Lamentations and contrasts this with the answer of the minority, then one will have to admit that the answer of the majority has grown out of reflection upon the text of Lamentations. The answer of the minority, on the other hand, reflects the immediate impression which the text makes. About this there can hardly be any question. If someone who has had no prior acquaintance with the Book of Lamentations reads the text, such a person will agree with the answer offered by the minority. One can say even more and still be certain. The answer of the majority rests primarily upon Lam 3 and apparently already presupposes the interpretive judgment that this chapter forms the culmination, or the mid-point, of the book as a whole. It must be noted that only the larger group of interpreters speaks about an intent underlying the origin of Lamentations. If these laments are truly reaction to an event, "an outcry of a devastated people," then no statement about intent is required in the context of discussion about the origin of Lamentations. However, it is certainly the case that an element of intent stands behind the process by which Lamentations was transmitted. These laments were passed down, initially by word of mouth and subsequently in written form, in order that future generations could in some sense participate in the precipitating event (so also Re'emi).

In any case it is at least certain that the answer of the majority does not adequately correspond to the nature of Lamentations. As a whole, Lamentations has neither an explanatory nor an admonitory function. At best only 3:26-41 could be described in these ways; all the other songs are simply laments. There is an obvious connection between the determination of the intent of Lamentations on the part of the majority and their devaluation of the lament genre. Because they recognize no theological significance to the lament as such, it follows that for them the intent of the text must be other than—or at least more than—lamentation. They persist in this evaluation even when it contradicts the obvious character of the text.

All interpreters agree in holding the recognition of the catastrophe as a divine judgment and the corresponding confession of guilt as theologically significant. There is no need to list specific names, since there is no dispute among the interpreters here. Nor is there disagreement that those responsible for the composition of Lamentations stand in the line of succession to the pre-exilic prophets of judgment, and therefore in opposition to the prophets who tended to speak easy words of assurance.

At this point, however, it is important to make a distinction. One gets the impression that some interpreters think those responsible for the composition of Lamentations saw their task first of all as one of awakening an awareness of guilt as the true cause of the catastrophe. But such a view hardly corresponds to the texts. Rather, in Lamentations we hear the voices of those who, in the terrifying experience of the destruction of Jerusalem, have already come to the awareness that Israel itself was to blame for this collapse. No one first needed to be brought to this awareness, in order thereby to awaken a sense of guilt. Ackroyd likewise emphasizes that these laments presuppose the recognition and the confession of guilt: "The acceptance of judgment is inherent in the Lamentations" (p. 46). In similar fashion, Hillers speaks of an "Amen" to the announcement of judgment (see above, pp. 42-43). There is yet another significant difficulty. If 3:26-41 really issues a call for self-examination and for a return to Yahweh, for a "submissive spirit," then this really does not fit a situation in which the people, under the impact of the most extreme suffering, have already come to an awareness of guilt in the presence of Yahweh—a situation attested in all of the songs. One is simply not taking seriously these profound confessions of guilt as voiced in the other songs when, in view of such confessions, 3:26-41 is nonetheless read as a summons to admit guilt. An obvious conflict also arises between the middle section of chapter three and the other songs to the extent that 3:26-41 is seen as calling for silent submission in the presence of suffering and as prohibiting lament as such. (Cf. 3:39: "Of what do human beings complain? Let us all master our own sins!") This stands in obvious tension with the call, otherwise issued throughout Lamentations, not to leave off imploring Yahweh until such time as He once again turns in favor toward His people (e.g., 2:18-19—but also 3:49-50!).

In several works the attempt is made to determine the theological significance of Lamentations on the basis of tensions out of which these songs arose. With Gottwald, it was the tension between the Deuteronomic doctrine of retribution and the reality being experienced by the people. Why must the people suffer so terribly immediately after a serious attempt at reform? Albrektson objects to this interpretation, finding no difficulty with the view that the political catastrophe was perceived as a divine judgment upon the historical guilt of

Israel and so was seen as consonant with the doctrine of retribution. According to Albrektson, the significant tension underlying the theology of Lamentations is that between the doctrine of the inviolability of Zion, derived from the Zion-tradition, and experienced reality. Childs dismisses the interpretations of both Gottwald and Albrektson, and he does so on the same grounds for each. For Childs the real tension grows out of the "canonical shape" of the Book of Lamentations. This tension is the conflict between those for whom the catastrophe really did amount to some sort of definitive end and those who saw the avenue of divine mercy as still being open (p. 596). In his stance Childs starts from the view that chapters one, two, and four are dirges, following Jahnow: "The dirge has been replaced by Israel's true form of supplication" (p. 595). However, if chapters one, two, and four are not dirges but rather communal laments into which motifs from the dirge have been inserted, then this interpretation does not hold. Communal laments, every bit as much as personal laments, are prayers; both speak "the language of faith."

As with Childs, many see the real theological concern of Lamentations to lie in an overcoming of a religious emergency or a crisis of faith. Weiser stresses how "at the center stands the religious emergency triggered by the fate that has befallen the people" (similarly Rudolph, Kaiser, and others). This can be understood to mean that Lamentations is dealing with the specifically religious dimension of the catastrophe—a dimension brought about by a conflict between prior religious conviction and harsh reality, a dimension residing in some inner or "spiritual" domain, a dimension mirrored in the souls of those affected by the catastrophe. But his would not be compatible with the texts, much less with the way of speaking about God throughout the whole of the Old Testament. The Old Testament does not know of some religious domain separate from the rest of reality. When Lamentations asks "have you totally rejected us, are you indeed so angry with us?" (5:22), it is not a "religious emergency" which is being expressed, but rather a crisis of being as such. If God had fully rejected them, then that would mean the end of their very lives. It is a matter of a crisis on the plane of existence as such when the survivors ask, "Is there yet some hope?"

Similarly, when several interpreters emphasize that Lamentations served to enable a theological assimilation of what had happened (Schmidt, Boecker), their views likewise do not correspond to the text—if they mean to be speaking of a purely spiritual process or of some conceptual undertaking. The issue in the text is much more one of survival as such.

In sum, Lamentations did not arise in order to answer certain questions or to resolve some problems or conflicts. These songs arose as an immediate reaction on the part of those affected by the collapse. Those so affected then expressed themselves in lamentation. The "meaning" of these laments is to be found in their very expression. Questions of a reflective sort arose out of these laments only secondarily; such questions are of subordinate importance to the phenomenon of lamentation itself. The real significance of laments resides in the way they allow the suffering of the afflicted to find expression. Hillers also understands the matter in this way:

> Thus Lamentations served the survivors in the first place as an expression of the almost inexpressible horror and grief they felt.... Lamentations is so complete and honest and eloquent an expression of grief that even centuries after the events which inspired it, it is still able to provide those in mute despair with words to speak (p. xvi; similarly Re'emi).

Devaluation of the Lament

In contrast to the above comment by Hillers stands a noticeable tendency, discernable in almost all commentaries upon and investigations of Lamentations, to devalue the lament or to speak of it with depreciatory reserve. This devaluation of the lament does not directly stem from the interpreters of these texts themselves; it is rooted in a preunderstanding. It is thought inappropriate to lament before God; lamentation is not compatible with proper behavior toward God. Lament disturbs or detracts from a pious attitude toward God. This point of view repeatedly and vehemently comes to the fore especially in the commentary by Brandscheidt. Such a depreciatory attitude toward the lament reflects the fact that lamentation has been severed from prayer in Christian piety throughout the history of the church. In the Old Testament lamentation is an intrinsic component of prayer, as is shown in the Psalter with its high percentage of psalms of lamentation. In the Christian church, on the other hand, the lament no longer receives a hearing. This transformation took place without being discussed in the official theologies of the church. Nowhere is there a reasoned rejection of lamentation as an intrinsic component of prayer; the severing of lamentation from prayer took place without comment. One of the consequences of this state of affairs is that, in Christian interpretation of Lamentations, the laments are simply not allowed to be laments. Either they are recast as something else ("they are not really laments, but rather...") or they are devalued for what they are. This devaluation of the lament is carried out in a number of different ways.

1. It can be stated quite explicitly. Haller says that, over against the laments, the prayer motifs reflect a "higher point of view," that they "rise to a higher plane." For Plöger, "in a song of lamentation the element of lamentation itself has no independent significance, regardless of how extensive this element might be." Brandscheidt puts it similarly: "The issue involved with the lament is not the lamenting over a disaster as such, but rather the disaster as pictured against the background of a recognized guilt" (231). With Weiser one finds remarks such as the following: "What is significant about 1:12-16 is not the...expression of plaintive sadness," or "The lament becomes the place in which God is sought" (16); with reference to 3:21-4 he speaks of "the danger which lies concealed in protracted lamentation," and in 3:25-30 he finds the admonition "not to lose oneself in mournful lamentation." Rudolph speaks in a similar vein: "One ought not carry on as do those people who are continually lamenting!" (236), and "However here as well the poet refuses to get stuck in mere lamentation" or "The prophet demands confession instead of grumbling" (255). Kraus writes concerning 3:39: "He rejects their murmuring (literally: their indulging in lamentation)." Once again Brandscheidt firmly holds that "...in 3:39 lamentation and accusation is forbidden as an unsuitable form of behavior for the pious."

2. A second form of such denigration is similar to the first, but it is not quite so blatant. This is the shifting of emphasis away from the lament as a means by which immediate reaction to suffering can find expression and toward some sort of spiritual or theological mastery of the situation. The element of suffering as such, and the language in which it comes to expression, become of secondary importance. This is the case, for example, in the investigations of Gottwald and Albrektson, investigations in which the phenomenon of lament attracts almost no notice at all. Much the same holds true with Childs and Johnson, as well as with Kaiser, for whom the lament as the "temporally bound" feature is not what is truly significant. The truly significant is what has grown out of that feature, namely its a-historical "teaching." "We elevate the content of these songs to the status of universal statements, because in this way all that is tied to the mere particulars of the time falls away. What gets distilled out of the content of these songs we designate as doctrine" (p. 304).

With several interpreters the lack of interest in the lament as such also comes to expression in the way they simply ignore the unique combination of the lament of a sufferer with the dirge, a phenomenon that occurs only here in the Old Testament.

3. For some interpreters the lament stands totally outside the domain of prayer; indeed it is explicitly differentiated from prayer. Thus, for example, with regard to 3:62-66 Weiser writes how "...out of the lamenting community there develops a community that prays in confidence." Here those that lament are not those that pray; rather, the former become the latter when they leave off their lamenting. Again, with regard to 1:18-22, Weiser writes that "...the lament here turns toward God and from this point on becomes prayer...the lament is no longer projected into the void." In a similar fashion Kraus says, with regard to 2:1, "...that the lament becomes a prayer." Along the same line go the words of Brandscheidt: "...out of the lamenter there comes a remorseful sinner."

4. The lament is really a confession, as Kraus asserts with reference to 2:1 ("The lament is an acknowledgement of the judgment of God") and 1:21-22 ("...a lament before God, which fundamentally is nothing other than a confession to God"). Weiser's observations sound much the same: "That Yahweh is the ultimate author of suffering is a theme raised by the lament to the plane of an acknowledgement of divine judgment" (referring to 2:1); referring to 1:21-22 Weiser says, "The lament is an acknowledgement of divine judgment" (p. 12).

5. Also rejected is the possibility that the lament could at the same time be an indictment of God (i.e., a charge directed against God) or a reproach (a rash unburdening of the heart). Kraus says, with regard to 1:20, "These questions are not to be taken as reproaches or as accusations against God." Weiser cautions, with regard to 1:18-21, "...as though the lament contained an accusation against God" (speaking similarly with reference to 2:20).

6. A lament can only be evaluated positively when something else is added on to it. Kraus writes, with reference to 5:16, "The lament acquires its real significance from the confession of sin, an element which protects the lament from losing itself in fruitless complaining." With regard to 3:43-51 he writes, "The lament becomes something valuable only in so far as it is constructed upon some other foundation." Here it is stated with uncompromising bluntness that the lament has no value in and of itself. Brandscheidt agrees: "Before the lament can be intoned, one thing must be clear to the people..." (p. 212), and "Lamentation is not prohibited to the people when they have the proper attitude toward God" (p. 234). This remark certainly must mean that, on the occasion of the conquest of Jerusalem, only those were permitted to lament who had the proper attitude toward God! Much the same is asserted by Kraus: "Those who came out of it alive have no cause to lament" [!]. Only once does one encounter a normal, fitting comment about lamenting, when Weiser remarks as follows with regard to 5:2-18: "The lament is the natural expression of a suffering individual."

With this pervasive, general, and multi-faceted devaluation of the lament, it is hardly surprising that none of our interpreters has noticed the contradiction between an understanding of the lament as comes to expression in the summons to lament in 2:18-19 ("Cry aloud to Yahweh, lament, O maiden Daughter Zion...!") and in the rejection of lament in 3:39-40 ("Of what do human beings complain? Let us all master our own sins...!").

In conclusion, when it comes to evaluating the theological significance of Lamentations, this much remains basic for our interpreters: Convinced that it corresponds to the text and is rooted in all of the songs of lamentation, they see as theologically significant the recognition that the catastrophe was God's judgment upon Israel. Associated with this recognition is the people's acknowledgement of their guilt.

Neither of these themes, however, is first introduced into Lamentations by the voices which there speak. Rather, these two themes arose directly out of the experience of the collapse, and the experience itself led in turn to the acknowledgement of guilt. Those who speak in the five chapters of Lamentations, or the composers of these songs of lamentation, presuppose this experience and this recognition. These two themes are intrinsic elements of the laments as initially intoned. These themes do not serve to instruct or to admonish. To the extent that they did this, they did so only secondarily.

Most of the answers to the question of the theological significance of Lamentations are shaped by the conviction that the middle section of chapter three, the admonition to acknowledge sins and return to Yahweh, forms the center of all these songs of lamentation. Where this view holds, it follows that little or no independent significance is accorded to the lament as such. However, this devaluation of the lament is simply incompatible with the fact that, by and large, the Book of Lamentations is composed of laments and needs to be read as such. Given how pervasive and multi-faceted the devaluation of the lament is in the history of the interpretation of Lamentations, one can readily conclude that we here find ourselves in the presence of a contrast between what the texts say of God and what the interpreters bring to light concerning God or the relationship between human beings and God. Only in the commentary by Re'emi is the lament not devalued; only here, rather, is it recognized as possessing its distinctive theological significance.

Chapter Three

On Interpreting Lamentations

Lam 1-5: The Collection

This interpretation of Lamentations differs from the usual sort. Typically, an interpretation of Lamentations starts by assuming that some author or poet planned out in advance what to say. Hence, the usual sort of interpretation aims to describe the basic ideas of the book against the background of the conceptualizing process assumed to have generated it. However, Lamentations is not literature—not even theological literature. This material came about as reaction to a concrete event. Therefore, Lamentations is closer to being "a direct account of suffering" (Kaiser) than it is to being poetry crafted by some author. This material generates no intellectualized theology, nothing that could be summed up as a teaching. What we have here are laments, and it is simply as laments that they are best heard.

They were intended to be heard, first and foremost, by the One to whom they were directed as prayers, by the One who is directly addressed in them: God. Initially these laments were handed on by word of mouth. Only later did they come to be written down, that they might also be heard by subsequent generations. Thus they became part of the tradition and the history of those subsequent generations. The result is that these laments, while initially significant as the never-to-be-repeated reaction of eyewitnesses to the precipitating event, **also** became venerable words to be contemplated by the descendants of those original lamenters.

If a lament is a reaction to a specific event, then the structure of the lament must in some fashion correspond to that event. The outline of the precipitating event must be discernible in the words of the lament. When one is dealing with an historical account, different factors come into play. An historical account is necessarily somewhat objective; it is marked by a sense of distance from the event about which it reports. Laments lack the objective perspective of historical narrative; an aura of immediate engagement permeates the lament. So, by their very nature, laments lack objectivity. Indeed, if laments were to arise out of disengaged reflection, then they would not exhibit the form-critical regularity that they do. This follows from the fact that a poet or writer, working in the mode of an historian, has the freedom to formulate thoughts about the event under consideration (in our case, the fall of Jerusalem). The historian can organize and arrange those thoughts as personally seems most fitting. With laments, however, the structure has to exhibit certain standard features; the genre of the lament as such imposes various structural constraints. This much has already been demonstrated in the way the Sumerian lament over Ur has a number of traits in common with the laments over Jerusalem. The important point is that it shares these traits despite the absence of any literary dependency. (One structural feature common to the lament genre—others could be mentioned—is the petition that follows upon the actual words of lamentation.)

Now, since each of the five chapters in the Book of Lamentations is a structurally unified text, interpretation of Lamentations must start out by directing attention to these units, to the individual songs or poems. The "book" of Lamentations, in other words, is a collection of separate songs or poems, each of which once stood independently and therefore is first of all to be investigated and understood on its own. We have the same kind of situation here that we have with the various groupings of psalms within the Psalter. If this is our starting point, then we must go on to ask how the separate texts relate to one another. This latter question initially runs up against two solid facts. The first is that chapters one, two, and four so closely resemble one another, in terms of their structure, that their commonality simply cannot be overlooked (so also

Dhorme). All three chapters are introduced by the typical cry of woe, '*êkāh* [ah!/alas!]. In all three songs elements of the dirge are joined to the basic communal lament. All three give the impression of standing quite close to the fall of Jerusalem and of going back to eyewitnesses of that terrible event. Agreements in matters of detail are also numerous. The assumption lies close at hand that these three chapters once formed an independent little collection in their own right. In any case, these three chapters form the kernel of the collection as it now stands.

The other solid fact is that the fifth song is a communal lament, or at least very closely resembles the communal laments in the Psalter (so also Gunkel and, following him, most other interpreters). At the same time it is obvious that the major section of chapter five, namely vv 2-18, closely resembles the songs of lament that comprise chapters one, two, and four— sometimes right down to the very wording. So, chapters one, two, and four form the core of the Book of Lamentations, and chapter five stands very close to this core. Since chapter five is also a communal lament, basically the Book of Lamentations is a collection of communal laments—laments whose distinguishing feature is the way they have also taken up motifs characteristic of the dirge. The adoption of these motifs took place because of the exceptional occasion out of which these songs arose.

The third song, on the other hand, falls entirely out of the pattern. In this song the lament of an individual plays a dominant role. This results in a fundamental difference in the form. The other four texts (Lam 1, 2, 4, and 5) are self-enclosed songs of lament; each is a unified composition with a recognizable starting point and an obvious point of conclusion. Conversely, chapter three is a composite work, one constructed out of several different types of psalms or psalm-fragments. In addition, a wholly different sort of expansion has been inserted into the song. For these reasons alone it is necessary to investigate the nature and the structure of chapter three apart from the other chapters. (That chapters one, two, and four belong together, while chapters three and five in some sense stand apart, was recognized as a problem for interpretation already by Thenius in 1855.)

The Lament and Its Significance

When one surveys the history of the interpretation of Lamentations, one finds that throughout this history the question of the true nature and significance of the lament has never been raised in a disciplined manner. Since Lamentations is the only book in the Bible to be called after this particular genre, it would seem only appropriate to raise the question of the nature of the lament. That the question has not heretofore been raised is probably grounded in the fact that everyone already seems to know what a lament is and therefore thinks it unnecessary to pursue the matter any further. However, the history of interpretation also shows that there is hardly any real agreement about the nature of the lament. On the contrary, notably differing forms of speech are designated laments by various interpreters, even to the point where texts which definitely are not laments are still so designated.

There is, however, a deeper reason why the question has not been pursued. Consciously or unconsciously, for many interpreters the very word "lament" carries a negative connotation. For many, it is not quite proper to lament; for many, it is better to learn to suffer without lamenting. This especially holds true in the area of one's relationship to God. In this domain the lament supposedly has no place at all; lamentation is widely thought to be without authentic theological significance. Such a stance is rooted in the history of prayer—more precisely, in the absence of lamentation in prayer as traditionally practiced in the Christian church (see above, pp. *81-85*). In the Bible, however, lamentation has genuine integrity; in the Bible, lamentation reflects the very nature of human existence. Just as pain and suffering are characteristic of human existence (Gen 3), so also the expressing of pain is intrinsic to life as we know it. Lamentation is the language of suffering. When a child is born, its first utterance is a cry. Throughout life, the heartfelt cry remains the immediate, pre-verbal expression of pain. The cry of Jesus on the cross (Mk 15:37 and par.) is most deeply human. Moreover, the cry too deep for words is common to all creatures capable of generating sounds, since all creatures share in the fate of being consigned to suffer (Rom 8:22). When pain becomes verbalized, the cry becomes a lament. As such, it initially appears in the form of a single word, or of a word expanded to a single phrase. One can find in Biblical narratives illustrations of the cry of lament in the form of one sentence (e.g., "If thus, why do I go on living?" [Gen 25:22]). To the extent that these narratives deal with pain and suffering, the lament appears in them as an intrinsic component. Examples of this include the laments of Cain (Gen 4:13-14), of Abraham (Gen 15:2), of Rebekah (Gen 27:46—in addition to Gen 25:22), of Samson (Judg 15:18), of Hannah (implied in 1 Sam 1:3-8), and of Hezekiah (implied in Isa 38:1-4, under the impact of the following vv 10-20). The list could go on. In such narratives one sees the lament in its primal setting, in the place in human life where it originally appears and to which it authentically belongs. The lament resembles a child's crying. (Cf. Gen 21:16-17: "...but the child began to cry aloud. Then God heard the child's crying."[1])

The lament can become separated from its original setting in life as directly experienced; it can be transformed into a self-standing unit of speech, a song or a poem of lamentation. This leads to the genesis of the structured lament, a distinctive genre whose identifying features correspond to the traits which typify suffering as such. Such a lament, transformed into a linguistic genre, can still closely resemble the primal cry of lamentation, but it can also bear little direct resemblance to its point of origin. It is a peculiarity of the lamentation-texts in the Old Testament that the laments which occur in them—be they poems, psalms, or songs—never really lose their tie to the primal setting of all laments. Nowhere in the Old Testament is a lament so reshaped as to become something that might have been generated solely in the mind of a poet. Never does an Old Testament lament become a true elegy, for example. Rather, Old Testament laments remain true laments, reactions to genuine instances of pain. This is shown, above all, by the laments of Job in the Book of Job. One can see the same, however, also in Deutero-Isaiah, in the psalms of lament in the

---

[1] Dr. Westermann's reading of this verse follows LXX; see the critical apparatus in **BHS**—*Trans.*.

Psalter, in Second Esdras/Fourth Ezra, and of course in the Book of Lamentations. In all of these places the lament has been preserved in the form in which it would once have actually been uttered.

To a modern person, terms such as "lament" or "lamentation" designate thoroughly secular or profane realities; they no longer have anything to do with one's relationship to God. The Old Testament laments identified just above, however, are all addressed to God. Even when this is not explicitly stated, as in the case of the child's crying in Gen 21:16-17, the text goes on to make clear that it is God who hears the lament. ("Then God heard the child's crying.") In the Old Testament, it is seen as only natural, as normal, that a lament is directed toward God. For those who lament in the Old Testament, God is the One who can take away suffering. That sufferers have been given the opportunity to pour out their hearts before God, precisely in the language of the lament, is seen in the Old Testament as itself an expression of divine mercy. Modern psychotherapy has long recognized that lamentation can have healing power, that openly expressing the pain of suffering can ameliorate its impact upon the sufferer. In the Bible, then, the liberating possibility is opened up for sufferers to bewail their suffering directly to God. In the Bible, sufferers are allowed to voice their laments directly to their Lord.

Excursus: The So-called Accusation against God

In form-critical parlance, one of the characteristic elements of the lament genre is the "accusation against God" [*Anklage Gottes*]. The Bible itself has no term for this feature; it appears as a sub-component of a larger whole, namely of the fully developed, threefold lament. Psalm 13 is an especially clear example of the lament as a fully developed genre. This same genre also shapes the Book of Job (Job laments his own fate —Job laments about his "friends"—Job laments directly to God).

The phrase "to pour out one's heart before God" captures the essence of what occurs in this particular component of the lament. In the "accusation against God," the lament is specifically directed toward God; this is the element of the genre where the lament is set before the heavenly throne. However, nothing like an actual charge—in the legal sense—is leveled against God. In other words, the "accusation against God" is not an indictment of God. Such a nuance is ruled out because an indictment presupposes a judicial forum, but the existence of any such forum—one before which God could be held accountable—is impossible in the Biblical understanding.

What we mean, then, by the phrase "accusation against God" can only be explained by reference to the texts themselves—that is to say, by reference to the texts in which this feature appears as an element of the fully developed lament. The characteristic feature of this element is that, in it, God is either the subject of the discourse or is addressed directly. Only when viewed in conjunction with the other two elements of the fully developed lament can these sentences be spoken of as "accusation against God." The lament conveys the full range of the language of suffering. Because the human being experiences suffering along three different axes, there are three elements intrinsic to the lament's structure.

In the Old Testament one encounters an "accusation against God" in those texts where an individual, or a community, has been afflicted with such severe suffering that it can no longer be comprehended. Specifically, this means where the pain can no longer be envisioned as resulting from a deliberate act of God. It means where the pain would be incomprehensible as a direct deed on the part of the Deity whom one worships. This extreme sort of situation most clearly forces the question "Why?". To ask "why" under the conditions just stated is the essential feature of the accusation against God. The essence of what we call the "accusation against God" is simply the query, "How could God have allowed this to happen?"—or, as direct address, "How could You, O God, have allowed this to happen?"

When people no longer dare to put this question before God in prayer—for instance, because of the rationalistic assumption that human beings simply cannot comprehend the acts of God—lamentation as such loses its meaning. One consequence of such a step is that lamentation is simply excised from the life of prayer, because the lament—and especially that element called the accusation against God—forces a confrontation with what is incomprehensible in the way God acts. However, the lament forces this confrontation precisely in order to allow sufferers to pour out their burdened hearts before God. Moreover, because the accusation against God takes place within the context of talking with God, all that is said remains encompassed by the sufferers' relationship to God. This is so even if the sufferers do no more than reproach God for the pain that afflicts them.

Where accusation against God is rejected as improper for the life of prayer, on grounds such as that it is irreverent to reproach God for anything, it necessarily follows that a whole aspect of reality—viz., all that which is too terrible to comprehend—is arbitrarily ruled out of one's relationship with God. When one speaks with God, one has to keep still about such matters. That, in turn, means one's speech with God must ignore a significant chunk of experienced reality.

Deliberations such as these clarify why, in the early church where human beings led hard lives and had to suffer heavy burdens, the lament once again found a place in the domain of prayer. Many early Christian songs had the character of laments. The same holds true in other cases where suffering reaches terrifying proportions and the question of how God can allow it to happen gets forced to the surface. In this context one cannot help but recall the immense suffering of the Jews during the Holocaust. Here questions were put to God that once again became, in effect, accusations against God. This can be seen in such deeply moving prayers and laments preserved from that time as, for example, the "Jossel Rackower Speaks to God" that came out of the Warsaw ghetto.

Another consequence of the refusal to incorporate accusations against God in the life of prayer is that, when faced with terrible catastrophes, the human being will simply deny God, both publicly and privately. One finds oneself no longer capable, at all, of praying to the God who allows such to happen. (Cf. Ps 73:2: "...I had almost stumbled.") In the place of turning away from God like this, the Bible knows of another possibility: the one who holds up the incomprehensible against God manages still, in that very process, to hold firmly to God.

The Lament in the Old Testament

The lament is of fundamental importance when it comes to speaking of God in the Old Testament.[2] If we regard the history of Israel as beginning with a mighty act of deliverance, we see how communal lamentation is a feature intrinsic to the account of that event [*viz*, the Exodus—*Trans.*]. Regularly, throughout the narratives of the Old Testament, lamentation is a feature in the sequence of events leading from distress to deliverance. Lamentation is a constant feature in explicit speech about God in the Old Testament. No significant changes occur in the lament throughout the history of God's dealings with the people of Israel. In the Psalter, the importance of the lament is demonstrated in the way lamentation comprises one end of the polarity (praise—lament) which dominates the material throughout that whole book. The lament is a chief component of the prayers contained in the Old Testament. Since Psalm-like motifs occur not only in the Psalter but throughout the Old Testament, the lament plays a considerable role in the whole corpus of the Hebrew Bible: in Deutero-Isaiah as well as in the other prophetic writings (cf., e.g., the laments of Jeremiah in Jer 11-20), in the Book of Job, in the Book of Lamentations, to a degree in the historical writings, and finally even in the apocryphal Second Esdras (also known as Fourth Ezra).[3]

Among the texts which we designate as laments, a further distinction ought to be drawn between the plaintive lament and the dirge. Associated with these two kinds of lament are two fundamentally different proceedings—proceedings which were also at one time differently designated. In fact, all these two types of lament really have in common is that human suffering comes to expression in each. This is the one element in common which widely leads them both to be called laments. However, attention must also be paid to the differences. The decisive difference between the two is that the dirge is profane

---

[2] For more information see the essay "Die Rolle der Klage in der Theologie des Alten Testaments," in my *Forschung am Alten Testament: Gesammelte Studien II* (ThB 55; Munich: Chr. Kaiser Verlag, 1974).

[3] The Psalm-like motifs which appear in so many places in the Old Testament are identified and listed in the *Einleitung in die Psalmen* of H. Gunkel and J. Begrich.

in nature while the plaintive lament is directed to God. In a plaintive lament the living bemoan their own suffering, while in the dirge the speakers bewail someone else, someone who is deceased. The dirge looks to the past; the plaintive lament looks to the future. Therefore the plaintive lament is a type of prayer, while the dirge is not a prayer at all. The life-setting of the dirge is the funeral in all its varying aspects. The life-setting of the plaintive lament is worship of God.

What is distinctive about the Book of Lamentations can best be seen against the background of the difference between the dirge and the plaintive lament as just described. The songs in this book cannot be dirges in any strict sense of the term. Their life-setting is not someone's funeral. If people still want to call these songs dirges, they can meaningfully do so only if they suppose that the songs refer, not to an individual, but to a community. (This happens elsewhere in the Old Testament; cf., e.g., Amos 5:1-2.) However, revising the understanding of the dirge in this way correspondingly forces an inaccurate description of these songs' genre. The clear formal elements of Lam 1, 2, and 4 militate against such a move. Undeniably, the life-setting of these texts corresponds to the life-setting of communal laments. Some disaster has befallen the city, and the survivors gather in a solemn assembly (Heb. *ṣōm*). To be sure, there is one significant difference here, compared to the pre-exilic communal laments voiced in response to earlier defeats of Israel and Judah. In this case the survivors have experienced the conquest of Jerusalem as the death of the city. Primarily, this difference stems from the fact that the destruction of 587 BCE included the demise of the two institutions which, more than any others, symbolized the very existence of the people: the Davidic monarchy and the Temple with its cult. In the combining of elements from the dirge with the basic form of the communal lament, this unique set of circumstances finds its corresponding verbal articulation.

The Form of Lamentations

A basic principle of form-critical analysis is that the structure of a genre must correspond to its life-setting, which is to say to the occasion out of which the genre grew and with reference to which it is intelligible. All of this is clear in the case of the dirge. Every line of a dirge reflects the fact that it is a direct response to someone's death and burial. In the dirge, as in the life-setting which produced it, there is an announcement of the death, a summons to wail and to engage in mourning rites, a description of the state of distress that has befallen the survivors, and eulogies for the deceased set in contrast to the distress of the survivors. These various motifs of the dirge do not appear in any fixed sequence (see above, pp. 63-66).

The structure of the plaintive lament likewise corresponds to its life-setting. In its aspect as a communal lament, its life-setting is the solemn assembly convened in response to a public emergency. The salient features of the communal lament have already been carefully described—more than once.[4] The occasion for such a solemn assembly was always some calamity that had befallen—or was about to befall—the land or the city. Given the kind of situation which constituted its life-setting, the communal lament sought to implore God for help. Thus the lament always ends in a petitionary prayer. A prayer presupposes an invocation of God, and in every plaintive lament some sort of invoking of God is either implied or openly expressed. Psalms which belong to the genre of the lament thus never consist entirely of lamentation. The dirge, on the other hand, is made up of various mournful motifs from beginning to end.

That the dirge and the plaintive lament are fundamentally different genres becomes all the more obvious once it is recognized that, in the plaintive lament, both the section which contains the mournful motifs and the section which contains the petitionary prayer exhibit internal structuring. Through the lament, the sufferer brings to expression a sort of pain which has affected the total person. In keeping with this fact, in the lament one finds reflected the three dimensions constitutive of human existence as understood in the Old Testament. Suffering impacts upon the human being's relationship to self, to fellow human beings, and to God. These three relational aspects of existence find corresponding expression in the

---

[4] I would particularly recommend the lively description of the communal lament by H. Gunkel and J. Begrich in their *Einleitung in die Psalmen.*

plaintive lament. These fundamental relational aspects appear already in the narrative of the creation of the first human beings, in Gen 2. The same three dimensions can be discerned in the first lament, the lament of Cain. They are at least implicit in every lament in the Bible. All three can appear together in very brief compass, as they do in the lament of Samson (Judg 15:18). In fact, the lament's characteristic tripartite structure is consistently displayed, not only in the full array of plaintive laments (in both its aspects, as the communal lament and as the lament of an individual), but also in the structure of the Book of Job and in passages in Deutero-Isaiah (cf., e.g., 49:14-26). If it can now be shown that these same three components of the lament are displayed in Lam 1, 2, and 4, then we have yet another argument in favor of the view that the genre of the plaintive lament decisively shapes these texts.

The same holds true for the element of petitionary prayer. It has been some time now since I first drew attention to the fact that the petition, as a constitutive element of the lament as a genre, itself has two structural components: a plea that God take notice of the petitioner, and a plea for effective divine intervention. The reason why the petition has this dual structure grows out of the fact that the section of the lament containing the actual lamentation regularly bemoans God's apparent distance and inattention. Against the background of this motif, effective divine intervention first necessitates that God take notice of the petitioner. Again in the case of Deutero-Isaiah, we find that the petitionary prayers always have this dual structure (cf., e.g., 41:17; 49:15; 51:23; 54:7). The dual structure of the petitionary prayer plays an important role in Lamentations as well. In this case, however, the emphasis is predominantly on the plea that God simply take notice of the petitioners, since the petitioners do not yet dare implore God to intervene actively in their behalf. This same dual structuring of the petitionary prayer within the lament occurs also in the Lamentation over Ur (see above, p. 16).

Now, if the texts in the Book of Lamentations correspond to the typical communal lament in having the features of direct address of God (to be sure, often only as a secondary feature), of a tripartite arrangement within the section consisting of the

lamentation itself, and of a dual arrangement within the
section containing the petitionary prayer, then all of this shows
that these texts are not dirges. Rather, they are a distinctive
group of communal laments. Their distinctiveness lies, above
all, in the fact that they have also taken up themes characteristic
of the dirge (see above, pp. 10-11).

The Acrostic Pattern

The songs of Lamentations exhibit the so-called acrostic
form, which is to say that the individual lines of the poems are
sequentially introduced by words beginning with letters which
follow the order of the letters in the Hebrew alphabet. Just as
the Hebrew alphabet has twenty-two letters, so also the songs
are built upon a base of twenty-two stanzas. The stanzas differ
in the number of lines they contain, however. In the Hebrew
each stanza of chapter five consists of a single line, whereas
each stanza of chapter four contains two lines (for a total, in the
Hebrew, of forty-four lines). In chapters one, two, and three,
however, each stanza contains three lines, so that each of these
songs is sixty-six lines long in the Hebrew. [This arrangement
is most obvious in chapter three; it is somewhat obscured by the
versification in chapters one and two—*Trans.*] In the case of
chapter five, the initial words of the individual lines do not
follow the order of the Hebrew alphabet; here the
correspondence is only in the number: twenty-two lines/stanzas
for the twenty-two letters. In the Hebrew of chapter four,
each subsequent two-line stanza begins with the next letter of
the alphabet, while in chapters one and two each three-line
stanza so begins. In the case of chapter three, the opening word
of each of the three lines of each stanza begins with the letter
of the alphabet which marks that stanza. Thus, chapter three is
the most rigidly alphabetic of all. A slight irregularity occurs in
the sequencing of the letters, in that with chapters two through
four the *pē* precedes the *'ayin* which it customarily follows.
(Chapter one follows the normal sequence.) This probably just
signifies that, at the time these songs were put together, the
sequence of letters later regarded as normative had not yet
been firmly established.

Alphabetically arranged psalms also occur in the Psalter (Pss

9-10, 25, 34, 37, 111, 112, 119, 145) and show up in Nahum 1:2-8 and Proverbs 31:10-31. Among these Psalm 119 is the most rigidly alphabetic, as each of the eight lines in the respective stanzas begins with the same letter. Alphabetic poems are also attested in Akkadian, Ugaritic, and paleo-Canaanite (cf. p. 297 of Kaiser's commentary). A convincing explanation of such alphabetically arranged poems has not yet surfaced. Some have seen the form as rooted in notions of magic, some have theorized that an alphabetic arrangement is simply a mnemonic device, and some have suggested that the structure aims to convey a sense of wholeness. However, at least for the late poems any relationship to magic is out of the question, and the mnemonic hypothesis is inadequate because it only addresses the poems in their oral form, not in their written form. That the form conveys a sense of wholeness ("from A to Z") is difficult to accept because this would leave us with five different expressions of wholeness, each dealing with the same subject and all standing immediately next to each other. A simple aesthetic explanation works best: shaping the poems in this fashion must have had a pleasing effect on early audiences. The way Lam 3 and Ps 119 both intensify this artistic technique adds credence to the explanation on aesthetic grounds. Perhaps this sort of arrangement also indicates a growing sense of the Hebrew alphabet as sacred (so Wallis, p. 62)—but this suggestion is hardly necessary to the explanation.

Structuring a poem or a song alphabetically is, in any case, a relatively late stylistic feature. This sort of arrangement presupposes that the psalms were more apt to be read than heard. More than anything else, this is seen to be a late and artificial form because the usual situation for Hebraic poetry is for the form to be determined by the content. With acrostic poetry, obviously, the alphabet determines the form; the beginning of each line is determined by whatever letter falls to that line. Such a mechanical type of arrangement has no intrinsic connection with content. This is shown most clearly in the case of Psalm 119, which all Biblical exegetes recognize as a late psalm. Arranging material according to the alphabet is pedantic; it is a habit which would have been "nurtured in the circles of the bookish" (so Wallis [p. 62]; in a similar vein already Löhr). Therefore it is unlikely that these songs of lament first appeared as acrostics. Only during the course of their transmission will they have acquired this form. That the old songs were re-arranged as acrostics during the time when they were being collected and preserved is quite possible, whereas it is most difficult to imagine their being decked out in the niceties of alphabetic form immediately upon their coming into existence under the impact of the catastrophe of 587 BCE. (Löhr said long ago, with regard to Lam 3:15, "In our opinion the artificiality of the alphabetic arrangement is most unsuited to the deeply moving quality of the laments.")

That the acrostic form was imposed on the text at a later stage of its development will be confirmed through a number of specific, exegetic observations. As will be shown in the next chapter, the pressure to organize the material alphabetically had a considerable influence on the choice and the positioning of individual words, as well as upon the ordering of the sentences. It led to additions, to transpositions, and to insertions (even of genre-alien elements, as also happened at Ps 145:20). Löhr already found a number of places where disruptions could be identified, disruptions caused by the compulsion to organize the material along acrostic lines. Such disruptions make the interpretation of the songs considerably more difficult. If one interprets the text according to the sequence of the verses, proceeding on a verse-by-verse basis and disregarding the changes that could have been introduced under the necessity of adhering to alphabetic form, one constantly runs the risk of inferring conceptual relationships between sections, lines, or even clauses, where such are simply not present. One will thus have to explore for criteria which allow one to avoid falling into this trap.

The Question of Origin

In light of the above, we must next inquire about the origin of the songs of Lamentations. In the work of none of the previous interpreters have I been able to find any investigation into the question of whether these songs developed out of oral tradition or were the product of literary activity. Rather, even those who assume that these songs were used on occasions of ceremonial lamentation nonetheless consistently seem to imagine that they were first written down and only then, in their form as given texts, did they come to be "employed" in worship services or on occasions of ceremonial lamentation. As far as I can tell, no one actively considers the possibility of a phase of oral transmission prior to the time when these songs were written down.

For someone such as myself, who for a long time now has been occupied with interpretation of the Psalms, such a state of affairs is difficult to comprehend. People can have differing opinions about the various results of specific form-critical investigations. Still, I was under the impression that a general consensus had been reached to the effect that the psalms had arisen orally as cultic songs, by and large in the time before the exile. Moreover, that they had been passed on by word of mouth for a considerable period of time and that they had only gradually been reduced to written form was also, I thought, widely taken for granted. Whether this pattern might also hold for the songs of Lamentations, however, is a possibility which none of the prior researchers on Lamentations seems even to have considered. At the very least, one would have thought that Lam 5 might have been seen as fitting in with the general course of development for the psalms. I can only attribute this state of affairs to the impact upon researchers of the acrostic form.

Most interpreters take it as obvious that Lamentations is "literature" and should be read as such. However, our notion of what constitutes literature came to be formed only long after the written word had become a commonplace phenomenon. In Old Testament times, the written word was still something of a rarity, and therefore in most circles of activity—including the cultic—it was necessary to continue transmitting material orally even though there were some people around who could read and write. Hardly anyone disputes this fact. The continuation of oral tradition alongside a developing literacy, even for centuries, is attested in a number of cultures throughout human history—as the so-called Scandinavian school of Old Testament scholarship has often reminded us. That the same state of affairs held true in ancient Israel can be taken as certain. Moreover, in the Old Testament there are only a few texts, or groups of texts, where an earlier phase of oral transmission is any more likely than it is in the case of Lamentations. These texts arose out of a community's experience. The authors of these songs were hardly isolated individuals, drawing on their thoughts and feelings in order to write down their personal impressions and ideas. On the contrary, the Book of Lamentations arose out of the collective experience of a human community, a community which had survived the collapse of Jerusalem. The remnant of Israel speaks in these songs. To be sure, even at that time there had to be someone who actually took pen in hand and wrote down the songs. But this action hardly made that person an author or a poet, in either the modern or the classical sense of these terms. The one who did the actual writing down of the songs by no means played the major role in the creation of Lamentations. These songs are the experiences, the reactions, the insights, and the responses of the remnant. It is the survivors of the catastrophe, as a whole, who are speaking in Lamentations. ("Jerusalem remembers the days of her misery and anguish" [Lam 1:7]). The one who wrote down this material transcribed the words, the phrases, the clauses—the cries, the sighs, and the laments—as they were spoken and as they were heard. Our scribe also thought these thoughts and spoke these words, but did so as one of many. These are words in which the scribe participated as a fellow survivor of the catastrophe.

So, two facts regarding their origin can recognized in the songs in Lamentations. (1) They possess a structure which did not first appear in and with these songs themselves. Instead, this structure was already on hand as a feature of the communal lament. (2) The songs of Lamentations grew out of the same type of situation which produced the communal laments in general, namely the experience of some distress which affects the whole community. Many of those who survived the catastrophe of 587 BCE were familiar with communal-lament psalms, just as they were familiar with ceremonies of public lamentation on the occasion of a national disaster—the sort of ceremony which provided the life-setting for the communal lament. Those who lamented the fall of Jerusalem simply followed the established form. Although they seem to have deviated from that form in some important ways, nonetheless they basically shaped their laments along the classic lines. The strongest evidence for this is provided by Lam 5, a true communal lament.

Another, and perhaps even clearer, argument for the existence of an earlier phase of oral transmission for Lamentations is the fact that, by and large, the sentence structure and the syntax of these songs reflect an oral delivery more than they do a written provenance. One needs only a modest feel for style in order to see this. For the moment I content myself with giving a single example. Lam 1:1-11 is cast in the third person. Against this background, note how two nearly identical sentences break the pattern: "Look, O Yahweh, upon my distress, see how the enemy triumphs!" (v 9c), and "Just look, O Yahweh, and see how despised I am!" (v 11c). How could anyone contest that these were originally spoken sentences? (The same sort of phenomenon occurs with the "Woe to us that we have sinned!" at Lam 5:16.) These are sentences which would have been spoken in just this fashion. The observers at the ceremony are also participants in the liturgy. What they heard, and said, on that occasion became indelibly etched on their memories.

The two facts, mentioned above, which argue for an earlier phase of oral transmission can jointly be summarized by saying that these sentences which clearly betray an oral provenance themselves have an intrinsic connection with the established structure of the communal lament. Vv 9c and 11c of Lam 1 are pleas for God to take notice, while Lam 5:16 is a confession of guilt.

We are unable to reconstruct in precise detail the stage of oral transmission lying behind Lamentations as a written text. However, on the basis of the written text we can deduce the main contours of that earlier phase. As many interpreters of Lamentations have discerned, the descriptions of the decimated city and its suffering inhabitants are often so vivid and gripping that they could only have come from eyewitnesses. This much is certain. Many voices, finding expression in diverse ways, echo throughout these laments. The initially chaotic, multi-voiced nature of such laments finds an impressive parallel in the Lamentation over the Destruction of Ur, with its frequent repetitions. Naturally, the laments as actually passed on can capture only a small segment of this initially chaotic state of affairs. However, even in its written form the material that has come down to us strikes us as so powerful and authentic precisely because it still mediates a sense of genuine lamentation. We are still able to overhear the voices of the ones first affected by the calamity. The poet—or compiler— who wrote down these laments kept "his" own personality in check, just as did all those anonymous figures who transmitted ancient folklore. It is the people's dismay which finds expression in these songs. It follows as a matter of course, then, that the acrostic form cannot have been a feature of this material at its early stage.

Time and Place of Origin

It is impossible to determine precisely the time at which the individual songs of Lamentations originated, but fortunately such a determination is not an essential prerequisite for understanding them. On the other hand, it is important to recognize that—apart from chapter three—a firm *terminus a quo* has indeed been established: the conquest of Jerusalem in 587 BCE (see above, pp. 54-55). There is also a very likely *terminus ad quem*: the time when Deutero-Isaiah was active (ca. 550 BCE). Judging from the contents of Deutero-Isaiah's message, the latter must be assigned to a time after the various songs of Lamentations had come into being but before the time of the famous Edict of Cyrus (538 BCE). The laments which appear in Deutero-Isaiah's announcement of salvation so closely resemble the material in Lamentations that the latter is almost certainly presupposed in the former. This can be seen, for example, in the case of Is 51:17b-20:

> Stand up, O Jerusalem, you who have drunk at the
>   hand of Yahweh the cup of his wrath....
> Who will lament for you, who comfort you?
> Your children lie helpless at all intersections
> ...full of the wrath of Yahweh...!

Other prophetic words of weal stemming from the exilic or the post-exilic period also call to mind or presuppose the songs of Lamentations (e.g., Mic 4:9-14; Nah 1:9, 11-13; 2:1-3; Hos 14:2). Although the *terminus a quo* for the origin of Lamentations (apart from chapter three) is firm and the *terminus ad quem* is at least probable, one must still exercise caution in the matter of arranging the individual songs in a temporal sequence. As will be shown below, it is probable that only chapter three is to be assigned to a genuinely late date. It is also possible that chapter five is later than chapters one, two, and four. Of these latter three, however, it can only be said that they all stand temporally very close to the destruction of Jerusalem. If one wanted to assign more precise dates within the considerable span of time between the *terminus a quo* and the *terminus ad quem* as determined above, one would need objective criteria that are simply unavailable at the present time.

The greatest likelihood is that Lamentations came into being on the soil of Judah/Jerusalem. The general assumption that the songs stem from people who actually witnessed the destruction of Jerusalem itself argues for the vicinity of the catastrophe as the place of origin for the songs. There is essentially nothing that positively argues for an origin outside of Judah, somewhere among the exiles.

Excursus: Comparisons in Lamentations[5]

In its 264 extant lines the Book of Lamentations contains seventy five comparisons; one can rightly say that the work is saturated with comparisons. Obviously, then, comparisons constitute an important stylistic element in Lamentations. (Enno Littmann draws attention to the same feature in the Abyssinian laments which he investigated.) These comparisons make reference to characteristic features of human life or of natural processes; only once does one encounter a comparison with an historical event. Throughout, the comparisons drawn are simple and readily understandable. The comparisons drawn from the domain of human life fix on basic and elementary

---

[5] For background to this excursus, see my *Vergleiche und Gleichnisse im Alten und Neuen Testament* (1984), esp. pp. 80-96 ("Vergleiche in den Psalmen").

processes; the same holds true for the comparisons with features of the natural world. Nowhere do the comparisons refer to institutions specific to the life of ancient Israel.

One finds comparisons with the human body or with parts of the body, with food and drink, with clothing and jewelry, with buildings and habitations, with implements and weapons, with family members and with friends, with the hunt and with battle. With reference to the natural order, a few of the comparisons focus on plants or animals. Comparisons with the organic realm are rare, however; more often, the comparisons are with non-organic elements. The most frequently encountered comparisons have to do with fire; things are said to be like embers, to glow, or to burn. (All of this corresponds to the Lamentation over the Destruction of Ur, with its frequent reference to the lightning accompanying a thunderstorm.) There are also references to the sea, to the sky, to darkness, to clouds, to the abyss of the underworld, to wilderness, to dust, and to snow. The one historical comparison refers to the destruction of Sodom. All of this leads to the conclusion that the songs of Lamentations arose among simple folk.

Apart from a few exceptions, the contexts in which these comparisons occur are stamped by motifs drawn from psalms and from the dirge. Seventeen times one finds comparisons which reflect the contrast motif characteristic of the dirge. (This feature is just as common in Abyssinian and other songs of lamentation.) Here the comparisons serve to intensify the contrast between then and now, between the happy state of affairs formerly in effect and the sad state of affairs currently in place. (Cf., e.g., Lam 4:1a: "Ah, how lusterless is the gold; how marred the fine gold!") Such comparisons are typical of the contrast-motif as reflected in the dirge. In the Book of Lamentations, they cluster in 4:1-8 but are also found at 1:1, 1:6, 2:1, and 2:15. Altogether, one finds twenty comparisons attached to the contrast motif in the Book of Lamentations. In the case of the motif "description of misery," a motif common to both the dirge and the plaintive lament, the comparisons intensify sensitivity to the distress being described. (Cf., e.g., Lam 3:48: "My eyes let streams of water flow over the downfall of the daughter of my people." The same image appears in vv 11 and

18 of chap 2.) Altogether there are ten cases where the "description of misery" motif comes equipped with a comparison.

Most of the other comparisons in Lam 1-5 are typical of psalmic motifs. Among these, the largest group consists of comparisons characteristic of the motif "accusation against God." Such comparisons, totalling thirty in all, occur in all five songs. Note, for example, 2:1: "Ah, how Yahweh in his wrath overclouds daughter Zion!" 2:4 is similar: "He bent his bow like an enemy, the arrow in his right hand!" Comparisons serving to intensify the accusation against God appear so often in Lamentations because of the incomprehensibility of what Yahweh has done to Israel. This much comes to expression in a comparison employed at 2:13: "Verily, deep as the sea is your ruin, who can heal you?"

Further comparisons occur in motifs typical of the communal lament: nine times where the community states its resolve to take up lamentation, and twice where the community confesses its guilt. The same holds true in the case of motifs characteristic of either the personal lament or the individual's song of praise (a total of twelve comparisons in these two cases). Here it is necessary only to point out that the comparisons are consistently of the same sort as occur with the corresponding motifs when exhibited in the Psalms. Note, for example, Lam 3:24: "'My portion is Yahweh,' says my soul"—typical language for an avowal of trust. Or look at Lam 3:52: "Hunted, hunted me like a bird have those who are without cause my enemies"—again, typical for the motif of recalling an earlier state of distress. The comparisons in Lam 1-5 present a further argument that we are dealing in Lamentations, not with dirges, but with a special group of communal laments. In this context it is worth noting that the comparisons which appear in communal laments differ from those which appear in personal laments—an important point to be held up against any interpretation which ignores or conceals the difference between communal and personal laments.

A particular significance attaches to the initial comparison in the first song. ("Ah, how lonely sits the city that once was populous! She who once was great among the peoples has become like a widow.") The comparison of a city or a community with a woman occurs elsewhere as well; cf. Amos 5:1-2, and also the Lamentation over the Destruction of Ur. The significant feature of this comparison is precisely the analogy drawn between the suffering of a city and the suffering of a woman. This particular comparison, introduced at the very beginning, has an impact upon all the rest of the songs in Lamentations. This is most clearly seen in the way Jerusalem is characteristically referred to throughout as "daughter Zion." Through this particular comparison, the destroying of a city is brought under the rubric of an occurrence that is recognizably human. It is no longer a mere object that is destroyed. Rather, the quarters which provided shelter are transformed into something intrinsic to the human sphere and, as such, into something which by extension is itself human. So, here at the very beginning, we encounter a feature characteristic of all comparisons: the object which serves as the point of comparison comes to participate in the nature of that which is being compared. In the case at hand (the comparison of Zion and the woman), the world of objects and the world of human beings are both grasped as parts of God's creation and, as such, both are enabled to respond to what has been decreed by God. Herein lies the true significance of this comparison.

Chapter Four

Exegesis of Lamentations 1-5

Lam 1

1 Ah^a, how lonely sits^b the city that once was populous!^c
   She who once was great among the peoples has become
     like a widow;
   she who ruled over provinces has been subjected to forced
     labor.

2 She cries endlessly at night, tears running down her cheeks.
   From all her friends not one is left to console her;^{ab}
   all her neighbors have become unfaithful to her, they have
     become her enemies.

3 Judah has been carried away from misery and harsh
     servitude.
   She dwells among the peoples, finding no rest;
   all her pursuers overtook her in her distress^a.

4 The roads to Zion mourn because no one comes to
     festival^a;
   all her gates are laid waste^b, her priests sigh.
   Her maidens are distressed^c, she herself is bitterly sad.

5 Her oppressors are dominant, her enemies prosper,
   for Yahweh has smitten her on account of all her
     iniquity.
   Her children went away as captives before the oppressor.

6 From daughter[a] Zion has vanished all her splendor, **7aβ**all
the valuables that had been hers since of old.[b]
Her nobles have become like stags that found no pasture,
weakly they went off before their hunter.

7 Jerusalem remembers the days of her misery and anguish
(7aβ to 6a)[a],
how her people fell into the hand of the enemy and no one
helped her.
Enemies saw it all and laughed over her demise[b].

8 Jerusalem committed grave sins, therefore she became an
object of derision[a];
all who had honored her came to despise her, for they saw
her nakedness;
but[b] she groans and turns away[c].

9 Her uncleanness clings to her garment[a], she took no
thought for her future.
Thus she has dreadfully[b] fallen, without anyone to console
her.
Look, O Yahweh, upon my distress, see how the enemy
triumphs!

10 The foe stretched out his hand[a] toward all her treasures;
verily, she saw heathens invade her sanctuary,
the very ones whom you commanded that they should not
draw near[b] to your assembly!

11 All her people groaned, they searched for bread;
they exchanged their treasures for food, that they might
assuage their hunger.
Just look, O Yahweh, and see how despised I am!

12 Now then,[a] all you who pass by, look here and see!
Is there any pain such as mine, such as has been done to
me
—pain through which Yahweh has inflicted suffering upon
me[b] on the day of his burning anger?

13 From above he sent down fire, he let it penetrate[a] my
      bones.
    He spread a net for my feet, he dragged me back,
    he laid me low, suffering endlessly.

14 Heavy[a] is the yoke of my transgressions, fixed in place by his
      hand.
    They came over my neck, he broke my strength;
    Yahweh gave me over to hands which I could not withstand[b].

15 Yahweh cast off all my seasoned champions in my midst,
    he ordered a battle against me, to annihilate my young
      warriors.
    The Lord trod the wine-press of maiden daughter Judah.

16 For these things[a] must I cry, my eye (...)[b] flows with tears,
    for far from me is any consoler, one who could revive me.
    My children are devastated, for the enemy is too powerful.

17 Zion spreads out her hands, she has no consoler.
    Yahweh ordered Jacob's neighbors[a] against him as his
      oppressors,
    Jerusalem became an object of loathing in their eyes[b].

18 Righteous is he, is Yahweh, for I have rebelled against his
      word.
    Hear, all you peoples[a], and see my pain!
    My maidens and my youths had to go off into captivity.

19 I called to my lovers[a], but they left me in the lurch.
    My priests and my elders died there in the city,
    while they sought for nourishment to prolong[b] their lives.

20 Look, O Yahweh, for I am alarmed, my innards smolder[a]!
    My heart twists within my body, for I was rebellious;
    outside the sword wreaks havoc and within death[b] is
      everywhere.

21 Listen[a] to how I sigh, no one is there to comfort me!

All my enemies heard of my misfortune, they rejoiced that
   you had done it.
Let come[b] the day which[c] you proclaim.

22 Let it yet come upon them as it has upon me; let all their
   evil come before you!
And do to them as you have done to me because of all my
   sins!
For my sighs are countless, and my heart is ill.

Textual Notes
1a: There is no anacrusis with this *'êkāh* (contra Th. Robinson).
b: Perfect in tense but present in meaning; on the usage cf. 1
Sam 2:5 [often read as a present tense, though not in NRSV—
Trans.]. **c:** The athnach should follow *'ām*.

2a: Rudolph translates "...she has no one as consoler from
among all her friends." **b:** On the syntax see GKC § 152o.

3a: Literally, "between the straits"; perhaps read here *miṣṣārĕhāh*

4a: On the participial construction see GKC § 116h. **b:** On the
Aramaizing plural at "her gates are laid waste" [*šōmēmîn*], cf.
Lam 4:3. **c:** Read *nehûgôt* with the text-critical apparatus of BHS
(= niphal participle of *ygh*; cf. Zeph 3:18, and the comments
thereon by Gottlieb *et al.*)

6a: Read, with the Qere, *mibbat.* **b:** See the note at 7a.

7a: V 7 has four lines; of these the second line is to be stricken.
The third line originally followed the first line, while the
second line is an insertion (thus the critical apparatus of BHS
and the majority of interpreters). However, one can well
imagine v 7b as following directly upon v 6a, and it is therefore
transposed to that location in our translation (as an insertion).
b: With Ehrlich [*Randglossen zur hebräischen Bibel*] read *mišbattāh*
= "over her demise" or "that it was all over for her."

8a: The *hapax legomenon nîdāh* is derived from *nûdî* [sic] and is to be rendered as either "disgust" or "derision." **b:** On the contrastive use of *gam*, cf. Ps 52:7 [52:5 Eng.]. **c:** Literally, "she draws herself back."

9a: A plural of extension [GKC § 124a-c], hence appropriately translated as singular. **b:** On the use of the accusative to describe the manner or state of an action, cf. GKC § 118q.

10a: The phrase ["to stretch out the hand"] occurs only here with the sense of describing a hostile action. **b:** On the construction of the relative clause, cf. GKC § 155f.

12a: The meaning of the first two words cannot be determined; most exegetes read *lĕkū*—suggested in the critical apparatus of the older BHK. Rudolph suggests that with the first two words here we have here a marginal gloss ("not intended for you!" [*lô' 'ălêkem*]), one that was supposed to guard the addressees against harm and which probably displaced the original *lĕkū*. **b:** Reading with the Greek, which reflects the first-person singular pronominal suffix attached to the verb [cf. the critical apparatus to BHK]; Kraus, Rudolph, Plöger, and others read it this way as well.

13a: Read here, following the Greek, *hōrîdāh*.

14a: Read here, with Prätorius [*ZAW* 15 (1895) 143-44] and others, *niqšāh* = "he/she/it is heavy." **b:** On this use of the construct state, cf. GKC § 130d.

16a: There is no anacrusis with this '*al-'ēlleh* (contra Th. Robinson). **b:** Following the text-critical apparatus of BHS, one of the two '*ênîs* is to be stricken (dittography). Gottlieb's suggestion that the double writing here indicates a special emphasis must be rejected because generating emphasis in this fashion is meaningful only in the case of verbal forms.

17a: On the substantival use of *sābîb* cf. Jer 48:17,39. **b:** Read *bĕ'ênêhem* ("in their eyes") with Delitzsch, Rudolph, and others; [cf. the text-critical apparatus of BHS].

18a: Read here *hā'ammîm* with the text-critical apparatus of BHS.

19a: On the use of the definite article with a participle containing a pronominal suffix, as here, cf. GKC § 116f. **b:** Kraus here follows the Greek, which yields "and they found nothing" [cf. text-critical apparatus of BHS]—a thoroughly possible reading. Ehrlich [*Randglossen*] suggests, on the contrary, *wayyāśiū* [sic] ("and were disappointed").

20a: "...my innards smolder" (literally: "effervesce") refers to the effect of pain; on the form of the verb, cf. GKC § 55e. **b:** Gottlieb (in company with Gordis) designates the *k* preceding the *māwet* an "intensifying particle."

21a: Read here *šĕma'*, following the Syriac and in company with Rudolph, Kraus, Plöger, and others. **b:** Read here *hābē'*, following the Syriac and in company with Rudolph and others. **c:** A relative clause lacking the customary *'ăšer*

The Structure of Lam 1

A quick comparison of the judgment of two different commentators on Lamentations points out the difficulty of finding a clear train of thought in these sixty-six lines. On the one hand, Kraus comments that "...in Lam 1 there is simply no meaningful flow of ideas or deliberate, controlling structure..." (p. 22). Kaiser, on the other hand, states quite emphatically that "The initial song of the collection contains a clear structure" (p.310)! Depending upon whether one starts out from the assumption that Lam 1 stands in the tradition of the communal laments of the Psalter or, conversely, in that of the dirge, one will look for possible connections relating back to those two models—all the while, of course, being attentive to possible disruptions caused by the acrostic arrangement of the lines.

An initial glance at the entangled complexity of these sixty-six lines presses one to ask, first of all, if there are not some firmly fixed points in terms of which a basic orientation is possible.

1. The beginning and the end of the first section are clear; they can be recognized without ambiguity. The song is introduced by the mournful cry *'êkāh*. This element leads first of all to a sorrowful description, a community's direct complaint—here appearing as an extended description of misery. This description encompasses 18 lines, or vv 1-6. Such a sorrowful description typically follows an introductory mournful cry. In this case the description follows the pattern of the dirge, marked as it is by the latter's characteristic contrast between the former and the present state of affairs. The opening clauses also sound like a dirge: the city has become a widow, etc.

A new section begins in v 7 with the clause "Jerusalem remembers...." Here one moves away from the sorrowful condition of the city's present, described in vv 1-6, to the disaster which brought about the misery: "...how her people fell into the hand of the enemy." "Thus she has dreadfully fallen!" (v 9b). In this section, vv 7-12b, the descriptive pattern typical of a community's direct complaint is continued, even though the pattern is interrupted by extraneous motifs, specifically in vv 9c and 11c. The second section breaks off in v 12b with the imploring cry for compassion and aid; Jerusalem beckons and rhetorically queries, "Is there any pain such as mine?"

2. The next major, cohesive section begins with v 12c, a fluid transitional line. This section, an accusation against God, encompasses the ten lines stretching between vv 12c and 15. It connects with the first section through v 12b ("Is there any pain such as mine..."), which introduces a motif then developed in v 12c ("...pain through which Yahweh has inflicted suffering upon me on the day of his burning anger"). As the ensuing lines relate, Yahweh sent down fire, spread a net, and broke the strength of the lamenter (on this last theme, cf. also v 17b).

3. The third characteristic component of the lament, namely the complaint about enemies (clauses in which the subject is some enemy of the lamenter), does not occur as a distinct unit in Lam 1. However, fragments of such a component are found scattered about in individual clauses: in vv 5a, 7c, 10a-c, and 21b. Also belonging to this motif, or closely related to it, are complaints about former allies that have become enemies; these are also found in scattered fashion, in vv 2c, 8b, 17b, and 19a. So, the three characteristic components of the lament are all present: the community's direct complaint (vv 1-12b), the accusation against God (vv 12c-15), and the complaint about enemies (appearing in individual clauses scattered throughout the song). To these basic features are then added additional elements typical of the song of lamentation.

4. Twice an acknowledgement of guilt interrupts the community's direct complaint: in v 5b ("Yahweh has smitten her on account of all her iniquity") and in vv 8-9 ("Jerusalem committed grave sins, therefore...her uncleanness clings to her garment..."). In both of these places Israel's guilt is expressly identified as the ultimate cause of Yahweh's judgment.

An acknowledgement of guilt likewise twice occurs within the element of the accusation against God: in the comparison at v 14a-b ("Heavy is the yoke of my transgressions, fixed in place by his hand...") and in the acknowledgement of the justice of God's actions v 18 ("Righteous is he, is Yahweh, for I have rebelled against his word"). Taken together, these four passages show special emphasis being placed on this motif of acknowledgement of guilt.

5. Several times the element of petition also occurs: in vv 9c, 11c, 20a, 21a, 22a-b. In 9c, 11c, 20a, and 21a the petition is for God to take heed; in 22a-b the plea is for retaliation against the enemies. On the other hand, an otherwise expected plea for direct divine intervention on behalf of the people of God is lacking.

6. The element of direct address of God (invocation of Yahweh) appears in vv 9c and 11c, in each case associated with the plea for God to take heed ("Look, O Yahweh, upon my distress...!" and "Just look, O Yahweh, and see...!"). An invocation of Yahweh is a necessary component of the psalm of lament. Here this component is immediately followed by the element of petition. This happens because the song as a whole is introduced, not by the element of invocation, but by the mournful cry.

7. Particularly emphasized in Lam 1 is the description of agony, that part of the community's direct complaint which brings the subjective aspect to expression, describing not what is suffered but how it is experienced. This element originally belongs to the dirge, but it also occurs within the plaintive lament. "She cries endlessly at night, tears running down her cheeks....not one is left to console her" (v 2a-b); "...she herself is bitterly sad" (v 4c); "...but she groans and turns away" (v 8c); cf. vv 16a, 20a-b, 21a. A clause noting the absence of a consoler is frequently included; cf. vv 2b, 9c, 16b, 17a, 21c. Also belonging in this array of motifs is the summons to share in the pain ("Now then...look here...!" [v 12]; "Hear...and see my pain!" [v 18b; cf. vv 17a, 20a, 21a]).

8. Standing out as distinct among all the motifs mentioned so far is the clause with which the accusation against God (vv 12c-15) properly concludes (v 18a): "Righteous is he, is Yahweh, for I have rebelled against his word." Set over against the accusation against God, this is a justification of all that God has done to Zion. This motif stands in the place where, in the lament, one normally finds an avowal of confidence.

9. The conclusion (v 22a-b) is a plea for reprisal against the lamenter's enemies. One comes across precisely such a motif in many psalms of lamentation.

To summarize: With regard to its beginning and its first section, Lam 1 does closely resemble the dirge. Features typical of the dirge are the mournful cry at the beginning and the description of misery which follows in vv 1-6 and 7-12, a description shaped by the feature of contrast. But all of this really amounts to no more than isolated motifs. Even a summons to lament can occur in a dirge. However, when one comes across a community's direct complaint, such as the one here (vv 1-12) transformed into an extended description of misery, one is properly dealing with a component of the communal lament.

In its second section Lam 1 more obviously resembles the communal lament. Here one finds such typical communal-lament features as the three basic components (the community's direct complaint, the accusation against God, the complaint about enemies), the acknowledgement of guilt, the invocation of Yahweh and the plea for Yahweh to take heed, the plea for reprisal upon the enemies, the motif of the justification of God set over against the accusation against God—to say nothing of the arrangement of the motifs, which clearly corresponds to the structure of the communal lament. To be sure, there are some motifs here which are common to both the communal lament and the dirge, for example the description of misery. That the motifs do not occur in any fixed sequence, but rather show up in scattered clauses or verses, is due at least in part to the constraints imposed upon the material by its alphabetic arrangement.

So the judgment of Jahnow—viz., that with regard to its structure Lam 1 is a dirge into which several motifs of the communal lament have been incorporated—must be rejected. Rather, in Lam 1 the structure of the communal lament can quite clearly be discerned. It is into the latter's structure that isolated elements of the dirge have been inserted. This has happened primarily at the beginning of the chapter; as the chapter progresses, it happens less frequently or not at all. The ambiguity which surrounds components not exclusively belonging to the dirge surfaces primarily in the case of motifs characteristic of prayer: invocation of Yahweh, petition, confession of sins. Leaving out the motifs which properly belong to the dirge, a comparison of the remaining contents of Lam 1 with the motifs characteristic of the communal lament exhibits a wide-ranging agreement.

Communal Lament	*Lam 1*
invocation	invocation (but not at the beginning)
lamentation	lamentation
accusation against God	accusation against God
community's direct complaint	community's direct complaint
complaint about enemies	complaint about enemies

acknowledgement of guilt	acknowledgement of guilt
avowal of confidence or retrospection	(lacking) ("righteous is Yahweh")
plea for God to take heed	plea for God to take heed
plea for intervention	(lacking)
petition for reprisal against enemies	petition for reprisal against enemies

The agreement is so comprehensive that only two components characteristic of the structure of the communal lament are missing in Lam 1: the avowal of confidence (or, in its place, a retrospection of God's earlier saving actions) and the plea for God's direct intervention in behalf of the people of God. The absence of these two motifs in Lam 1 is due to the fact that the shock of the catastrophe went so deep as to forestall their articulation. The possibility of a retrospection on God's earlier saving actions has been brought to a standstill (likewise in Lam 2, 4, and 5); the element of avowal of confidence has been reduced to a single trace, in the clause at v 18a ("righteous is Yahweh..."). The fact that, in Lamentations, the dirge has been joined to the communal lament thus finds a correspondence in the way both of these motifs are lacking.

Exegesis of Lam 1

1-6: description of misery (communal lament), introduced by a mournful cry
  1-2: the lonely widow
    1a,b,c: contrast: the formerly populous city—the widow
    2a,b: description of pain
    2c: her friends have become enemies
  3: Judah was carried off, her pursuers overtook her
  4a,b: roads and gates are laid waste
  4b,c: priests sigh, maidens are distressed
  5a: her oppressors are dominant
  5b: Yahweh has smitten her for her iniquity
  5c: her children have gone away as captives
  6a: Zion lost her splendor
  6b,c: the nobles were carried off by enemies

The mournful cry *'êkāh* ("Ah!" or "Ah, how...!") occurs in other such distressed outcries as Isa 1:21 ("Ah, how the faithful city has become a whore!") or Jer 48:5 ("Ah, at the descent...one hears a cry of anguish" [*sic*, cf. Jer 48:17b—*Trans.*]). Not only does this term introduce the songs of lamentation in Lam 1:1, 2:1, and 4:1, but it also appears in the lament of David over Saul and Jonathan in 2 Sam 1:19, 25, 27 ("Ah, how the mighty have fallen!"). Biblical cries of lamentation are often repeated—something that also occurs in the Lamentation over the Destruction of Ur ("The people mourn!"; "...bitter is their lament.").

The mournful cry *'êkāh* was used by the prophets in their announcements of destruction or annihilation. This happened particularly in their oracles against foreign nations:

> Ah, how the oppressor has ceased!
>
> (Isa 14:4)

> Ah, how you have fallen from heaven!...
> Ah, how you have been smashed to earth,
>   you who enslaved all peoples!
>
> (Isa 14:12)

> Ah, how the hammer of the whole earth
>   is cut down and broken!
>
> (Jer 50:23)

(See also Jer 48:17; 51:41; Ezek 26:17; Zeph 2:15.)

Not only are all these clauses introduced by *'êkāh*, but they also exhibit an important trait of the dirge: the contrast between the former and the current state of affairs. Even in the judgment oracle at Isa 1:21 the elements of mournful cry and contrast appear together. At Jer 9:16-18 [9:17-19 Eng.] the dirge over Judah/Jerusalem goes as follows:

> Ah, call out the women who mourn,
> let them voice a dirge over us,
> that our eyes might flow with tears...
> Ah, how we are ruined...covered with shame!

This song of lamentation, which announces Yahweh's judgment over Jerusalem, anticipates the very situation which has actually come to pass in Lamentations. This Jeremianic text parallels Lam 1, not only in the use of the mournful cry, but also with the summons to lament and the description of agony—to say nothing of the fact that in both texts the one being mourned is the city of Jerusalem.

Verse 1

The section comprising vv 1-6 forms a cohesive unit with a clearly discernible structure. The mournful cry initiates the bewailing of a contrast between past and present: Jerusalem, once populous, now sits alone (theme expanded by use of comparisons in v 1b-c). Next comes a description of Jerusalem's distress (v 2a); no one consoles her (v 2b), her neighbors have proven unfaithful to her (v 2c). The three clauses of verse 3 likewise describe her misery, adding a comment about what happened to her: she was led away into exile. Vv 4-6 (except for v 5a-b) develop the description of Jerusalem's misery: her roads and gates are laid waste, the priests sigh, the maidens are distressed, the children are taken prisoner, the nobility is enfeebled, all her splendor is gone. This cluster of themes is interrupted at v 5a-b (v 5c would read better following directly upon v 4c) with the insertion of the motif of a complaint about enemies ("Her oppressors are dominant..."). However, since the clause at v 5a develops the theme of contrast, it can serve as part of the description of misery. V 5c, which specifies the ultimate cause of this misery, falls out of the otherwise related cluster of statements: "Yahweh has smitten her on account of all her iniquity." This clause addresses the scene from a reflective distance; here inquiry into the cause of the misery has intervened. All this misery has transpired because of Israel's guilt; Yahweh's people have been punished. By having v 5b stand out from its immediate context, the description of misery, even more attention is drawn to Israel's guilt. The same happens at vv 8-9, 14, 18b, and 20b.

Excursus: The Description of Misery

The description of misery, a feature which also occurs in the Akkadian psalms of lamentation, develops the basic lament along each of its three characteristic axes. In place of the usual "You, O God, have done...," one finds the same motif cast in the third person: " God has done...." In place of the customary first-person plural ("We are..."), one finds the misery described from a third-person point of view. Instead of the complaint about enemies, one finds description of the situation as brought about by the actions of the enemies. The description of misery is a development of the basic lament in the sense that, while the lament is structurally a tripartite reaction to a devastating incident on the part of those directly affected, the description of misery surveys the state of affairs that has resulted from the blow.

The description of misery is also a characteristic element of the dirge. There it appears in the motif of contrast, juxtaposing the state of affairs before and after the calamity [*viz.*, the death]. In contrast to the personal form of address in the lament ("we...you..."), in the dirge one finds no direct address of God but rather an impersonal bewailing of the situation. In the lament, however, the personal form of speech becomes possible where the deity is directly addressed.

The plaintive lament, normally addressed directly to God and hence cast in first-person and second-person forms of speech, can also be expanded by means of the description of misery. When reference is made to the calamity that has been brought about by God, there can follow a description of its wider impact. In the communal laments of the Psalter, such expansion by means of a description of the misery tends to be only suggested or implied.

They have poured out their blood...
and there was no one to bury them.

(Ps 79:3)

You have broken down its walls,
so that all can pluck [its fruits]...it is grazed bare.

(Ps 80:13-14 [80:12-13 Eng.])

All day long my disgrace is before me....

(Ps 44:16 [44:15 Eng.])

It is noteworthy how, in several communal laments outside

the Psalter (*viz.*, in Isaiah 63/64 and in Jeremiah 14)—laments which appear to be looking back upon the destruction of Jerusalem—the description of misery is an element which more clearly comes to the fore.

Jer 14:1-6 —
   The misery occasioned by a drought is described.

Jer 14:18 —
   If I go out into the field, there I see lying about people
      slain by the sword;
   if I go back into the city, there I see people tormented
      by famine....

Isa 64:9 (64:10 Eng.) —
   The holy cities are destroyed,
   Zion has become a wilderness,
   Jerusalem a desolation.

Isa 64:10 (64:11 Eng.) —
   The temple...has become a victim of the flames...it lies
      in ruin....

Both texts closely resemble what we see in Lamentations. Even the element of a description of agony is to be found here:

My eyes flow with tears day and night,
they can find no peace....
                                      (Jer 14:17; cf. Lam 2:11)

Ps 80:6 (80:5 Eng.) contains a trace of the same motif:

You have them eat tears as bread,
tears to overflowing you give them for drink.

To the best of my knowledge, this element of the description of misery—as well as the allied feature of a description of agony—has not yet been investigated in the context of form-critical study.

Following the mournful cry at the beginning of v 1 are three lines bewailing the contrast between the current and the former state of affairs. These three lines unfold in readily intelligible sequence. Formerly Jerusalem was a "populous city," "great among the peoples," a renowned city that ruled over a considerable territory ("who ruled over provinces"). Now this city is "lonely" (emptied of inhabitants), its reputation has been diminished ("...has become like a widow"), and it stands under foreign domination. The Lamentation over the Destruction of Ur exhibits exactly analogous development: "Oh thou city of great name, now hast thou been destroyed." Thus, in the three lines of v 1 the motif of contrast—focusing on the earlier glory of the city of Jerusalem in terms reminiscent of the songs of Zion—resounds in just the same fashion as does the praise of the former glory of the fallen hero in dirges. Further resembling the manner of speech in dirges, the devastated city is spoken of as a person: "She sits alone...she has become like a widow." The close connection between dirge and plaintive lament is especially apparent in this introductory verse, with its identification of the city as a person. What we have here is a personifying of a collectivity, of a people taken as a whole. We have seen this sort of move already in Amos 5:1-2 and Jer 23:1-4, as well as in the Lamentation over the Destruction of Ur.

Verses 2-3

The notion of "personifying" here would be inappropriate if by that one meant nothing more than the equating of a some*thing* with a some*one*, of an object with a person. The essential point of this comparison is that, through it, the history of a people is accorded a characteristic usually reserved for a personal story. A whole people acquires the traits of an individual, someone whose destiny involves the possibility of suffering.

2a-b: All of this is said explicitly in v 2a-b ("She cries endlessly at night, tears running down her cheeks..."). Here the initial comparison is being developed. Suffering, pain, weeping—in reality all of these are features of the individual human being's existence. If they are here ascribed to a city as a whole, then we have before us a specific instance of the "corporate personality." The city is personified; the city itself suffers. Such personifying does not fit well with our modern perception of historical or political events; we tend not to personalize events in this way. However, just such a personalized understanding of a political entity (the city) is characteristic of Lamentations as a whole. The tone which determines the whole resounds already here in the opening verses of the first song. As our exegetic work proceeds, we will need to pay careful attention to this particular way of conceptualizing a city. It is important that we not overlook how different this is from our own practice.

Part of the suffering of the city is the fact that "no one...consoles her." The city suffers in solitude. The motif that Jerusalem is unconsoled runs like a thread throughout this whole song of lamentation (vv 9b, 16b, 17a, 18b, 20c, 21a). The Hebrew verb *niham* has a broader range of meaning than the English "console."[1] *Niham* designates comforting words, to be sure, but it also refers to actions that alleviate or mollify suffering. This fuller range of meaning lies behind the reference to Job's friends, when they are said to come to console Job. It is also the thrust of the opening clause of Deutero-Isaiah's proclamation "Comfort, comfort my people!" (see also Pss 22:12 [*sic*, 23:4?]: 72:12 [*sic*, 71:21?]; 107:12 [*sic*, 86:17?]; Isa 63:5 [*sic*, 66:13?]; Job 29:12 [*sic*, 29:25?—*Trans.*]).

In the motif "there is no one to console...," which occurs several times, we see reflected a distinct understanding of the nature of community: a sufferer has a right to expect to be consoled. It is inhuman not to console a sufferer. This expectation holds not just in the realm of private, inter-personal relations. It holds just as well in the area of relations between groups. Despite the realities of ethnic conflict and inter-group hostility, the Bible retains a recollection that people are essentially neighbors to one another. Their antagonisms are rooted in a secondary order of reality.

2c-3: The description of misery passes over to recollection of the event that brought about this disastrous state of affairs.

---

[1] Cf. entry *niham* in *THAT*, II:59-66.

Israel was left in the lurch by its neighbors (v 2c). As a consequence, the city was captured and the populace had to go into exile. The expression "away from misery and harsh servitude" refers to the gruesome time during which Jerusalem was besieged and subjected to the enemy. Then came the worst of all: "Judah has been carried away" into exile. Conceptually, v 3c belongs before v 3b; many tried to escape from the misery and impending exile, but they were pursued, captured, and led away. Now Judah "dwells among the peoples," finding no rest, displaced among alien peoples. Intertwined in the description of misery in vv 1-3, then, we have both a depiction of a situation and a report on how such a state of affairs came about. The emphasis falls on describing the disastrous situation which resulted, but allusions to the chain of events which led up to this situation are a steady accompaniment to the main flow of thought. Both themes are tightly interwoven, and the lament encompasses both. It is the fate of a city which is being bewailed here, but that fate played itself out in stages around the central calamity. The whole sequence of events is involved when "Jerusalem remembers" (v 7). The fate of the city is like the fate of an individual human being.

Verses 4-6

The description of misery is continued in vv 4-6, but now in such a fashion that the distress of the city (v 4a-b) and its inhabitants (vv 4c-6, except for v 5a-b) receives individualized treatment.

4a-bα: First the city's misery is described. The city as a whole is encapsulated in the word-pair "roads...gates." Precisely these two features of the city are mentioned because of their visibility, and because the speaker wants the hearer to be able to envision the destruction. The roads are personified; they "mourn" because no one treads upon them. The gates, now "laid waste," are where the people were accustomed to gather. The scope of the destruction is captured in a contrast: "...because no one comes to festival." Festivals are intrinsic to the life of a city. Here, in remarkably few words, the extinguishing of a city's life is pictured; anyone who hears these words can capture the whole scene in the mind's eye.

4bβ-6: Next the misery of the city's inhabitants is described. Mentioned in particular are priests, maidens, children, and nobles or aristocrats along with their splendor and their valuables—i.e., everything that gave the life of the city its glitter. Artistry is evident in the way these groups are enumerated. Only a few of the groups within the populace as a whole are mentioned by name, but the totality of the population is implied in the way one readily calls to mind those associated with the groups explicitly mentioned (e.g., with "children" one thinks also of parents, etc.). Artistry is also evident in the way the miserable circumstances (they sigh, they are oppressed) under which the city's inhabitants must now exist are brought into association with the events that generated these circumstances: the children must also fall into the line of march of the exiles, all the city's treasures have been plundered (vv 5c, 6a). Parenthetically, the clause "all the valuables that had been hers since of old" (v 7a) ought to be read as immediately following v 6a; when read as part of v 7, it overloads the stanza. In conjunction with the overthrow, the city's nobles were hunted down like wild animals under pursuit (v 6b-c). The terror of the conquest still reverberates in the misery which followed in its wake. To top it off, it was Yahweh who smote the city (v 5b). The first two lines of v 5 are not actually part of the description of misery; rather, they identify the ultimate cause of the misery. In the midst of the description there is inserted a recognition of guilt (see also vv 7-11).

Verses 7-11

Vv 1-6 hang together as a unified segment of the text; the same can be said for vv 13-15. For the intervening vv 7-11 (& v 12) one must first search for a context that can give unity to the material. The community continues its lament here, but the lament is interrupted by other motifs. The opening words constitute a new point of departure: "Jerusalem remembers the days of her misery and anguish." In contrast to what has gone before, in vv 7-11 (& v 12) the emphasis falls initially on a bald recounting of the collapse (v 7a-c—also v 9b). Attention then shifts to the acknowledgement of guilt in v 8a (continued in v 9a), and to the plea for God's gracious intervention (v 9c, v 11c). In order to grasp the connections here, one must first of all read this material without the lines interspersed in vv 8b-c, 10, and 11a-b. That is, we must start by reading the material as follows:

7a: introduction: "Jerusalem remembers..."
7b,c; 9b: report of the collapse
8a; 9a: acknowledgement of guilt
9c; 11c: plea for Yahweh's gracious intervention

This is the sequence of events to keep in mind as we proceed to the verse-by-verse analysis.

7a: "Jerusalem remembers...." The act of remembering deals with events of the past, the recalling of which is an actualizing of the same due to their significance for the present.[2] Such remembering often takes place in connection with lamentation (Num 11:4-5; Pss 42:5,7 [4,6 Eng.]; 137:1; Lam 3:20). On such occasions the mind actualizes events—particularly experiences with suffering—which made such a deep impression that they were indelibly fixed in the memory. Actualizing a defeat in this way—here the conquest of the city—can assist in overcoming the bitterness of the suffering that was experienced, even if a long time has passed since the initial ordeal. Working through an earlier experience of suffering in just this way is a very important feature associated with the Book of Lamentations.

There is another significant feature attached to the act of remembering. In the act of remembering, a community—of whatever sort—preserves its history and thereby also its identity. If a community loses its ability to remember, it loses its soul.

7b-c: "...how her people fell into the hand of the enemy and no one helped her." It is a notable feature in both the Book of Lamentations and the Lamentation over the Destruction of Ur that the specifically military actions which led to the defeat recede sharply into the background. Of such actions there is hardly any mention (other than in 4:17-20). Presumably it would have been just too painful to relive these actions again, even if only in memory. So, instead, one sees brought to the fore the motif of abandonment ("...and no one helped...").

[2] Cf. entry *zkr* in *THAT*, II:511.

Why was there no one to help against the overwhelming power
of the enemy? Israel's defeat was followed by exultation and
mockery on the part of her enemies: "Enemies saw it all and
laughed over her demise" (v 7c; cf. v 5a). So now, if memory
recalls the fall of Jerusalem, thoughts turn to the mocking by
the victors. It is quite common for laments about suffering to
pass over to laments about the dishonor which followed in the
wake of defeat. The theme of mocking by enemies appears also
in Pss 44:14-17 [13-16 Eng.]; 79:4; 80:7 [6 Eng.]; 89:42. To be
dishonored and despised by others was perceived to be just as
painful as the actual blow which had been absorbed. This sort
of situation is reflected more than once in the Book of
Lamentations.

8a-9b: The three lines of v 7 form a unity shaped by the
"Jerusalem remembers..." at the beginning of the verse. The
section which follows, comprising vv 8a-9b, is held together by
the acknowledgement of guilt in v 8a and the implication of the
same in v 9a. In both these places the substance of the clause in
v 5b is reiterated: "Yahweh has smitten her on account of all her
iniquity." When derision is spoken of as a direct consequence
of sin (v 8a), the intervening element of divine punishment can
be left unmentioned because it has already been identified (v
5b). The confession of sin in v 8a is repeated in v 9a, except that
the second time it is found in a metaphor which adds emphasis
to the theme. As in vv 1-2 so also here Zion is depicted as a
woman. This time emphasis falls on her being clad in a precious
garment. However, "her uncleanness clings to her garment" (v
9a)—i.e., she carries the marks of her disgrace around with her
in her skirts. The motif of contrast echoes throughout this
imagery. The word "uncleanness" designates menstrual blood,
which rendered a woman impure (in a cultic sense) in ancient
Israel. She cannot free herself of this uncleanness; it is out in
the open where everyone can see it. Such impurity leads to a
woman's denigration, and hence "she has dreadfully fallen" (v
9b).

One aspect of her guilt is the fact that she cast the admonitions
of the prophets to the wind: "She took no thought for her
future" (v 9aβ—cf. Isa 47:7: failing to pay heed to how matters
will end). Jerusalem's fall brings her into derision (v 8a), a

theme developed in v 8b: "all who had honored her came to despise her, for they saw her nakedness." The clause which now follows ("but she groans and turns away" [v 8c]) is a description of both her pain and her disgrace. Once again it is noted that she is "without anyone to console her" (cf.v 2a-b). So the five lines comprising vv 8a-9b, introduced by v 7, obviously form a unit. This is also indicated by the stylistic device of *inclusio* (i.e., v 7b = v 9b).

9c; 11c: The pleas for Yahweh to take heed, in v 9c and v 11c, frame the section comprising vv 10a-11b. Between v 9c and v 11c, on the one hand, and vv 10a-11b, on the other, no intrinsic connection exists. However, vv 9c and 11c are very closely tied to one another. They form the matching clauses of a structural parallelism. The motif in both of these lines is the plea for Yahweh's gracious intervention. This motif is a typical feature of the psalm of lamentation. Structurally, it is the element which contrasts with the actual lament.

> 9c: Look, O Yahweh, upon my distress, see how the enemy triumphs!
> 11c: Just look, O Yahweh, and see how despised I am!

In both the communal and the individual psalms of lamentation, a plea follows upon the lament as such. Structurally, the transition from lament to plea is the most important feature of the psalm of lamentation. The whole lament strives toward the plea. The dirge, on the other hand, exhibits no plea. In both the cases at hand, an invocation of Yahweh is attached to the plea. These two sentences could just as well stand in one of the many psalms of lamentation in the Psalter. The plea for divine intervention relates directly to the material which precedes it—*viz.*, the speaker's distress as depicted in the unfolding lament and the triumph of the speaker's enemies as described in the sections complaining about enemies (vv 2c, 5a, 6c, 7c). V 11c adds a comment about being despised, picking up on the motif of dishonor attached to suffering as initially voiced in v 8a-b. Both the community's lament about its own situation and its complaint about its enemies become transformed in the plea. They appear as reasons why God should intervene in behalf of the sufferer(s). This is also a characteristic feature in the Psalter's psalms of lamentation (e.g., in Ps 9:14 [13 Eng.]).

10a-11b: The five lines that fall between the similarly worded vv 9c and 11c exhibit no clear flow of ideas. They are aspects of a description of misery: the three clauses of v 10 reflect the element of a complaint about enemies, while the two clauses of v 11a-b are direct laments. Jerusalem is the subject that dominates in these lines. Quite possibly this section was attached to its foregoing through catch-word association: "...how the enemy triumphs" (v 9c)—"the foe stretches out his hand..." (v 10a). What this section does is develop the description of misery in vv 1-6 and the isolated sentences of the preceding lament about enemies (vv 7c & 9c). The structural disruption evident here was probably caused by the need to develop the material along alphabetic lines.

Clauses such as those in v 10a-c, derived from the element of complaint about enemies, are scattered throughout the whole text of Lamentations. All the same, it is noteworthy that they actually bear very little weight. Nothing more is really said than that the enemies plundered Jerusalem of its treasures (v 10a)— something that always happened when a city was conquered— and that they trespassed upon the sacred precinct (v 10b-c), which was a violation of Israel's law. What is not said, however, is that they destroyed the temple! To be sure, the hearer is meant to understand that trespassing upon the temple precinct already effects its defilement (cf. Dt 23:3; 2 Chr 36:17-19). All in all, however, the element of complaint about enemies plays a very modest role in Lam 1.

The hunger of Jerusalem's inhabitants is described in v 11a-b (cf. 2 Kgs 25:3). Here the structural disruption is particularly evident, for these two lines are actually a part of the description of misery in vv 1-6. They were attached to their present context only subsequently, as becomes apparent when one examines the descriptions of misery in the other songs. The severity of the famine is the point of emphasis here: "all her people groaned, they searched for food" (v 11a). Here the whole of the surviving population is mentioned for the first time. They are brought together by the common predicament of famine. Like wild animals, they must forage for something to eat; their treasures avail them not, except as means to procure food (v 11b). This sentence is so starkly descriptive of the scene in a conquered and occupied city that it cannot be other than an actual recollection. People who have actually lived through such grim circumstances report that this is indeed what it is like. Those who have not experienced for themselves the famine that grips a defeated city cannot fully understand the situation. Describing famine from the standpoint of a detached observer simply must fail to capture its gruesome reality.

Verses 12-18a

The accusation against God which lies before us here is not an actual indictment of God. It is a fervent lament directed toward God. A fundamental characteristic of the material in this section is the way both vv 12a-b and 18b contain a summons for the hearer sympathetically to participate in the speaker's pain. They separate the material into two sections. With v 12a-b a unified section is introduced; this first section runs through v 15c. Directly or indirectly, God is the subject of each clause in this section. The accusation against God in vv 12-15 corresponds to the direct complaint of the community in vv 1-6. Taken together the two sections form the corresponding parts of a larger unity.

In v 12a-b the accusation against God is introduced by Zion's directing a summons to passers-by. Like a beggar Zion pleads for compassion: "Look here and see! Is there any pain such as mine?" These few words make startlingly clear the awful misery of the one who has been overthrown, the one whose deepest agony is that none other than one's own God has done all of this (v 12c).

What God did to Jerusalem is now specified in vv 13-15, in twelve clauses distinguished by their basic "God did 'x'" structure. There is no real development of ideas here; the clauses form no discernible sequence and have no recognizable relationship to one another. The one here speaking has simply collected statements traditional for the accusation-against-God section of a communal lament and set them down next to one another. The piling up of so many clauses is intended to add emphasis, but one might well ask whether this supposed intent has actually been achieved. Perhaps the constraints of the alphabetic arrangement also has something to do with the heaping up of clauses here.

Within the group of clauses marked out by vv 12-15 (v 17b-c fits here as well), one can discern two distinct sub-groups. There are clauses which directly state what Yahweh did to Judah / Jerusalem, and there are clauses describing Yahweh's acts through metaphors. For the first sub-group v 12b-c, the reference to the "pain through which Yahweh has inflicted suffering upon me on the day of his burning anger," serves as a superscription. The expression "day of burning anger" occurs frequently in prophetic oracles of judgment (cf., e.g., Isa 13:13; Zeph 2:2; Jer 4:8,26; Hos 11:9). Yahweh delivered Jerusalem over to her enemies: "Yahweh gave me over to hands which I could not withstand" (v 14c; cf. also, e.g., Ps 78:61). Moreover, "he ordered a battle against me, to annihilate my young warriors..." (v 15b-c); "Yahweh ordered Jacob's neighbors against him..." (v 17b); "he cast off all my seasoned champions..." (v 15a). These are all direct statements about acts of God in definitive historical events. It was Yahweh who caused Judah's military collapse and brought about the overthrow of Jerusalem.

Essentially the same is also said in metaphors derived from Israelite tradition. Some of these metaphors properly belong to the genre of the lament, in particular laments about illness: "from above he sent down fire, he let it penetrate my bones" (v 13a — the verb is unclear in the Hebrew text; cf. 4:11); "he laid me low, suffering endlessly" (v 13c); "he broke my strength" (v 14b). Added to these are clauses which complain about Yahweh as the enemy: "he spread a net for my feet, he dragged me back" (v 13b); "the Lord trod the wine-press of maiden daughter Judah" (v 15c). Both of these motifs depicting Yahweh as an enemy also occur in accusations against God in the Psalms (on the treading of the wine-press, e.g., cf. Isa 63 and Joel 4:13).

Formulating the element of the accusation against God in the third person softens somewhat the accusations that are directed toward God; a certain sense of distance is hereby created. One can find traces of such neutralizing of the accusation against God also in v 14a: "heavy is the yoke of my

transgressions, fixed in place by his hand." Here two distinct
transactions are brought together in one metaphor. On the
one hand there is a confession of sins: "heavy is the yoke of my
transgressions...." On the other hand, the yoke's pressing down
and weighing heavily refer to the punishment which God lays
upon Israel for her sins: "...fixed in place by his hand." That
such dampening of the element of accusation against God is
intentional is shown by the way the accusation is framed on
both sides by confession of sin, in v 14a and then again in v 18a
("...I have rebelled against his word"). One could just as well
read v 18a immediately after v 14a, which would yield a stylistically
attractive chiasm:

> Heavy is the yoke of my transgressions,
> fixed in place by his hand (14a);
> righteous is he, is Yahweh,
> for I have rebelled against his word (18a).

As will be shown, the line at v 18a is the actual conclusion
of the accusation against God which comprises vv 12-15 and
picks up again in v 17b-c. Following v 18a, and corresponding
to v 12a, we encounter in v 18b a summons to participation.
Again as at v 12a, this summons introduces a new section. Only
as the concluding clause of a section does v 18a ("Righteous is
Yahweh...") receive its appropriate emphasis, for it closes off
the whole complex comprised of vv 12-17b (except for v 16 and
v 17a), a section shaped by the element of accusation against
God. Although the sequence of thought is disrupted in the text
as it has been transmitted to us, behind that text we can
nonetheless find an intelligible arrangement:

> 12a-b: summons to participation
> 12c: introduction to the accusation against God
> 12c-15: accusation against God
>   (enclosed by the acknowledgement of guilt in v 14a
>   and v 18a)
> 18a: conclusion of the accusation against God, an
>   acknowledgement of the justice of God's ways
> 18b: summons to participation

The summons to participation is an element taken from the dirge. It frames the accusation against God, which is itself further tied together by the acknowledgement of guilt. In the conclusion, at v 18a, the accusation against God is deliberately juxtaposed to an acknowledgement of divine justice, a motif which corresponds to the acknowledgement of guilt. Then there follows, in v 18b, a renewed summons to participation; this, together with v 12a-b, makes up the framework. The whole is an eloquent example of how the plaintive lament can be associated with themes from the dirge. Only loosely tied in to this particular context is the description of agony in vv 16-17a, a feature which occurs in both the element of a community's direct complaint and the element of accusation against God. This feature attaches to the material in v 15 by means of the *'al-'ēlleh* ["for these things..."].

The lines at vv 16c, 17b, and 17c exhibit no meaningful connection. V 17b-c is a supplement to the accusation against God and would therefore be expected to fall between vv 15 and 16; 17b and 17c belong together according to the suffering — dishonor schema. V 16b, on the other hand, properly belongs in the context of the community's direct complaint in vv 1-11. The sentence ("My children are devastated, for the enemy is too powerful") could serve as the transition from the community's direct complaint to the complaint about enemies. Since the element of the community's direct complaint occurs elsewhere in Lamentations only in a cluster of at least three lines, here it has the effect of being displaced. This is just another indication that the proper sequence of verses has been disrupted, most likely through the compulsion to arrange the material alphabetically. On the other hand, the disruption is so slight that the conclusion of the unit comprising vv 12-15 + 17b-c is unmistakably recognizable at v 18.

This clause at v 18a ("Righteous is he, is Yahweh, for I have rebelled against his word") can properly be appreciated only when seen in the context here assigned to it. Just how important the acknowledgement of guilt is for Lam 1 has already been shown (with ref. to vv 5 and 9). Here, at the high point of the whole song, this motif is brought into conjunction with an acknowledgement of the justice of God's ways such that the whole preceding lament is set off: God *must* act in this way, because we have transgressed against his word. When seen in this way, the clause also intimates a significant "nevertheless." That is to say, despite our lamenting we still hold fast to the conviction that God is just. This "nevertheless" corresponds to the so-called *wāw adversativum* in the psalms of lament— the grammatical element which marks the transition from expressions of pain to statements of trust. Quite often, following the *w āw adversativum*, one finds an avowal of trust. To be sure, those doing the lamenting here are not yet able to break through to such an avowal. Still, a suggestion of such is to be found at the proper place here in v 18a: despite all that has transpired, Yahweh is nevertheless in the right! Here we also see how Lamentations comes close to Deutero-Isaiah, who in his contestations (cf., e.g., Isa 43:22-28) likewise emphasizes the necessity of God's acting in the way God has in fact acted.

Verses 18b-22

The summons to participation in v 18b introduces the concluding section of Lam 1, a section which contains as sub-units vv 18b-21a and 21b-22c. The first sub-unit offers essentially just repetitions of themes already encountered above. Here as well the proper sequence of the verses is disrupted. The emphasis clearly lies on the plea for God's gracious intervention, voiced in v 20a and repeated in v 21a. Otherwise the individual themes follow one upon another without intrinsic connection.

18b-21a: That we here begin a new sub-unit is shown by the summons to participation ("Hear, all you peoples, and see my pain!"). This summons is grounded in the specific words of lamentation in vv 18c-19c. The youth among the populace must go off into exile (v 18c — a theme which stems from the community's direct complaint and which repeats what is said in vv 3a and 5c); their friends have left them in the lurch (v 19a); famine haunts them (v 19b-c — again a theme which stems from the community's direct complaint; cf. v 11a-b); death rages both within and without (v 20c — cf. v 7b-c). Despite the presently disordered arrangement of the material, one can still see how these clauses aim at persuading God to turn graciously toward the people (vv 20a, 21a). When such themes occur in the context of a plea they are always briefly worded; they consist of only one or two lines.

> 20a: "Look, O Yahweh, for I am alarmed, my innards smolder!"
> 21a: "Listen to how I sigh, no one is there to comfort me!"

Here, at the song's end, the lament becomes a plea. The final emphasis falls on this plea. In keeping with such a shift the individual clauses of lamentation, clauses which aim at persuading God to respond graciously, no longer have the same third-person form as do the clauses in the description of misery in vv 1-6. Instead, they are all here put into first-person form (a feature anticipated already in v 14a). This feature of first-person speech persists to the end of the song.

The pleas for God to take note, in vv 20a and 21a, are similar to the pleas in vv 9c and 11c. It is particularly noticeable, with the repetition of these pleas here at the end, how the customary second element of such a plea—a plea for God directly to intervene on behalf of the people of God—is lacking. To ask for this much is no longer being dared. Rather, in v 20aβ-b one finds another description of misery ("I am alarmed, my innards smolder..."). This description is offered in the hope that God will thereby be persuaded graciously to turn toward the people. Once again a confession of guilt follows ("...because I was rebellious"). The sequence of themes in these clauses follows effortlessly upon the plea in v 20a .

The next line ("outside the sword wreaks havoc and within death is everywhere"—v 20c) follows somewhat abruptly. It would fit very nicely after v 18c as the conclusion to the community's direct complaint. In any case, its meaning suggests that it belongs there. Moreover, v 21a would better follow directly upon v 20b. Apparently the necessity of arranging the material alphabetically has once again forced a dislocation. Removing v 20c would leave the remaining material—consisting of vv 20a, 20b, and 21a—with a plea for God's gracious attentiveness at both the beginning and the end; this would create a consistent and comprehensible little unit. "Outside...

within" is a standard word-pair meaning "everywhere" (cf. Deut 32:25; Isa 14:18 [*sic*, Jer 14:18?]; Ezek 7:15 — and also the Lamentation over the Destruction of Ur).

21b-22c: The final section consists of a plea for reprisal to be exacted against Israel's enemies (vv 21c-22c). This plea is introduced by a line of complaint about enemies (v 21b).

V 21b voices the theme of mockery on the part of the enemies (as in vv 5a and 7c): "All my enemies heard of my misfortune, they rejoiced...." The "misfortune" is the collapse of Judah. The text does not specifically identify the misfortune. Rather, it speaks of it indirectly, noting "...that you had done it." This is a conceptual contraction; it serves as a bridge to the petition directed to Yahweh in the immediately following clause. The "you" of "...that you had done it" promptly becomes the "you" who is asked nonetheless to work retribution. Specifically, "Let come the day which you proclaim." (The Hebrew text is somewhat unclear at this point, but in any case the reference is to the day on which retribution is meted out to Israel's opponents.)

In v 22a-b the petition against the enemies continues. "Let it yet come upon them as it has upon me; let all their evil come before you!" The foe has likewise committed transgressions, and so the foe should be punished by Yahweh just as the people of God have been punished: "And do to them as you have done to me...!" The petition of v 22a is repeated in v 22b in order to append the motif "because of all my sins." Reprisal against enemies is the traditional concluding theme of psalms of lamentation (e.g., Pss 79:12 and 83:14-15; also 6:11 [10 Eng.]— an individual psalm of lament). In the present case, however, this theme has been expanded in the way the plea for reprisal against enemies has been drawn into conjunction with the theme noting what God has done to the people of God ("...that you had done it [v 21b]...because of all my sins" [v 22b]). In other words, the traditional theme of a plea for reprisal to be enacted against enemies has indeed been adopted, but here it is associated with an awareness of the singular set of circumstances. The plea for reprisal grows directly out of the experience of having been decimated. No one yet dares voice a plea for Israel's restoration.

The description of agony in v 22c is not intrinsically related to its immediately preceding lines. "For my sighs are countless, and my heart is ill" (cf. Jer 8:18). The clause has been appended here simply to bring the number of lines in the stanza to the requisite three.

Excursus: The Change of Voices in Lam 1

Many exegetes attempt to break up Lam 1 on the basis of its change of voices. So, for example, Rudolph writes, " The song naturally falls into two units of the same size: vv 1-11, and vv 12-22. In the first unit Zion is primarily spoken of in the third person... In the second section Zion herself does most of the speaking, with only v 17 speaking about Zion" (p. 209). As do Kraus and others, Rudolph concludes "that the song is meant from the outset to be performed." In other words, it is to be spoken by distinctly separate voices. When divided up according to whether Zion speaks as subject or Zion is spoken of as object, one section (Zion as subject) comprises vv 9c, 11c-16c, and 18-22, while the other section (Zion as object) comprises vv 1-9b, 10a-11b, and 17. However, breaking up the material in this way yields no intelligible sense; the arrangement of the material can hardly be explained in this fashion.

To be sure, Rudolph (joined by others) is correct in observing that "the change of voices gives the poem a somewhat dramatic movement" (p. 209). However, this dramatic movement can be accounted for in another fashion. In the first section, in vv 1-11, Zion's misery is described. A change of voice occurs only in vv 9c and 11c, in the plea for God's gracious attentiveness or in the transition from the lament to the plea. Here the change of voice is to be explained by reference to the content; the element of petition to Yahweh acquires its own distinctive form. In the second section, in vv 12-22, a different state of affairs holds. This whole section is predominantly prayer; here Zion is spoken of in the third person only in v 17. Constituent elements of this section include the confession of sins in v 18, the plea for God's gracious attentiveness in vv 20a and 21a, and the petition directed against enemies in v 22a-b. The preponderance of the element of description of misery inclines the petitionary language in the second section toward a lamenting style of prayer; this is the style in which Zion turns toward God. Such an inclination toward lamentation stamps the whole section. So, according to our explanation the change in subject is due to the content. This explanation applies to the whole song.

The change from singular to plural, or vice versa, likewise plays no role in dividing the text into its constituent units. Those who speaking in this text are at the same time both the lamenters and the lamented. Zion, taking up her lament as a solitary and defenseless woman, also represents a multitude—the whole city and its inhabitants. Correspondingly, Zion herself can say "my sighs are countless" while someone else can speak of her suffering and note that "she groans and turns away." Zion both laments and is lamented. The change between singular and plural is a way of expressing the fact that the lamenters can be viewed as either a unit (Zion) or as a conglomeration (see also our remarks on 3:48, 49, and 51, below).

The distinctive feature of Lam 1 is the way it emphasizes two motifs which stand in polar relationship to one another. One pole is the expression of agony, with its *leitmotif* of being inconsolable. The other is confession of guilt, a motif repeated several times. The polar relationship of these two major themes finds clearest expression in v 18a, the clause that—from a form-critical perspective—stands where one would expect an avowal of trust ("Righteous is he, is Yahweh, for I..."). Those voicing the lament here clearly know that the terrible fate which has befallen them has been inflicted upon them because of their own guilt. Yet they do not stop with confirming that their punishment was deserved. Instead, they lay out their bitter agony before God. They do so in order that, despite their guilt, God might graciously turn toward them once again.

Lam 2

1   Ah, how Yahweh in his wrath overclouds[a] daughter Zion!
     He has cast down the majesty of Israel from heaven into the dust[b]
     and remembered not his footstool on the day of his anger.

2 Yahweh has laid waste without pity[a] all the meadows of Jacob,
   in his rage he has torn down the strongholds of daughter Judah.
   He thrust to the ground, he defiled[b] the kingdom and its princes.

3 He has shattered in fiery anger[a] all the might of Israel,
   drawn back his right hand in the face of the enemy[b]
   and raged in Jacob like a flaming fire, devouring all around.

4 He bent his bow like an enemy, the arrow in his right hand,[a]
   like a foe he smote[b] and slew all the well-equipped.
   In the tent of daughter Zion he poured out his wrath like fire.[c]

5 Yahweh became like an enemy, he devastated Israel,
   he demolished all his[a] palaces, destroyed his fortresses
   and heaped up in daughter Judah distress upon misery[b].

6 He tore down like a garden his booth,[a] laid waste to his tabernacle.
   Yahweh made holiday and sabbath to be forgotten in Zion
   and in his glowing anger spurned king and priest.

7 Yahweh has rejected his altar, disdained his sanctuary,
   he gave over to the hand of the enemy the walls of her palaces[a],
   they have made an uproar in the temple of Yahweh as on a day of festival.

8 Yahweh intended to destroy the walls of daughter Zion,
   he stretched out the line,[a] he did not hold back his hand from destroying.
   He caused to mourn both rampart and wall[b], together they sank down.

9 Her gates sank into the dust, he destroyed and shattered[a] her bars.

Her king and her princes are among the Gentiles, there is
no longer any guidance[b],
nor do her prophets find revelation from Yahweh any
more.

10 The elders of daughter Zion sit silently[a] on the ground,
they have strewn dust on their heads, girded themselves
with sackcloth;
the maidens of Jerusalem have dropped their heads to the
earth.

11 My eyes are dissolved in tears, my innards are in ferment,
my bowels[a] are poured out on the ground over the downfall
of the daughter of my people[b],
as children and nurselings languished[c] in the squares of
the city.

12 They kept crying[a] out to their mothers, "Where is bread
and wine[b]?"
as they languished, mortally wounded, in the city's squares,
as they breathed their last at their mothers' bosoms.

13 To whom shall I compare you,[a] with what shall I liken you,
O daughter Zion?
What can I liken to you, so as to console you, O maiden
daughter Zion?
Verily, deep as the sea is your ruin, who can heal you?

14 Your prophets have announced to you mere whitewash[a],
they have not exposed your guilt, to avert your fate;
nay, they have prophesied to you lying and misleading
speeches.

15 All who passed on the way clapped their hands at you;
they hissed and wagged their heads over daughter
Jerusalem.
Is this the city of which one said, "crown of beauty, the
delight of the whole world"[a]?

16[a] All your enemies flung open their mouths against you,
they hissed and gnashed their teeth, they said, "We have
annihilated![bc]
Verily, this is the day for which we hoped[d], we have attained
it, have experienced it."

17   Yahweh has carried out what he planned, has fulfilled his
word,
just as he announced it long ago. Without pity has he
trampled underfoot,
has allowed the enemy to exult over you, has given strength
to your oppressors.

18   Cry aloud[a] to Yahweh, lament, O maiden[b] daughter Zion!
Let tears flow like a brook, by day and by night!
Allow yourself no rest, your eyes no respite!

19   Arise, loudly[a] lament at night, at the beginning of the
watch!
Pour out your heart[b] like water before the presence of
Yahweh!
Lift up your hands to him for the life of your children
(who perish of hunger at every street corner)[c].

20   Ah, Yahweh, look and consider to whom[a] you have done
this!
Should women eat their offspring, their dandled[b] little ones?
Should priest and prophet be slain in the sanctuary of
Yahweh?

21   Young and old lie prostrate in the dust of the streets.
My maidens and my youths fell by the sword[a].
You have slain them on the day of your anger, you have
slaughtered without pity.

22   You summoned as though for a festival those round about,
those who threatened[a] me,
there was no one on the day of Yahweh's wrath[b] who
survived and escaped.

> Those whom I nurtured and reared — my enemy has obliterated them.

Textual Notes

1a: Instead of our "how [Yahweh] overclouds [Zion]," L. Kopf (*VT* 8 [1958] 188-89) here translates "how [Yahweh] has dishonored [Zion]," citing an Arabic cognate; this alternate translation possibility is followed by, *inter alia*, Rudolph, Hillers, Gottlieb, and Kaiser. **b:** There is no mythological allusion here; this is merely a metaphorical expression meaning "very far down" (cf. Rudolph *et al.*).

2a: With the *Qere* read *wĕlō' ḥāmal* ("and had no pity"). **b:** Read *ḥillēl* with MT; the same motif occurs at Ps 79:1.

3a: Perhaps read "in his anger" with the versions; [see the critical apparatus to BHS.] **b:** Luther translates "as the enemy came"; Rudolph does the same. (On the metaphor cf. Ps 74:11.)

4a: Read *ḥēṣ bîmînō* (with Rudolph, Kaiser). **b:** Expand the verse by adding *ḥikkāh* (with Hillers, Kaiser). **c:** The critical apparatus of BHK³ suggests transposing the two stichoi of this colon; in BHS this suggestion is lacking.

5a: Despite Löhr and the suggestion of the critical apparatus in BHS, it is not necessary to change the suffix (cf. Kraus, Gottlieb). **b:** Hillers here draws a comparison with the Lamentation over the Destruction of Sumer and Ur (cf. ANET 617:361-62 and 619:486-87).

6a: The initial words of the verse are not intelligible as they stand; the translation can be little more than a surmise. (The Greek has "vine" [ἄμπελος] rather than "garden.") By and large, interpreters find none of the suggested emendations convincing. Re'emi translates, "He has broken down his booth like that of a garden." In all likelihood we are here dealing with an abbreviated comparison (thus Gottlieb). A similar comparison shows up in the Lamentation over the Destruction of Ur: "My house...like a garden hut, verily on its side has caved in" (ANET, 457:122).

7a: This is probably a reference to the temple; Rudolph emends the text to read "the most costly of her treasures" (= the temple's utensils).

8a: "He stretched out the line" clearly presupposes that a measuring line was used in conjunction with pulling things down (cf. 2 Kgs 21:13 and T. J. Meek's "he marked it off by the line"). **b:** Rudolph's "outer fortification" is perhaps a more precise translation.

9a: The *šibbar* is stricken by many as a variant. **b:** The *'ēn tôrāh* is a self-standing clause, which Rudolph renders "instruction is lacking."

10a: This is an instance of the so-called circumstantial verbal clause (GKC § 156d); emendations to the text at v 10a are unnecessary.

11a: The versions here read *kĕbōdî* ["my glory"], but there is no compelling reason to change the Masoretic Text. **b:** On the phrase *'al-šeber bat-'ammî*, cf. Jer 6:14 and 8:11. **c:** Perhaps MT's *bē* is to be read *bĕ*, cf. the critical apparatus to BHK.

12a: The imperfect is to be taken as a frequentative. **b:** There is no reason either to strike or to emend the *w āyā yin* ("and wine").

13a: The wording corresponds very closely to Isa 40:18. The two verbs in this colon must have a similar meaning ("to vouch for someone"—cf. the "commended" [so NJPS; same verbal root-*Trans.*] at Job 29:11).

14a: "Mere whitewash" occurs also at Ezek 13:10, but there is still no reason to assume literary dependency here (*contra* Cothenet, Kaiser).

15a: The last three words are not a subsequent addition but rather a deliberate citation of Ps 48:3.

16a: In this acrostic the *pē* precedes the *'ayin;* several manuscripts have therefore reversed the order of vv 16 and 17. **b:** It is not necessary to append a pronominal suffix to the verb. **c:** The verb is *billaʿ,* as in vv 2 and 5 (cf. Isa 49:19 and Jer 51:34). **d:** Kaiser speaks of an asyndetic word order in cases of agitated speech.

18a: Read *ṣaʿaqî lāk* (or *libbēk*). **b:** Read *hĕmî bĕtūlat* = "lament, O maiden!"

19a: *Rānan* is otherwise attested mainly with the meaning "rejoice" (cf. Jer 14:12). **b:** Cf. Ps 62:8 and 1 Sam 1:15; this expression is found not only in Hebrew but occurs also in English and German. **c:** The last line is a subsequent addition (cf. Lam 2:11b and 4:1).

20a: Unspoken, but implied, here is "to the people whom you have chosen as your own." **b:** The *ṭippuḥîm* is a *hapax legomenon* (cf. the contrasting use of the same root in v 22c).

21a: Hillers compares to v 21 some lines from the Lamentation over the Destruction of Ur (cf. ANET, 459:215-18).

22a: On *mĕgūray* = "who threatened me" cf. Jer 6:25. **b:** "Day of Yahweh's wrath" is a fixed expression.

The Structure of Lam 2
As in Lam 1, so also in Lam 2 each successive verse begins with the next letter in the sequence of twenty-two letters in the Hebrew alphabet. Again as with Lam 1, each verse of Lam 2 contains three lines. Hence this chapter also consists of sixty-six lines. It is also the case here, as with Lam 1, that the constraints imposed by the alphabetic arrangement of the verses has led to various transpositions and expansions, as well as exercising an influence upon the specific choice of words employed.

1. Even though at first glance the structure of Lam 2 appears to have little in common with the structure of Lam 1, upon closer analysis the similarity is indeed considerable. Here also one must start out from the features that are clear, for it is on the basis of these features that the overall configuration is recognizable. A division of the whole lament into three parts is determinative also for Lam 2. The large complex of material at the beginning, vv 1-9a, is [in form-critical terminology] an accusation against God, transformed into a third-person description of misery. In most of the clauses here the subject is God; most of these clauses have the form "God has done...." Since the accusation against God surfaces once again in vv 21c-22a (note the direct address!), the framework of Lam 2 is an accusation against God.

2. The section comprising vv 9b-12 is a description of misery, corresponding to a community's direct complaint but here formulated in the third person. There is a fluid zone of transition between the accusation against God and the community's direct complaint; in vv 8c and 9a both these elements are tied together. Vv 9b-12 deal with the effect of the divine wrath.

3. The clauses of the accusation against God in vv 1-9a follow one another without recognizable sub-division. One can arrange this material only according to the content of the various clauses:

> In wrath God has brought about the collapse, he has
> destroyed the land, the cities, the buildings and the temple,
> has overthrown the land's leadership, has terminated its
> worship. God fought like an enemy against the very people
> of God.

The community's direct complaint in vv 9-12 is tied in with a first-person description of misery in v 11a-b, while in the rest of the clauses the complaint proceeds by enumerating the miseries of the various groups of people affected.

4. The confession of guilt, an element that is particularly emphasized in Lam 1, appears to be lacking in Lam 2. However, such an element is implicit in the attribution of guilt directed against the false prophets in v 14 and then reflectively expanded in v 17. The complaint about enemies in vv 15-16 is thus framed by a confession of guilt. This third type of complaint is thus here kept short and tightly circumscribed.

5. V 17 is once again accusation against God. This time it has a comprehensive and summary character. One would have expected to find v 17 following v 8, for there it is already affirmed that God has carried out his plan, has already confirmed the prophetic message of judgment.

6. Special emphasis lies on the summons to engage in lamentation, in vv 18-19. Here begins a turning point, since there soon follows plea addressed directly to Yahweh (cf. v 20a : "Ah, Yahweh, look and consider...").

7. Properly speaking, our lamenting prayer concludes with this plea for God to take heed, for the clauses which follow v 20a are basically just repetitions of laments already voiced (and, to be sure, cast in all three of the basic types of complaint). These concluding clauses have the function of motivating Yahweh to respond favorably to the plea voiced in v 20a . ("...to whom you have done this!" [v 20aβ]; "Should women...?" [v 20b]; Should priests...?" [v 20c]; "You have slain them on the day of your wrath...!" [v 21c].)

In broad outline, then, the structure of Lam 2 corresponds to that of the communal lament. Only the mournful cry at the beginning really belongs to the dirge. In keeping with this is the quite extensive transformation of the lament into description of misery. The summons to lamentation in vv 18-19, resembling a feature of the dirge, becomes rather a call to invoke the aid of Yahweh. All in all, the sequence of themes reflects the pattern of the communal lament:

1-8(9a): description of misery, corresponding to an accusation against God;
9b-13: description of misery, corresponding to a community's

    direct complaint;
15-16: a complaint about enemies;
14,17: a confession of guilt;
18-19: summons to voice a plea to Yahweh;
20a: direct address, plea for Yahweh's gracious response;
20b, 21a, 22b: motive clauses;
21b, 22a: accusation against God: It is You who have done it!

Exegesis of Lam 2
Verses 1-9a

Despite the constraints imposed by its alphabetic arrangement, 2:1-9a forms a distinct block of material. All of the clauses in this section have the same basic form ("God has done...") and therein correspond to the so-called accusation against God, an element which one also finds in the psalms of lamentation. That the feature of direct accusation (accusation cast in the second person) stands closely behind this accusatory speech (cast in the third person) is shown at the end of the chapter, in vv 21c and 22a. No more than the situation reflected in these concluding lines is needed to establish that the Book of Lamentations is a special collection of communal laments. This holds even though, in 2:1-8, the contrast motif as known from the dirge obviously stands in the foreground (cf. the "How you have been destroyed...O celebrated city!..." of Ezek 26:17ff; cf. also Ezek 19:1-9, 10-14; 27; 28:11-19 [on these references see above, p. *20*).

If one surveys these deeply moving lines as a whole, the first feature to strike one is how the *leitmotif* (viz., the wrath of Yahweh) of this section reappears at the end, in v 21c. This is the theme of the opening line ("Ah, how Yahweh in his wrath overclouds...!"), to which one must add the following references: "...the day of his/your anger" (vv 1c and 21c); "in his rage" (v 2b); "he has shattered in fiery anger..." (v 3a); "raged...like a flaming fire" (v 3c); "...poured out his wrath like fire" (v 4c); "and in his glowing anger spurned..." (v 6c); "...on the day of Yahweh's wrath" (v 22b). At hardly any other place in the whole of the Old Testament is there so much talk about the wrath of God.

When the Old Testament talks about the wrath of God, it is not referring to an attribute of God. This sort of language is used to describe a way in which God reacts to some sort of event. Some incident triggers an angry reaction on the part of God. Such reaction on the part of God is then experienced by specific human beings, or by some particular human group. Only on the basis of an experience of this sort is it possible to speak of the wrath of God. In other works, speech about the wrath of God is grounded in interpretation of some concrete event that has transpired. The prophets who speak of the wrath of God "speak not of some emotion on the part of God but rather of an anger that is evident in a blow directed against the people of God and so capable of being experienced, in terms of its effect."[1] Because of this dimension, speech about the wrath of God in Lam 2—as well as throughout the Book of Lamentations—stems from a different realm than does the superficially similar speech about the wrath of God in the prophets of judgment.

The second noticeable feature of this section is the way the experience of the wrath of God focuses entirely on one event: the destruction of Jerusalem, the city of Yahweh. A description of the circumstances surrounding that destruction is almost totally lacking in this section. Instead, the lament concentrates wholly on the event that led to the speakers' present situation. One could put it this way: Those who speak in this fashion are like people who are thunderstruck. They have been struck completely numb by an incomprehensible turn of events.

1: This section starts out with a lament to the effect that God has brought about the collapse: "Ah, how Yahweh in his wrath overclouds daughter Zion!" It was Yahweh who "cast down the majesty of Israel from heaven into the dust"—a contrast typical of the dirge. Yahweh has shattered Israel's strength. Expressed in simile, Yahweh has raged like a flaming fire (vv 3c, 4c) and torn down his booth like a garden (v 6a)—though this latter comparison is anything but obvious. Moreover, Yahweh has dealt with Israel as though dealing with an enemy. Like a foe,

---

[1] Cf. my "Boten des Zorns," in my *Forschung am Alten Testament: Gesammelte Studien III* (ThB 73; 1984) 100.

Yahweh has laid waste to Israel (v 5a) and slain all who were "well-equipped" (v 4b). Again like an enemy Yahweh has bent his bow, an arrow in his right hand (v 4a). In short, "he did not hold back his hand from destroying" (v 8b). Elsewhere in the Old Testament the theme that God has become an enemy is stated so bluntly and so extensively only in the laments of Job. There, only one individual has been smitten and laments; in Lam 2 the people have been struck down, and they lament in tones reminiscent of the dirge. In both cases, however, the laments are reaction to incomprehensible suffering. The theme of the deity as an enemy also shows up in the Lamentation over the Destruction of Ur: "How long, pray, wilt thou stand aside in the city like an enemy?" (line 374).

Lam 2 goes on to say that Yahweh did not do what the God of Israel was supposed to do. The Helper and Savior of Israel has not come to the people's aid. Yahweh has "drawn back his right hand in the face of the enemy" (v 3b); Yahweh has not been mindful of his people in their time of need (v 1c). In these clauses there is a suggestion of a theme characteristic of the communal lament but otherwise absent from Lamentations, namely some retrospection upon God's earlier saving acts (cf., e.g., Ps 80). The lack of this particular theme is characteristic of Lamentations. Israel's collapse has been so dreadful that recollection of God's earlier saving deeds is stifled. In the two aforementioned clauses there is only a hint of this theme. Why, it is wondered, did God not come to Israel's aid? (On v 1 cf. also 1 Chr 28:2; Pss 49:5 and 132:7.)

2-9a: The extent of the destruction brought about by God is now unfolded. The land has been laid waste. "Yahweh has laid waste without pity all the meadows of Jacob" (v 2a); he has "...laid waste to his tabernacle" (v 6a), destroyed the inhabited sites. "In his rage he has torn down the strongholds of daughter Judah" (v 2b); "he demolished all his palaces, destroyed his fortresses" (v 5b); "he gave over to the hand of the enemy the walls of her palaces" (v 7b); he has destroyed Zion's ramparts and walls, her gates along with their cross-bars (vv 8-9a; on the motif of mourning Jerusalem's ruins, cf. Isa 52:9-10). In sum, "Yahweh has rejected his altar" (v 7a). Moreover, Yahweh has allowed the leadership to fall: "he thrust to the ground, he defiled the kingdom and its princes" (v 2c); "in his glowing anger [Yahweh] spurned king and priest" (v 6c). God has destroyed all that the people relied upon for safety, security, order, and a sense of direction. All of this has disappeared with the destruction of the sanctuary and the elimination of the festivals, for it was from these that blessing went out over the land (cf. Ezek 24:21-24).

This elaborately developed accusation against God in Lam 2, for all its distraught quality, nonetheless on the whole exhibits a carefully conceptualized arrangement. It has developed out of mournful reflection upon the devastating loss on occasions when the fall of Jerusalem was solemnly memorialized. None of all that which God granted and entrusted to the people of God upon their entrance into the land has proven to be a secure possession, something of which Israel could freely dispose. Israel has learned by experience that, if the people of God do not prove faithful to their Lord, God can take away all that was given.

Verses 9b-13

While the accusation against God, in vv 1-9a, reproaches Yahweh for the destruction of the land (not only of the inhabited sites with their structures but also of the leadership), in vv 9b-13 the people who have lived through the calamity bemoan their suffering. This shift is signaled by the deliberate way in which vv 8c-9c build a transition. In v 8c, as in the preceding clauses, Yahweh still appears as subject ("he caused to mourn..."). The object of Yahweh's action, rampart and wall, mourn like human beings, however; in this they join the sufferers of whom vv 9b-13 then deal. Rampart and wall were built by human beings in order to surround and protect their builders. Destroyed, they now lament along with those human beings; they are no longer able to fulfill their purpose. The clause at v 9a fits closely with that at v 8c, since gates and cross-bars are actually part of the walls. Destroyed, the gates and their bars sink into the dust. Here the accusation against God echoes once again: it is Yahweh who has destroyed them! God has become like an enemy to the people of God!

9b-c: In v 9b the theme of the discourse is once again king and princes—i.e., the leadership of the people. This time, however, there is a subtle difference. Now the leaders are also a part of the suffering populace; they are among those who have been exiled to foreign lands. Appended in v 9c is mention of the prophets. Supposedly those who impart instruction to the people, they themselves have ceased to receive instruction from Yahweh. Prophecy has come to a halt.

10a-13: Now comes a description of the misery, and that in two phases. First the survivors are described as mourners (v 10); the description picks up on the language and the gestures of a dirge. The elders sit silently on the ground; they have strewn dust on their heads and girded themselves with sackcloth (v 10a-b). Jerusalem's maidens have deeply lowered their heads (v 10c). As happens so often in Biblical poetry, a totality is here indicated by means of two catchwords. In this case the catchwords are "elders" and "maidens." Together they stand for all who survived the calamity, the remnant of the people. There is another description of misery in v 11a-b. This description differs, however, in that here the distress of the immediately affected comes to the fore. The deeply moving agony of these eyewitnesses focuses on a single phenomenon, namely the suffering of the little children (vv 11c-12c). They "...languished in the squares of the city," cried out to their mothers for food, and died while being cradled at their mothers' bosoms.

Considering all the terrible misery experienced by the survivors (cf. Lam 1 or 5), why is this one type so extensively described, taking up as it does not only the four lines of vv 11c-12 but also (by way of introduction) the two lines of v 11a-b? Why is this regarded as the worst aspect of the calamity? One can properly answer this question only from a consideration of the whole of Lamentations and when viewed from within the context of its historical occasion. The precipitating event was the "day of wrath" on which Israel experienced the punishment of God. Although the event was recognized as punishment, it remained incomprehensible in its severity. The severity of the event was nowhere more evident than in the suffering and death of small children. The four lines encompassing vv 11c-

12c bring out this aspect. The theme is even carried over into v 13, the verse which brings this section to a close: "To whom shall I compare you...O daughter Zion? ...Verily, deep as the sea is your ruin, who can heal you?" With the perishing of young children by starvation, something unspeakable has taken place. The explanation that this was a divine punishment does not suffice, for what is the place of small children in that! Those who witnessed this dying of the small children on the streets of Jerusalem can no longer be consoled. These three lines (v 13a-c), which emphasize the incomparability of the misery, are not of a piece with the traditional lament. Rather, these lines indicate a new awareness which began to dawn among the survivors in response to this unprecedented situation. These survivors directly experienced where the disobedience of the people finally led: to the incomprehensible suffering of the innocent, namely the children. We find this same awareness also dawning in the proclamation of Deutero-Isaiah and in a number of anonymous prophetic words of weal. The gist of the awareness is that, if the covenant history of God and Israel is to continue, then it can no longer do so in the form of the history of a people that strives for power and greatness—realities that, in the final analysis, can be achieved only by means of warfare.

In the Israelite remnant's recognition that their suffering was incomparable, another important facet becomes evident. It makes a significant difference whether the history of an armed conflict is written by those who where active participants in it or by those who, as noncombatants, nonetheless were forced to witness the unspeakable misery of innocent and uncomprehending victims—above all, the children.

Verses 14-17

We now come, following the accusation against God in vv 1-8 and the community's direct complaint in vv 9-13, to the complaint about enemies. This third of the three characteristic elements of the communal lament is here framed by the theme of attribution of guilt. It is significant that this attribution, directed against the false prophets (v 14), follows directly upon the lament about the incomparability of the suffering (v 13). Normally one would expect to find in this position an acknowledgement of guilt on the part of the speakers, a theme which runs so clearly and unmistakably throughout Lam 1. There is good reason, however, for the difference here. Lam 2:1-8 is controlled by the dominant motif of "wrath." In the Old Testament, this motif always appears as an interpretive reaction to something that has happened. Where one finds passionately agitated speech about the wrath of Yahweh, present by implication is also reference to the cause of the divine wrath: Israel's guilt. This is the sort of situation we find in Lam 2:1-8. That Israel's guilt is not made explicit, in the form of an open confession, is certainly due to the fact that the speakers are still somewhat stunned by all that has happened. Be that as it may, however, they are at least able to point out one aspect of their past in which the guilt of those days now lies clearly revealed to all. The false prophets lied; they held up visions of weal to the people when, in fact, no weal was to be expected. In this context one need do no more than recall Hananiah, Jeremiah's opponent. What prophets such as Hananiah announced, it turns out, was "mere whitewash." Once reference to the false prophets has been made, it becomes possible also to speak openly—albeit briefly—of Israel's guilt: "they have not exposed **your guilt**, to avert your fate." Exposing Israel's guilt is what those prophets should have done. Indirectly included in this charge is also a reference to the pre-exilic prophets of judgment. They did indeed carry out their proper task, but they went unheeded.

Corresponding to the accusation which the prophets of judgment raised against their people is the announcement of judgment in v 17a-b: "Yahweh has carried out what he planned, has fulfilled his word, just as he announced it long ago." Both aspects of the prophetic word of judgment [viz., accusation and announcement of punishment] find reflection in these several lines of our lament. They attest to a transformation in the thinking of those who survived the catastrophe. They now recognize that what the prophets of judgment said has indeed come to pass. Such a recognition then gets taken up in the proclamation of Deutero-Isaiah and becomes a feature of exilic and post-exilic restoration prophecies.

The framing of the complaint about enemies (vv 15-16) by

the attribution of guilt directed against the false prophets (v 14) and the associated confirmation of judgmental prophecy (v 17) is deliberate. It is not the enemy's military action against Jerusalem as such that is mentioned in v 16. Rather, attention is directed to the arrogance with which the enemy boasted about the deed: "All your enemies flung open their mouths against you...they said 'We have annihilated...we have attained!'" Such arrogance was unjustifiable, for the enemies were in fact but the instrument for carrying out Yahweh's plan: "Yahweh has carried out what he planned..." (v 17a). The constrained nature of the complaint about enemies in this case is grounded in the fact that Yahweh, the Lord of history, was at work in this defeat of Israel. Here is another sense in which the proclamation of Deutero-Isaiah is in accord with Lamentations.

Again as happens so often elsewhere in the Old Testament, some reference is made to the disgrace attached to suffering (v 15). In word and in gesture, the passers-by express their astonishment and their disdain. "Is this the city of which one said, 'crown of beauty'?" This too suggests the contrast motif characteristic of the dirge. The particular expression here used ["crown of beauty"] obviously plays upon a song formerly sung in praise of Jerusalem (cf. Ps 48:2), a song now silenced.

Verses 18-22

Vv 18-22, which conclude the second song in the Book of Lamentations, form a unit centered around the plea for God to take heed, in v 20a. Leading up to this plea, in vv 18 and 19, is a summoning of Zion: "Pour out your heart...before the presence of Yahweh!" The words which follow the plea are intended to persuade Yahweh to turn favorably toward the people of God.

18-19: "Pour out your heart before Yahweh!" These two verses form the high point of the whole song comprising Lam 2. They consist of a chain of imperatives, eight in six lines. Form-critically speaking, these lines correspond to the imperatively-worded summons to praise known from the Psalms. Standing behind this chain of imperatives is also the theme of a summoning to lamentation as known from the dirge (see above, pp. *15-16*). In the case at hand, however, the imperatives actually uttered have been altered somewhat from the traditional ones in order to prompt the people to turn to Yahweh in supplication. In terms of their content, these imperatives more closely resemble the call to wait patiently upon Yahweh (cf., e.g., Ps 62:9 [8 Eng.]: "Trust in him...pour out your heart before him"). The sequence of imperatives here used, summoning to lamentation, exhibits an unprecedented intensity. In the wake of all that Zion has had to undergo, to plea for God once again to take heed no longer appears as a matter of course. An undeniable sense of distance has intruded (cf. Lam 5:22). It is against such a background that the imperatives in vv 18-19 become understandable. To those sunk in despondent mourning, a challenge is directed. Dare once again to call upon Yahweh! This avenue to hope is always open!

With this summons, our lament passes imperceptibly over into petition. At the outset lamentation still dominates, in no small part because the summons to engage in lamentation is a theme characteristic of the dirge. For parallels, cf. Jer 9:9 [10 Eng.]: "Take up weeping and wailing for the mountains, and a lamentation for the pastures of the wilderness," as well as Isa 23:1-14 and lines 39-72 of the Lamentation over the Destruction of Ur (see above, p. 32). From the very beginning, however, ours is a lament directed to Yahweh (v 18a). What follows the opening imperative is, in effect, an encouragement to persist in lamentation. Don't cease lamenting now!

The ensuing clauses consistently encourage persistence in imploring God. The phrase "to pour out one's heart before God" in v 19b encompasses both lamentation and supplication, as can also be seen in the superscription to Psalm 102. Similarly, the gesture of raising the hands (v 19c) connotes both lamentation and supplication. The same association of themes is implied in the line at v 19c which reads "...for the life of your children." The Hebrew preposition here rendered "for" is *'al*. This preposition's semantic range includes both the notion of pleading *for* some desired outcome and pleading *about* some existent state of affairs. The distinctive wording of the clause at v 19c is also significant. Here one does not yet dare to plead for restoration; one only implores that the children who are still alive not perish.

20-22: There follows, in v 20a , the petition "Ah, Yahweh, look and consider!" One can sense a certain hesitation here, in that this petition is voiced only once, without the customary poetic repetition. All the same, a significant transition occurs at this juncture in the lament. Here, for the first time, Yahweh is addressed directly. Here, for the first time, the lament becomes a prayer! The feature of direct address of Yahweh then reappears in vv 21c and 22a. The interweaving of dirge and lament in Lamentations, with its merging of the one form into the other, is nowhere more evident than here in 2:18-22. After the calamity of 587 BCE, cultic activities in Jerusalem were reduced to little more than solemnized lamentation. In such a situation, a gradual shift away from the intoning of dirges toward the voicing of supplications to Yahweh became inevitable. However, because this plea for God's gracious response remained only a short step removed from gloomy despair, there immediately follows (v 20aβ) an intimation of a reproach as the speaker goes on to ask Yahweh to consider "to whom you have done this!" With this, the feature of lamentation returns. With it comes a note of direct accusation, only intimated in v 20a but spelled out in vv 21c and 22a: "You have slain...you have slaughtered...you summoned...." These words of accusation differ from the ones we saw in vv 1-8. At the beginning of the chapter we were dealing with a description of misery; at the end we are dealing with accusation against God. This shift best reveals the distinctive nature of this particular song. What has transpired remains incomprehensible, but something new emerges in the way the lamenters now turn directly to Yahweh. They no longer persist in looking to the past.

The next two clauses, v 20b-c, are of a piece with the petition introduced in v 20a in that they are intended to persuade Yahweh to respond favorably to the supplication. What the survivors had to suffer was so terrible that one can recall it only with horror—the famine which drove people to engage in acts of cannibalism (v 20b), the desecration of the sanctuary through the murder within it of priests and prophets (v 20c).

In v 21a-b the description of misery that constituted the bulk of 9-13 is picked up once again. This time, however, the description is expanded to include the whole populace, all those whose sacrificial deaths are to be lamented: young and old, maidens and youths. The note that they "lie prostrate in the dust of the streets" finds an echo in Deutero-Isaiah (Isa 51:20). The destruction of a city means not only the death of its inhabitants as individuals; it also amounts to the tearing asunder of a community.

For our understanding of this last section of Lam 2, it would be better to transpose v 22b ("there was no one on the day of Yahweh's wrath who survived and escaped") so that it connects directly with v 21b, since the description of misery that encompasses vv 20b-21b here finds its proper conclusion. With this transposition, the resulting juxtaposition of v 22c with v 22a would also work better. The accusation against God which is initiated in v 20a is continued in v 21c ("you have slain them on the day of your anger...") and brought to a conclusion in v 22b. Here again we encounter the *leitmotif* of vv 1-8, the "day of your anger." This, in fact, is the guiding theme for the whole lament. There is only one feature that reaches beyond this theme, namely that the lamenters are addressing God. Their final word is "Ah, Yahweh, look and consider!"

In sum, the distinctive feature of Lam 2 is the intensity with which it juxtaposes, on the one hand, speech about the wrath of God—or the experiencing of the same—in vv 1-8 with, on the other hand, a summons to lament, to pour out one's heart before God. One finds such a sharp and intense juxtaposition of these two features nowhere else in the Old Testament. The way these two features are set side by side, as the contrasting terms of a singular polarity, renders the second chapter of Lamentations a unique testimony to how, in the Old Testament, one can speak to God.

Synopsis of Lam 2

    1a : introduction: mournful cry, "Ah, how...!"
    1-8: accusation against God, transformed into a description of misery
        1aβ: "...Yahweh in his wrath overclouds Zion!"
        1b: "...from heaven into the dust..."
    2-7a: main section of accusation against God
    7b-c: connection with complaint about enemies, "they

have made an uproar in the temple"
8c: transition to the community's direct complaint, the mourning of rampart and wall
9-13: community's direct complaint
8c-9a: rampart and wall, gate and cross-bar
9b-c: no longer king, princes, prophets
10a-c: mourning of elders and maidens
11a-b: description of misery
11c-12c: community's direct complaint, the children are dying
13: description of misery, the incomparable suffering
14-17: guilt and punishment, complaint about enemies
14: guilt of the false prophets
15-16: mockery of the passers-by, triumph of the enemies
17: punishment: Yahweh has caused to come to pass what he had announced beforehand
18-19: summons to lamentation and to supplication before Yahweh
18a: "Cry aloud to Yahweh...daughter Zion!"
18b-19a: "Let tears flow...!"
19b-c: "pour out your heart" before Yahweh
20-22: plea for Yahweh to take heed, along with motive clauses
20a: plea for Yahweh to take heed, accusation against God
20b-c: "Should women...? Should...in the sanctuary?"
21-22: motive clauses: community's direct complaint, accusation against God, complaint about enemies

Lam 3

1 I am the one who[a] experienced affliction under the rod of his[b] anger;

2 he drove me, he led me into[a] unilluminated darkness.

3 Yes, against me he turned his hand again and again, day after day.

4 He made my flesh and my skin wither, he broke my bones.

5   He surrounded and encompassed me with bitterness and hardship.[a]

6   He has made me dwell in thick[a] darkness like those long dead.

7   He has walled me in without means of escape, clasped me in heavy chains.

8   Even though I shrieked and cried out, my plea was not heard[a].

9   He has obstructed my way with ashlar, convoluted my pathways.

10 He became a lurking bear to me, a lion in a dense[a] hiding place.

11 He turned me aside[a] from my way and mangled[b] me, he made me desolate.

12 He bent his bow and set me up as a target[a] for his arrow;

13 he emptied the contents of his quiver into my vital organs.

14 I have become the laughing-stock for all my people, their constant lampoon.

15 He sated me with bitterness, saturated me with gall.

16 He made me gnash my teeth on gravel[a], trampled me down[b] in the dust.

17 You cast out my soul from peace. I forgot what happiness was,

18 and I thought, "Perished is my span[a], my hope in Yahweh."

19 To recall[a] my affliction and my disquiet[b] is gall and venom.

20 Yet you will certainly bear in mind[a] that[b] my soul is bowed down within me;

21 this fact I will take to heart, and therefore will I have hope.

22 The mercies of Yahweh are not at an end[a]; his compassion does not cease,

23 it is new every morning. Great is your faithfulness!

24 "My portion is Yahweh," says my soul[a]; therefore will I hope in him!

25 Good is Yahweh to the one who trusts[a] in him, to the soul that seeks him.

26 It is good...[a], quietly to wait upon the help of Yahweh.

27 It is good for a person to bear the yoke while still young.

28 Let such a one sit silently and alone when the Lord imposes it.

29 Let such a one put mouth to dust—perhaps there is yet hope.

30 Let such a one offer the cheek to the smiter, let such a one accept a full measure of humiliation.

31 For Yahweh does not reject humankind[a] forever.

32 Rather, having afflicted, he then[a] has compassion according to the fullness of his mercy;

33 for he does not torment and afflict[a] anyone capriciously.

34 That one should tread under foot all the prisoners of the land,

35 to pervert someone's rights in the presence of the Most High,

36 so that one is oppressed on the occasion of a lawsuit—shall Yahweh not see this?[a]

37 Who could have spoken, and have it happen, without Yahweh having commanded it?

38 Does not both evil[a] and good[b] come forth out of the mouth of the Most High?

39 Of what do human beings complain?[a] Let us all master our own sins[b]!

40 Let us test and examine our ways[a] and return to Yahweh!

41 Let us raise our heart upon[a] our hands to God in heaven!

42 We have transgressed and rebelled; you have not forgiven[a]!

43 You have wrapped yourself in anger, pursued us, carried us off without[a] pity,

44 you have enveloped yourself in clouds, such that no prayer can penetrate!

45 Refuse and trash have you made us amidst the peoples.[a]

46 All our enemies flung open their mouths against us,[a]

47 Terror and pit[a] became our lot, devastation[b] and destruction.

48 My eye lets streams of water flow over the downfall of the daughter of my people!

49 My eye overflows without repose, it will not cease[a],

50 until Yahweh looks down from heaven and sees.[a]

51 My eye makes my soul miserable from much weeping[a] over my city.

52 Hunted, hunted me like a bird have those who are without cause my enemies.

53   They hurled me, alive, into the pit,[a] they cast stones upon
       me.

54   Water cascaded over my head; I thought, "I am lost[a]!"

55   Then I called upon your name, O Yahweh, from deep
       down in the pit;[a]

56   you heard my cry. Conceal not your ear to my cry for help[a]!

57   You were near when I called you, you said, "Do not fear!"[a]

58   You have taken up my cause[a], O Lord, you have saved my
       life!

59   You have seen the violation of my rights, O Yahweh,
       vindicate[a] my cause!

60   You have seen all their vengefulness, all their plans against
       me![a]

61   You have heard their taunts, O Yahweh, all their plans
       against me!

62   The lips of my adversaries and their rumorings are against
       me all day long.

63   Notice[a] that, when they sit down and when they rise up[b], I
       am their taunt-song[c].

64   You will requite them, O Yahweh, according to the work of
       their hands!

65   Give them hardness of heart, let your curse come upon
       them!

66   You will pursue them in anger and blot them out from
       under the heaven of Yahweh.[a]

Textual Notes

1a: The text intends a relative clause despite the absence of the usually preceding relational particle *'ăšer.* **b:** According to Löhr, third-person pronominal reference to God is a characteristic feature of late Biblical-Hebrew literature.

2a: This is an accusative of direction (*accusativum loci*).

5a: "With bitterness and hardship" follows Rudolph.

6a: On the intensifying plural, as used here, cf. GKC § 124e and also Ps 143:3.

8a: The Hebrew term *śātam,* which occurs only here, translates literally as "[my plea] was closed up."

10a: This is another intensifying plural (see above, note 6a).

11a: The Hebrew term here used, *sōrēr,* translates literally as "he entangled [my paths]." **b:** The meaning is uncertain; several translate "and crippled [Ger. *lähmte*] me."

12a: The translation "as a target" for *kammaṭṭ ārā '* corresponds to the use of this expression at Job 16:12.

16a: The Hebrew term *ḥāṣāṣ* is elsewhere attested only at Prov 20:17. **b:** This verb [*kpš*, hiph'il] is a *hapax legomenon.*

18a: The Hebrew term [*nēṣaḥ*] literally means "duration," here contextually rendered "[my] span [of time]."

19a: The verbal form is the infinitive construct. **b:** The translation of *mārūd* as "disquiet" is compatible with our translation of this same term as "anguish" in 1:7.

20a: To read the verbal form here as a second-person masculine is preferred by Löhr and Kraus; Rudolph and Plöger take it as a third-person feminine. **b:** Reading with Meek, the conjunctive *wĕ* implies the notion "that."

22a: Read the verb as *tāmmū* (following S & T; cf. McDaniel).

24a: MT is to be followed [*contra* the critical apparatus of BHK³].

25a: Follow the *Ketib* (singular).

26a: Strike the *wĕ.*

31a: A direct object is implied at the end of the line but is missing; "humankind" is an expansion in the spirit of the one suggested by Budde and others [viz., *Menschen*].

32a: "Then" renders the force of the *wāw* as the beginning element of the second clause.

33a: Read *wayyōgeh* with the text-critical apparatus of BHS.

36a: This is a question despite the absence of the usual interrogative *hē.*

38a: *Rā'āh*, conventionally rendered "evil," here implies the notion of "trouble." **b:** "Good" gets its precise meaning here by contrast with the implied "trouble" of **38a.**

39a: On the translation see Löhr *et al.* **b:** Read *yĕhî* in place of MT's *hāy;* a literal rendition would be "Let him become master over his sins!"

40a: The Greek presupposes a singular noun here—a possible reading of the original text.

41a: Following the majority of commentators, *wĕ'al* is to be read in place of MT's *'el.*

42a: Rudolph translates, "**We** have sinned...and therefore **you** could not forgive" (similarly Plöger, Boecker, and others). However, this is to read a nuance into the text which is not actually there. Rather, with v 42 a fragment of a communal lament begins, a fragment to which a confession of guilt quite naturally belongs. Only with such a confession is the continuation in v 43 intelligible.

43a: It is not necessary to read *wĕlō'* (so Plöger and others) in place of MT's *lō'*.

45a: This verse clearly identifies vv 42-51 as part of a communal lament.

46a: The verse corresponds to 2:16a.

47a: For parallels to the word pair which occurs here cf. Isa 24:17 and Jer 48:43. **b:** The Hebrew term is a *hapax legomenon*.

49a: *dāmāh* = *dāmam*

50a: The section comprising vv 48-51 reaches its goal in v 50: "until Yahweh looks down...." This is so clear from the context that a transposition of vv 50 and 51 (as sometimes suggested) is not necessary.

51a: The text of MT is corrupt at this point; read *bĕkōl* (as with Kraus, Plöger, and others).

53a: Translated literally, the reading here would be "They cast my life into the pit."

54a: The text literally says "I am cut off."

55a: Cf. Ps 130:1.

56a: The *lĕšaw'ātî* at the end of the verse is an expansionary gloss (so, correctly, Kraus, Kaiser, *et al.*).

57a: Cf. Pss 56:10 [9 Eng.]; 102:3 [2 Eng.].

58a: Read the singular *rîbî*, or perhaps *napšî*; the plural is elsewhere attested only at Ps 18:44.

59a: With Gottlieb, the imperative is not to be changed to a perfect, despite the reading of G and S.

60a: V 60 could be a doublet to v 61 (so Plöger), but MT can just as well be transmitting the original text here.

63a: *Contra* Rudolph *et al.*, the imperative is to be maintained. **b:** The expression "their sitting down and their rising up" conveys the notion of a totality (cf. Ps 139:2). **c:** Contrary to the rule, the *nun* is not assimilated.

66a: It is not necessary to change the phrase "the heaven of Yahweh," for this is a fixed expression.

Noteworthy with regard to the acrostic form of Lam 3 is the fact that the three lines comprising a triad begin with the same word on three occasions: vv 16-18 [*wāw*, "and"], 25-27 [*ṭôb*, "good"], and 31-33 [*kî*, "for, that"]; the same prepositional element [*lamed*] opens the three lines at vv 34-36.

The Nature of the Composition

Many of its interpreters recognize that Lam 3 is a composition whose various parts are of different types. The issues of just how Lam 3 was combined out of these parts, and how the ensuing composition as a whole is to be explained, are contested. Here, at the outset, we will take up these issues only in broad outline. Lam 3 contains three basic parts. These basic parts can be recognized as independent units—albeit somewhat truncated—on the basis of parallels. Interspersed among these three basic units are two expansions, vv 26-41 and vv 59-63. The expansions are the work of the hand responsible for Lam 3 as a total composition.

The independent units are the following: (a) vv 1-25, form-critically a personal psalm of lamentation, to which vv 64-66 have been appended as a (fragmentary) conclusion; (b) vv 42-51, a (fragmentary) communal psalm of lamentation; (c) vv 52-58, a personal psalm of praise (again, in fragmentary state).

Determinative for the whole is the personal psalm of lamentation. This is so, first of all, because it forms the beginning and the end. Secondly, both the expansions are to be reckoned as attached to this unit. Thirdly, the composer of the total composition transformed what was originally a personal psalm of lamentation by adding at the beginning a sentence ("I am the one who experienced affliction...") which does not stem from the language of that genre. (Already in 1904 Löhr suspected that originally independent psalms of lamentation were to be found in vv 1-25 and 52-66.) Both of the other units, a communal psalm of lamentation (vv 42-51) and a personal psalm of praise (vv 52-58), have been worked into the final composition in such a way that the beginnings and the endings of both—that is to say, their specifically liturgical parts—have been left out. Only in this way could they be made to fit in with the whole. Demonstration of just how, and with what intent, these two units stemming from other genres have been blended into the personal psalm of lamentation which now encompasses them must await the detailed exegesis below. The center of the total composition is formed by the expansion in vv 26-41, a section which in fact belongs to no established psalm-genre.

The total composition is held together by its acrostic form. Each block of three verses begins with the same letter of the Hebrew alphabet, while each successive block begins with the next letter. Imposing such an arrangement on the whole composition can only be judged as arbitrary. Such a judgment implies an important methodological consequence, however. Specifically, the structure of the material can be properly recognized only if one pays attention to organizing features which preceded the imposition of the alphabetic scheme. Initially, therefore, one must look for such groupings of material as can be identified within the context of recognizable psalm-genres. Only then can one proceed to inquire about the possible connections between the various parts.

Exegesis of Lam 3
Verses 1-25

The lament of the individual ("I am the one who...") which now lies before us is separated into the following parts: v 1, an introduction; vv 2-17a, an accusation against God; vv 17b-19, a personal complaint; vv 20-25, an avowal of confidence. This sequence of themes corresponds to the normal pattern for the genre of the personal lament. Lacking at the beginning, however, is the customary invocation of Yahweh. In other words, the introduction normal for a personal lament has been altered. The length of the accusation against God is also worthy of note. The other characteristic focus of the lament, namely complaint about enemies, appears only in the concluding part, in vv 59-63. A plea generally follows the avowal of confidence. As with the invocation of Yahweh, however, such an element is missing in our text. In its place we get the expansion in vv 26-41. Vv 64-66, which bring our composition to a close, are once again characteristic of the personal lament.

1: The opening clause ("I am the one who experienced affliction under the rod of his anger...") forms an independent unit. The one who is going to speak in the following verses here appears before the audience as someone who has suffered under the wrath of God. The nature of this suffering is then described, which transforms the lament directed toward God into a description of misery intended to capture the attention of the hearers. Direct address of God is transformed into third-person description ("He has done..."). As is shown in the last clause ("You cast out my soul from peace"), however, all of this is really meant to be accusation against God.

Both features—the fact that the accusation against God is transformed into a description of misery and that the sufferer recites this description in the presence of others—find a parallel in the Book of Job, particularly in its chapter 30. There, in the presence of his friends, Job contrasts his present misery to his earlier good fortune. ("And now my soul is poured out within me, and days full of misery seize me" [30:16].) Moreover, Lam 3:14 ("I have become the laughing-stock for all my people...") is very close to the wording of Job 30:9 ("And now I have become their laughing-stock...").

So here at its very beginning, the personal lament is transformed into a description of misery. At the same time, in the place usually reserved for invocation of Yahweh an address is directed to hearers, the address introduced by the words "I am the one...." Once these features have been recognized, one can assume that corresponding transformations of the personal lament will also become evident as Lam 3 continues. Indeed, the language actually employed in the expansion in vv 26-41 is without parallel in the Psalms. As teaching and as admonition, the words of this expansion also address the hearers; in this they correspond to v 1. The composer thus sets these words of parenesis at the center of a small, psalm-like collection of material. The words are intended to convey fundamental tenets of the tradition out of which the composer speaks. Vv 26-41 are consciously assigned their central role through the placement of the avowal of confidence in the immediately preceding vv 20-25.

2-17a: Throughout, the subject of these sentences is Yahweh. The one doing the lamenting consistently appears as the object of Yahweh's actions. The basic motif is repeatedly "God has smitten me." Parallels to such a concentration of accusations against God are hard to find except in Lam 2:2-8 and the Book of Job. The lines comprising these sixteen verses stand without intrinsic connection to one another. Such a lack of structure would hardly be imaginable within the context of a cultic ceremony of lamentation; it can only be explained if one assumes for these verses a strictly literary provenance. In other words, this concentration of accusations can only have entered the text in conjunction with the alphabetic ordering of the lines. In interpreting the material, one must first arrange it according to themes which obviously belong together.

> God is angry with the speaker (v 1) and turns a deaf ear to the speaker's plea (v 8).
> God has afflicted and driven the speaker into a state of anxiety and distress—in short, to "darkness" (vv 2,3,5,6,7; on v 6 cf. Ps 143:3).
> Several clauses refer directly to physical suffering, such as "He made my flesh and my skin wither..." (v 4; cf. also vv 15-16).
> God has become the speaker's enemy ("Yes, against me he turned his hand again and again..."); the same point is made in the analogy of God to a hostile warrior (vv 12-13) or to attacking animals (vv 10-11—cf. Pss 17:12 & 22:13-14 [12-13 Eng.]).

God has made the speaker into a laughing-stock (v 14).
The section concludes with an accusation against God, cast
  in direct address ("You cast out my soul from peace"; cf.
  Jer 16:15).

These sixteen verses consistently display the language of the
personal lament. Parallels to each of the clauses could be found
in the psalms of personal lamentation in the Psalter as well as in
the laments of Job and Jeremiah. Especially when one compares
it against the material found in Lam 2:2-8, the content of this
accusation against God adequately refutes the view that the one
here speaking embodies or represents the suffering people as a
whole. Each of the afflictions here mentioned is one that affects
an individual, whereas in the accusation directed against God in
Lam 2:2-8 each clause deals with the fate of the people. The
sufferer who says "I am the one..." in 3:1 is an individual human
being relating personal experiences.

14, 17b-19: The same holds true for the personal lament. In
v 17 there is a smooth transition from accusation against God
to personal lamentation ("You cast out my soul from peace...I
forgot what happiness was..."). The two themes hang closely
together.

It was the blows from the Almighty that caused the speaker
to forget happiness, to become a laughing-stock (v 14; cf. Ps
69:13 [12 Eng.]), and to see pleas to God rendered futile. These
few clauses of personal lamentation are shaped by reflection
and molded by description of misery. ("Perished is my span..."
[v 18]; "to recall...is gall and venom" [v 19].) Similar to v 18 is
the reflective clause in Ps 73:15.

The accusation against God obviously ends with v 17a. Only
hints of personal lamentation appear in the following verses,
which tend rather toward recollection: "I forgot..." (v 17b);
"and I thought..." (v 18a); "to recall..." (v 19a) and "you will
certainly bear in mind..." (v 20a). The emphatic *zākōr- tizkōr*
["You will certainly bear in mind..."] of v 20 stands in contrast
to the simple *zĕkār* ["to recall"] of v 19. Such a contrast
corresponds to the function of the so-called *wāw adversativum*
as found in the personal psalms of lamentation. To v 20 ("Yet
you will certainly bear in mind that my soul is bowed down

within me") one can compare Ps 42:6. Here we can see that the opinion of many interpreters—viz., that the composer of Lam 3 made use of no more than isolated expressions or themes from the psalms of lamentation—does not stand up under scrutiny. It is much more the case that Lam 3:1-25 corresponds, point for point, to the structure of the personal psalm of lamentation. In keeping with this, it is significant how, precisely at the transitional point which is v 17, the preceding description of misery gets transformed into petitionary address.

20-25: Following the lamentation as such is an avowal of confidence, one which is especially elaborate and yet meaningfully structured. Already in the transitional verse (v 20) the lamenter achieves renewed confidence ("Yet you will **certainly** bear in mind..."). Similar in spirit to this affirmatory clause is v 21a ("this fact I will take to heart..."). The traditional avowal of confidence itself follows in v 21b ("...therefore will I have hope"). The same theme is continued in v 24 ("My portion is Yahweh... therefore will I hope in him!"—cf. Pss 16:5, 73:26, 142:6 [5 Eng.]).

Bracketed by the avowal of confidence are two sentences rendering praise to God: "The mercies of Yahweh are not at an end; his compassion does not cease, it is new every morning. Great is your faithfulness!" (vv 22-23). These sentences correspond to the motif of praising the goodness of God as found in the psalms of praise (e.g., Exod 34:6-7 or Ps 103). A special touch of artistry is evident in the way both motifs are intertwined in the concluding v 25: "Good is Yahweh to the one who trusts in him, to the soul that seeks him".

Such association of the avowal of confidence with clauses rendering praise to God occurs more than once in the personal psalms of lamentation (e.g., Pss 6:5 [4 Eng.], 13:5, 37:28, 86:15, 102:13 [12 Eng.]. The intertwining of both motifs in v 25 brings the section comprising vv 20-25 to a definitive close. A new section, the expansion, starts with v 26.

In vv 20-25 we can observe a phenomenon which occurs fairly often in the later psalms, namely the transformation of the language of cultic petition into the language of reflective devotion (cf. Pss 8 and 139—and the remarks on these in my book *The Living Psalms*). What happens here is that recollection of a former avowal of trust becomes the stimulus for expression of praise. Such reflective devotion, growing out of psalmic motifs and developing in consonance with them, is to be distinguished both from didacticism (sapiential speech), as is found in 3:27, and from doctrinal instruction (a form of midrash), as found in 3:33-38. The fact that all three appear in the expansion comprising vv 26-41, and without distinctions being drawn among the types, is a strong indication that this expansion arose in very late Biblical times.

If one compares vv 17b-25 with the preceding vv 2-17a, a basic difference between the two sections readily becomes apparent. Vv 17b-25 are so arranged that each of its clauses has a necessary function; in these verses one can discern a clear train of thought. The accusation against God (vv 2-17a), however, consists of a bald juxtaposition of a number of complaint clauses exhibiting no intrinsic connection to one another. Vv 2-17a are held together only by the fact that they all express similar motifs and exhibit the same general "God-has-done" structure. Furthermore, the fact that vv 17b-25 could be read, sentence for sentence, as a part of a personal psalm of lamentation in the Psalter—despite the fact that such an aggregation of essentially the same motif does not actually occur in the Psalter—directs our attention once again to the artistry of the compiler of this material, the one who organized it in acrostic fashion. In the case of vv 2-17a, on the other hand, the compiler simply gathered themes characteristic of the accusation against God and arrayed them in alphabetic order.

In sum, the structure of vv 20-25 sketches out as follows:

20: Transition from the lament to the avowal of confidence (*wāw adversativum*);

21: continuation of the element of reflection: resolve to hope (continued in v 24);

22-23: praise of God, the ground of hope, praise of the goodness of God, which is ever new;

24: the traditional avowal of confidence: Yahweh is my portion;

25: conclusion, which unites both themes.

Verses 26-41

The section consisting of vv 26-41 is clearly an expansion, since v 25 closes off a section of the psalm of lamentation and vv 42-51 are a fragment of a communal lament. The intent of this expansion becomes apparent in its conclusion, the admonition to return to Yahweh (vv 39-41). The expansion finds its proper culmination in these concluding verses, especially since the expansion begins, in v 26, with an indirect admonition pushing in the same direction.

The expansion falls naturally into three parts. (1) The first part is a transitional element moving away from the avowal of confidence in the preceding vv 21b & 24. This element occupies vv 26 and 31-32; the counsel to wait upon Yahweh (v 26) is grounded in the praise of God's goodness (vv 31-32). (2) There follows, in vv 27-30, a general admonition to bear up patiently under suffering, with a theological rationale for doing so appended in vv 33-38. (3) The third, and concluding, part is the admonition to return to Yahweh, in vv 39-41.

One difficulty with the arrangement of vv 26-32 is the fact that two different statements of rationale stand in sharp juxtaposition: "For Yahweh does not reject humankind forever..." (vv 31-32), and "for he does not torment and afflict anyone capriciously" (v 33). This difficulty disappears as soon as one sees vv 31-32 as the rationale for v 26 and vv 33-38 as the rationale for vv 27-30. Such an understanding also obviates the need for any transposition of the verses.

26, 31-32: V 26 recommends putting one's hope in Yahweh (cf. also Pss 25:3, 146:5, 147:11), a recommendation grounded by reference to the goodness of God in vv 31-32, verses whose meaning clearly ties them back to v 26 (cf. also Pss 77:8-9 [7-8 Eng.], 103:9, and Jer 3:12). However, while the praise of the goodness of God in vv 22-23 speaks the language of the Psalms, vv 31-32 are didactic prose. A recommendation to put one's hope in Yahweh (v 26) is a theme familiar from the Psalms. One finds quite similar wording, for example, at Ps 40:5 [4 Eng.]: "Happy are those who make the Lord their trust.") The admonition to wait for the Lord occurs in such diverse places as Pss 27:14, 37:7&34, 42:6&12 [5&11 Eng.], Prov 20:22, and Job 35:14[1]. That one is dealing with didactic speech in the case at hand, however, is shown not only by the prosaic language of vv 31-32 but also by the addition of "quietly" in v 26 (a feature explained below).

27-30: Characteristic for the composition of the expansion is the sequence of vv 25-27. In keeping with their alphabetic arrangement, all three verses begin with the same Hebrew word, *ṭôb*. In the Book of Proverbs there is a series of sayings which likewise begin with *ṭôb* (the so-called sayings of appraisal).

Through this use of the same word at the beginning of each verse, the transition from one unit of speech to the next is made less abrupt. V 25 concludes the unit comprising vv 20-25. It is still a part, therefore, of the avowal of confidence. V 26 voices the recommendation to put hope in Yahweh. The addition of "quietly" here suggests, however, that we are no longer dealing with an expression of faith but rather with a distinct mode of human conduct—as is customarily the case with the sayings of appraisal. While the sufferer is being counseled to embrace a hopeful attitude in v 26, what is being conveyed in vv 27-30 is impersonal and timeless advice.

In terms of content, the transition from v 26 to v 27 is indeed abrupt. Being counseled to wait, quietly and trustingly, does not adequately prepare us for "it is good...to bear the yoke while still young." This latter statement is cast in the didactic, admonitory speech of parenesis. This form of speech then continues for several more lines by means of catchword association, imitating the sayings of appraisal in the Book of Proverbs. It is good when someone has to go through hard times even as a youth. Such a person is advised not to resist the yoke but rather to bear it in silence. V 28 speaks no longer just of young people but rather of a generalized sufferer. Advice is given on how such a one should behave; such a one should bear

---

[1] On the theme of waiting for Yahweh, see also my article "Das Hoffen im Alten Testament: Eine Begriffsuntersuchung," in my *Forschung am Alten Testament: Gesammelte Studien I* (ThB 24; 1964) 219-64.

the yoke silently and alone, with mouth bowed down to the dust. The mode of conduct here being described is designated a "submissive spirit" by N. K. Gottwald (similarly R. Albertz; cf. also the didactic admonition of, e.g., Ps 37:3). This person of submissive spirit is not only to suffer blows in silence but also to accept being shamed (v 30). Some mention of hope is made also in v 29 ("Let such a one put mouth to dust—perhaps there is yet hope"), but the mood differs significantly from v 25. The qualifier "perhaps" is especially significant. In an avowal of confidence such a qualifier would have no place; there the expression of confidence is voiced without hesitation. One never finds an avowal of confidence hedged this way in the Psalms, for example. (That is quite likely why Luther, in his translation of Lam 3:29, instinctively left out the "perhaps.") However, the addition of such a qualifier is quite in keeping with the spirit of parenesis. More than once, for example, one finds such qualification in the conditional promises of Deuteronomic language (e.g., Amos 5:15). The transition from psalmic speech to parenesis is a feature of the post-exilic era, when the Psalter became a devotional book and pious wisdom made inroads into its content.

33-38: The material that follows, in vv 33-38, serves as theological warrant for the preceding. Here we are even farther removed from the language of the Psalms; what we have before us is didactic midrash. When God afflicts someone, that does not happen simply because God takes pleasure in doing so, "for he does not torment and afflict anyone capriciously" (v 33). At this point one expects some answer to the question of why God does so afflict human beings. However, the expected answer surfaces only in vv 39-41—and then it occurs in the form of an admonition. The lengthy intervening section, vv 33-38, develops the theme of v 33: God does not afflict capriciously. The theme is brought to a conclusion in vv 37-38: God is responsible for everything that happens; all comes from the hand of God. These verses also express what Luther called the "strange work of God" [*opus alienum Dei*]. A similar set of verses occurs at Isa 45:6-7. In terms of their function, vv 34-36 develop the theme of v 37: God sees the evil that human beings do. Thus vv 34, 35, and 36a are all dependent on v 36b. Conceptually, the sequence runs "Shall Yahweh not see that...that...that...." These sentences are further held together by the *lĕ* with which each of the three lines begins—another feature of the song's alphabetic arrangement. The question "Shall Yahweh not see this?" receives added emphasis through the "in the presence of the Most High" of v 35b. In other words, emphasis is clearly being placed on the notion that God sees the evil deeds of human beings. The one who speaks in these admonitory and didactic terms is addressing people who have suffered injustice and been put to shame, people whose right has been perverted (v 35) and who have been trampled underfoot (v 34). Hidden behind vv 34-36 is the lament of someone who has suffered unjustly. All these sentences can also be found in the personal psalms of lamentation, and especially in the section known as the complaint about enemies—a section missing from the portion of the lament found at the beginning of Lam 3. This element of complaint about enemies is presupposed in the parenetic expansion in vv 26-41, but the didactic form has strongly altered its appearance. To the one suffering from hostile attack the speaker is in effect saying, "If you must suffer all this, also know that Yahweh sees it all." The theme that "...one is oppressed on the occasion of a lawsuit" refers to the actions of enemies. Such actions find mention in the accusations which the prophets directed against Israelite society as well as in the complaints about enemies in the psalms of lamentation. The reference here is clearly to the societal domain; the focus of attention is the oppression of the weak by the dominant. It is the oppressed who cry out to Yahweh in the psalms of lamentation, who say "Vindicate me, O Lord!" Some have wanted to interpret the "prisoners of the land" as referring to Israelites taken captive in war. However, the overall trend of the passage (vv 34-36) runs against this interpretation.

The expansion begins in vv 26-30 as parenesis and also ends as such in vv 39-41. The intervening verses (31-38) are explanatory and didactic; they speak the language of midrash. Another indication of this intervening section's midrashic character is the way it tends to rely upon scriptural turns of phrase. "Yahweh does not reject forever" (v 31) and "he has compassion according to the fullness of his mercy" (v 32) refer to Psalmic expressions (see above, comments on vv 22 & 23); vv 34-36 are a paraphrase of a complaint about enemies; v 37 alludes to Gen 1 or to Ps 33, v 38 to Isa 45, and v 39 to Gen 4:7. It is also noteworthy how this midrash, Lam 3:33-38, makes use of the late divine epithet 'ĕlyōn ("the Most High," vv 35 & 38; cf. Dan 3:26,32 [4:2 Eng.], etc.). Finally, with regard to vv 33-38, it remains firmly established that this little midrash, a piece of didactic instruction, differs not only from the other chapters in Lamentations but also from the beginning and concluding sections of chapter three in the way it clearly exhibits a conceptual structure, or train of thought (cf. the excursus above, pp. 73-76).

39-41: "Of what do human beings complain?" This query brings to clear expression all that was intended in the preceding didactic material directed to the lamenter as well as in the admonition at the beginning of vv 26-30. Here, in a concluding admonition based upon the preceding explanation, further lamentation is disallowed. Instead, lamenters are advised to turn away from their sins ("Let us all master our own sins!" [v 39b]), to examine their ways and return to Yahweh (vv 40-41). In these few sentences of admonition is stated the goal of the whole expansion, the unit comprising vv 26-41. V 41 emphasizes the call to leave off lamenting and the admonition to engage in self-examination and to repent. This is to be done wholeheartedly! As has already been explained, God must exact punishment for sins. So the point here is to examine one's own conduct. The two Hebrew verbs employed in v 40 (ḥpś and ḥqr) are closely related in meaning: to investigate, to look into, to examine. Both occur regularly in wisdom material (e.g., Prov 2:4; 20:27; Job 5:27; 28:3, 27; Ps 139:1, 23; Sir 13:11; 42:18). The way these terms are used indicates that the admonition to examine one's own ways is directed to individuals and focused on the realm of personal conduct, not directed to the people as a whole or meant in a socio-political sense. The self-examination being called for properly leads to recognition of one's own sins (v 39b), which in turn leads to a return to Yahweh. The admonition to return to Yahweh, then, is the goal of the expansion comprising vv 26-41.

With this material we are clearly in the presence of a different sort of language and a different type of pathos than we find reflected in chapters one, two, four, and five. Those other chapters see the only possibility of rescue as lying in a turning to Yahweh in prayer. Thus one finds there passionate calls to engage in lamentation (see esp. 2:18-19) and not to give up beseeching Yahweh. Here in 3:26-41, however, lamentation is disavowed. Now one is supposed to bear in silence the suffering imposed on one, not to engage in lamentation. In the place of lamentation comes self-examination. Here one is called to turn away from one's sins and turn toward Yahweh.

This admonition to turn away from one's own sins and toward Yahweh is one of the chief themes of Deuteronomic parenesis[2]. Such parenesis speaks a language different from that prevalent in the laments which arose in response to the catastrophe of 587 BCE. It is also directed to quite a different situation, a situation far removed from the horror of Jerusalem's destruction. As indicated in vv 34-37, this paranesis is promulgated in a time of steadily increasing hardship. In such a time, the chief issue at hand is simply the ability to carry on, silently and submissively, and to resist the temptation to fall into apostasy. The time for such parenesis is a time when public lamentation over Jerusalem has been restricted to occasions for commemorating the disaster of 587 BCE. Actual worship services focusing on repentance and atonement have by now come into being. We have here come down to the time of Ezra and Nehemiah.

The upshot of these observations is that any interpretation of Lamentations which sees the kernel of the whole composition in chapter three, and especially in vv 26-41 of that chapter, must be rejected. This section is hardly the key to the understanding of the other songs; it is hardly the theological prism for the whole collection. Rather, in this post-exilic expansion we are dealing with a deliberate attempt to shift the songs away from their original focus on the destruction of Jerusalem, an effort to bring the songs into closer harmony with a later situation.

---

[2] See also my *Prophetic Oracles of Salvation in the Old Testament* (1991).

In sum, vv 26-41 comprise a secondary expansion that has been shaped to resemble an avowal of confidence, a component of the personal psalm of lamentation. All the parts of our unit fit within this framework. Even the parenesis is compatible with this paradigm, as is the concluding admonition to return to Yahweh (vv 39-41). The theme of guilt is handled differently here from the way it is handled in communal laments. There the talk is of guilt that the whole people, as such, have brought upon themselves within the context of a particular span of history. This is the sort of guilt spoken of by the prophets of judgment, and it is also the sort of guilt being referred to in chapters one, two, four, and five. Here in the expansion, however, the point of reference is the sins of the individuals addressed in the parenesis, sins with regard to which the addressees are to engage in self-examination and of which they are to repent. In all the sections discernible within chapter three, only the fragment of a communal lament occurring in vv 42-51 has to do with the fate of the people as a whole and the situation immediately following 587 BCE. Attempts to relate the other sections of this chapter, and especially vv 26-41, to the whole of Israel as caught up in the crisis of 587 BCE simply have no warrant in the text.

The structure of the expansion, vv 26-41, can be summarized as follows:

26: transition: encouragement to hope, grounded in vv 31-32 (Yahweh does not reject forever);
27-30: admonition to bear up patiently under suffering;
27: it is good to bear the yoke while still young;
28: admonition to endure suffering in silence;
29: admonition to silent submission: perhaps there is yet hope;
30: admonition to endure being shamed;
(31-32: grounds for v 26 [see above]);
33-38: theological grounding, a midrash;
33: God does not torment humankind capriciously;
34-36: examples of suffering, drawing on motifs from the complaint about enemies;
37-38: evil and good alike come from Yahweh;

39-41: goal: admonition to return to Yahweh;
39: rejection of lamentation, gaining mastery over sin;
40a: summons to self-examination;
40b-41: admonition to return to Yahweh.

Verses 42-51

With v 42 clauses from a communal lament abruptly—and fragmentarily—begin. Some interpreters call vv 42-51 a penitential psalm, specifically the one that seems to be called for in vv 39-41. This is unlikely, and for two reasons. First of all, vv 42-51 is a section showing an exact correspondence to the structure of the communal lament. Only a single half verse, 42a, suggests confession. As can be seen from Ezr 9 and Neh 9, the penitential prayer has a wholly different structure. Admittedly, v 42a makes reference to a common guilt. However, the admonition to return to Yahweh, in vv 39-41, is directed to people as individuals. The most one can say is that the compiler of vv 1-66 displayed an acute power of association in placing v 42 next to vv 39-41.

This is a communal lament in abbreviated form; it is lacking both an introduction and a conclusion. Its structure is as follows:

42-45: (confession of sin and) accusation against God;
42a: confession of sin, without development;
42b-45: accusation against God (complaint against God);
46: complaint about enemies;
47: community's direct complaint;
48, 49, 51: description of agony;
50: intimated plea for God to take heed.

In v 42a the smitten people confess, "We have transgressed and rebelled." In v 42b, however, they set out their accusation against God when they add "You have not forgiven." This statement presupposes that the people have admitted their guilt and have prayed for forgiveness (cf. the "you have enveloped yourself in clouds, such that no prayer can penetrate" of v 44). Yahweh has become Israel's foe ("You have...pursued us, carried us off without pity" [v 43]). Being shamed follows in the wake of suffering ("Refuse and trash have you made us amidst the peoples" [v 45]). It is noteworthy how this accusation is cast as a form of direct address, unlike the third-person accusation in vv 2-16. This stylistic difference alone would be enough to show that, originally, these were independent texts. Casting the accusation in the form of direct address parallels the communal laments as found in the Psalter and Lam 5 (see also Lam 3:17, and our comments thereon).

A fragment from a complaint about enemies gets appended in v 46 ("All our enemies flung open their mouths against us"). We encounter a piece of a community's direct complaint in v 47 ("Terror and pit became our lot, devastation and destruction"— the sentence gives the impression of being the conclusion to a longer direct complaint). In short, the truncated lament comprising vv 42-47 stands as a parade example of the way the lament is characteristically divided into three parts [direct complaint, complaint about enemies, accusation against God].

A description of misery is often included within the element of direct complaint, and such happens here in vv 48-49 and 51. That the description is cast in the first-person singular does not mean there has been a change of speaker, nor even that the communal lament has been abandoned in favor of a personal lament. Rather, the use of "I" in these verses brings out the fact that the misery is experienced at a personal level. The tears being referred to are those of a representative human being in deep distress. The "I" is speaking as one of the "we". Since v 48 is almost identical with 1:16 and 2:11, it is certain that all three stem from the communal lament.

The section consisting of vv 48-49 and 51 ("My eye lets streams of water flow...from much weeping over my city") resembles the songs of lamentation in chapters one, two, and four. The phrase "over the downfall of the daughter of my people" occurs also in 2:11, in conjunction with that description of misery in the wake of the city's demise. These similarities help explain why 3:42-51 was incorporated into the final collection. Specifically, we have seen that vv 42-51 are a truncated version of a communal lament, one which—like Lam 5— resembled the songs of lamentation comprising chapters one, two, and four. In its original and complete form, then, 3:42-51 would have functioned as a binder between chapters one and two, on the one hand, and chapters four and five, on the other. With regard to the origin of these songs of lamentation, what apparently happened is that, after the fall of Jerusalem, pre-exilic communal-lament songs were simply taken over in somewhat altered form (cf. Lam 5). The material now found in 3:42-51, though in its fuller form, was most probably a part of this stock of pre-exilic communal laments.

The conclusion to this section is found in v 50 ("...until Yahweh looks down from heaven and sees" [cf. Isa 63:15]), even though this verse has been inserted between vv 49 and 51. Focusing on the train of thought, v 50 clearly follows v 51 ("I must lament [weep] until...").

With this the communal lament breaks off. It lacks an invocation of God and an introductory plea at its beginning, just as at the end it lacks a corresponding petition seeking God's intervention and a closing word of praise or promise to remain true to God (cf. Pss 74, 79, 80—note esp. the repetition of these closing motifs at the end of Ps 80). However, all the other components of the communal lament are present. Not only are they present, but they appear in the sequence determinative for the genre of the communal lament as found in the Psalter. Most interpreters of the Book of Lamentations maintain that the poet constructed Lam 3 out of various psalmic motifs, selecting these motifs from any number of psalms and drawing upon diverse psalmic genres. In the case of 3:42-51, this view is simply inaccurate. Rather, we have here a genuine communal-lament psalm, one still preserving the proper sequence of its parts, except that the customary beginning and ending have fallen off. This communal-lament psalm, shortened with regard to the aforementioned sections to make it fit better into the encompassing composition, was taken over from oral (perhaps written) tradition. The same holds true for vv 52-58.

Verses 52-58

This section of the third chapter has a structure which corresponds, line for line, to the descriptive psalms of praise or psalms of thanks. However, as with vv 42-51 so also here the opening and closing sections are missing. Immediately below is the pattern for the arrangement of these psalms set alongside an outline of Lam 3:52-58.[3]

Psalmic Structure	*Lam 3:52-58*
announcement	(lacking)
introductory summary	(lacking)
retrospection upon state of distress	52-54: my enemies hunted me
report of rescue	55-58: report of rescue
I called	Then I called upon your name
He heard	You heard my call
He rescued	You were near when I called you
	You saved my life
vow of praise	(lacking)
descriptive praise	(lacking)

Contrary to frequently expressed opinion, here as well we are not dealing with motifs taken over from the song of thanks, but rather with a genuine representative of that genre. For the same reasons that applied in the case of vv 42-51, the customary beginning and ending of this song of thanks are missing. In consonance with the other sections of Lam 3 (except for vv 42-51), this is the psalm of an individual. If one were to bracket out vv 26-41 and 42-51, the result would be an individual's song of praise following upon the personal lament of an individual (both elements in abbreviated form). This sequence finds parallels in several psalms, especially in Ps 22 where a descriptive psalm of praise (vv 23ff [21bff Eng.]) follows a section of lamentation (vv 1-22 [1-21a Eng.]). Pss 31 and 40 can also be mentioned in this context.

52-54: In the way its ideas are developed largely by means of comparisons ("Hunted, hunted me like a bird have those who are... my enemies" [v 52]), this retrospection upon a prior state of distress resembles the corresponding feature in other psalms of the same genre. On the motif of being caught in a pit or a net,

---

[3] For the structure of the psalms of praise or psalms of thanks, cf. Pss 18, 30, 40, 66:13-20, 116, etc., and see also my *Praise and Lament in the Psalms* (1981).

see also Pss 7:16 [15 Eng.], 9:16 [15 Eng.]), 35:7, 57:7 [6 Eng.]).[4] The reference is to bystanders who, without reason, are hostile to the one being persecuted. The one being persecuted in turn feels unfairly treated (as in v 35; cf. also Ps 69:5 [4 Eng.]). The added persecution on the part of these enemies brings the victim to the brink of death ("They hurled me, alive, into the pit, they cast stones upon me" [v 53]). Such a retrospection, identifying the enemies of the lamenter as evildoers, is a common aspect of the complaint about enemies. The feature of a personal complaint is mirrored in v 54 ("Water cascaded over my head; I thought, 'I am lost!'"—cf. Jon 2:4 [5 Eng.] and also Christoph Barth's fundamental study *Die Errettung vom Tode in den individuellen Klage- und Dankliedern des Alten Testaments* [1947]).

55-58: With its three distinct parts (I called—he heard—he [or you] rescued me), this report about being rescued exhibits a fixed and widely attested structure. For example, the same structure underlies the so-called "historical creed" of Deut 26:5-10. On the motif of calling to God from out of the depths, see also Pss 88 (esp. vv 2-8, 14 [1-7, 13 Eng.]) and 139 (esp. vv 7-12). In v 56 the theme that God hears such cries is rendered explicit ("you heard my cry"). In these four verses, with their language of praise as shaped in the cult, God is addressed directly. This is another indication that vv 52-58 once stood as part of an independent psalm. V 57 brings out the theme of God's favorable hearing ("You were near when I called you, you said, 'Do not fear!'"[5]). While they are still in a state of extreme distress, those who are imploring God hear the admonition not to fear. The mere fact that God is no longer silent begins to ameliorate their situation.

This passage (vv 55-58), which has many parallels in the Psalms, also shows how two components belong to the element of the plea directed to God as it occurs in the psalms of lamentation. There is the plea for God to hear the prayer, and

---

[4] See also my book *The Parables of Jesus in the Light of the Old Testament* (1990).

[5] Cf. Joachim Begrich, "Das priesterliche Heilsorakel," in *Ibid., Gesammelte Studien zum Alten Testament* (ThB 21; Munich: Chr. Kaiser Verlag, 1964) 217-31 [= *ZAW* 52 (1934) 81-92].

there is the plea for God actively to intervene. Both components also occur in the report of the rescue, as here. Since the report of the rescue is a natural outgrowth of the plea as it occurs within a lament, the structure of the one is reflected in the structure of the other ("You heard my plea—you have saved my life").

Here the psalm breaks off. In fact, precisely those sections which would identify this material as psalmic in nature are lacking: the summons to praise and the renewed promise to give praise. Words of praise thus do not appear in vv 52-58.

Our psalm was taken out of its original context in the cult so it could be inserted into its present setting as part of Lam 3 (as happened with vv 42-51, but unlike vv 1-25).

Verses 59-66

59-61: These three verses have the same structure. A similar invocation of Yahweh introduces each verse: Yahweh, you have seen...seen...heard. By implication, the object of Yahweh's action is also the same in each case: "...the violation of my rights." Again, this violation in each case comes at the hands of the speaker's enemies: "...their vengefulness...their plans... their taunts." All three verses belong to the element of the complaint about enemies, an element which leads to a plea for requital, as here in v 64. With its threefold "you have...," this group of verses attaches closely to the similarly formulated v 58 ("...you have saved my life!"). The technique of manufacturing a connection between units by means of formal similarities seems to be a trademark of the compiler of this material; recall the similar move in vv 39-41. From the fact that a report of rescue appears in v 58, it follows that a new unit appears in vv 59ff. Specifically, this new unit is a complaint about enemies. Its function is to establish grounds for Yahweh's intervention against those enemies. Each clause in vv 59-61 has its proper place within the element of the complaint about enemies as a feature of the personal lament.

62-63: When one reads the concluding vv 59-66, one must first bracket out vv 62-63 in order to see that the final plea, in vv 64-66, attaches directly to v 61 ("You have heard their taunts...you will requite them...!"). It is also the case that vv 62-63 exhibit language uncharacteristic of the psalm of lamentation; they are prosaic and only serve to fill space prior to the conclusion in vv 64-66. The compiler evidently sensed that the final petition for reprisal against the enemies stood in tension with the clause reporting the rescue (v 58b). The clause in v 58a ("You have taken up my cause...") also implies that the speaker has been liberated from the depredations of enemies. The prosaic vv 62-63 represent an attempt to soften the tension between report of rescue and petition for requital. These verses explain how the enemies continue to be "...against me all day long"; they urge Yahweh to "notice that, when they sit down and when they rise up, I am [still] their taunt-song." In the light of these considerations, the petition against the enemies in vv 64-66 becomes justified. The hand of the compiler is clearly evident in clauses such as these. We have here an illustration of how the compiler took originally independent bits of material and wove them together to achieve the final composition.

64-66: The petition for requital against enemies that concludes the chapter is prepared for by the complaint about enemies in vv 59-61 and is made understandable by the transitional claims voiced against them in vv 62-63. Nowhere in the Psalter does a complaint about enemies, complete with a following petition for requital to be visited upon those enemies, serve as the conclusion to a song of praise. Thus vv 64-66 can only be taken as the conclusion to a psalm of lamentation.[6] As typically happens in the psalm of lamentation, here at the conclusion Yahweh is implored to intervene against the enemies of the lamenter and to visit upon them precisely what they had intended for the lamenter. The actual plea appears in v 65: "Give them hardness of heart, let your curse come upon them!" (The petition against enemies originated in the curse.) Vv 64 and 66 intensify the petition by expressing the certainty that God will indeed grant it ("You will requite them, O Yahweh...You will...blot them out"). The particular wording of these themes

<hr/>

[6] Cf. H. Gunkel / J. Begrich, *Einleitung in die Psalmen* and my *Praise and Lament in the Psalms.*

from the complaint about enemies in 3:59-66 clearly sets this conclusion apart from the corresponding sections in chapters one, two, and four. (An ending of this sort is lacking in chapter five.) The words directed against the enemies are sharper and more vehement here. Since vv 59-66 can properly be the conclusion to neither the preceding psalm of praise in vv 52-58 nor the communal lament in vv 42-51, it follows that these verses must be the conclusion to the whole chapter. This means vv 52-58 also serve as the conclusion to the personal lament in vv 1-25. Thus portions of a personal psalm of lamentation make up the framework for the full composition, 3:1-66. It is probable that the compiler here made use of an already existent psalm of lamentation, one which began with vv 1-25 and ended with vv 59-66 (except for vv 62-63). At the very least, the enemies who appear in vv 59-66 were intended by the composer to be understood along the lines of the enemies who appear in the personal lament. Both convey a sense of sharp opposition between the pious and the wicked ("let...curse come upon them!"). Not a single clause in this final unit needs to be seen as referring to the external enemies of the Israelite state.

Structure of Lam 3

The major units of chapter three are the following:

1-25: lament of an individual (lacking beginning and ending)
26-41: expansion: parenesis and didactic explanation
42-51: fragment of a communal lament
52-58: fragment of an individual's psalm of praise
59-66: concluding section: complaint about enemies and
   plea for requital.

In detail, the structure of chapter three is as follows:

1-25: lament of an individual (lacking introduction and
   conclusion)
   1a: introduction: I am the one who...
   1b-17a: accusation against God (description of misery)
   1b,8: God is angry with the speaker and seems not to hear
      the speaker's supplication

2-16: God has caused the speaker to suffer: has driven the
speaker into darkness and distress (vv 2,3,5,6,7), has
inflicted bodily pain (vv 4,5,16), has made the speaker
into a laughing-stock (v 14), indeed has become the
speaker's enemy (vv 3,10,11,12,13)

17a: "You cast out my soul from peace" (second-person
address)

14,17b-20: speaker's direct complaint

14: "I have become the laughing-stock..."

8a: "my plea [to God] was not heard..."

17b-18: "I forgot what happiness was...perished is...my hope..."

19: "to recall my affliction...is gall and venom"

20-25: avowal of confidence

20: reflective transition: "yet you will...bear in mind..."

21: resolve to hope (continued in v 24)

22-23: praise of God: God's mercy is ever new

24: avowal of confidence: "My portion is Yahweh"

25: conclusion, tying together theme of hope and praise
of God

26-41: expansion: admonition and didactic explanation

26: transition: recommendation to hope, grounded in vv
31-32 ("Yahweh does not reject...forever")

27-30: admonition to bear suffering with patience

33-38: didactic expansion, a midrash

33: God does not torment capriciously

34-36: development on theme of suffering (using motifs
characteristic of the complaint about enemies)

37-38: evil as well as good comes from Yahweh

39-41: goal of the expansion: admonition to return to
Yahweh

39: rejection of lamentation, call to mastery over one's sins

40a: summons to examine one's conduct

40b-41: admonition to return to Yahweh

42-51: communal lament (without introduction or conclusion)

42-45: accusation against God ("You have wrapped yourself
in anger...")

46: complaint about enemies: the enemies mock us

47: community's direct complaint: destruction became
our lot

48, 49, 51: description of misery

50: intimated plea for favor ("until Yahweh looks down...')

52-58: individual's psalm of praise (lacking introduction and conclusion)

52-54: retrospection upon earlier distress ("hunted, hunted me...")

55-58: report of rescue: I called—you heard—you rescued

59-66: conclusion: complaint about enemies and plea for requital

59-61: complaint about enemies, preparing for the petition against the enemies ("You have seen the violation of my rights...you have seen their vengefulness...")

62-63: prose transition ("[they] are against me all day long")

64-66: "You will requite them, O Yahweh...and blot them out..."

Summarizing Conclusion

Lam 3 is constructed out of different components, all held together by the alphabetic sequence of its verses. Through utilizing this acrostic arrangement, the compiler has succeeded in giving 3:1-66 the appearance of being a literary unit, as being one with the songs of lamentation which comprise the other four chapters of the Book of Lamentations. Moreover, our compiler has so carefully woven together the various components which once stood as independent texts that the literary seams can hardly be recognized. However, one can safely assume that some little collection of psalms once stood behind this composition, just as happened in a number of cases with the Psalter. For example, the small collection which now comprises Pss 120-134 arose out of an earlier core of psalms all having the same genre. Or think of the psalmic texts in the Books of Chronicles, where pieces taken from different psalms have been woven together. (In the case of 1 Chr 16:8-36, for example, vv 8-22 are derived from Ps 105:1-15 while vv 23-33 come from Ps 91:1b-13a.) In the same vein, Ps 66 has been constructed out of three originally independent psalms (vv 1-8, 9-12, 13-20). The only real difference, in the case of Lam 3, is that the compiler constructed a whole out of independent additions as well as out of three different psalms.

What the compiler intended to achieve with this composition can only been deduced from the nature of the compositional process. Here the most important section is the expansion consisting of vv 26-41. That this section is pivotal for the whole composition follows already from the clause at the very beginning, the "I am the one who...." By using this opening in place of the original introduction for the psalm of lamentation, the compiler gave to the whole the character of an address, a character which is then all the more pronounced when it comes to the expansion. It is only in keeping with this change of focus that the liturgical portions of the three constituent psalms have been left out. The composer of Lam 3 is not interested in the liturgical function of the constituent psalms, but rather in their didactic content.

The expansion combines admonition and instruction. Of the two, however, proportionately greater emphasis falls on the element of admonition. This is seen in the way the admonition to recognize one's own sins and return to Yahweh concludes the section, in vv 39-41. The renunciation of further lamentation which occurs here is a deliberate correction stemming from a later, post-exilic time. The admonition to examine their ways and return to Yahweh is directed to individuals—and as such is likewise an indication of the piety of a later time. That more emphasis came to be placed on the lament of the individual in later times is shown in the way this genre predominates over the communal lament in the Psalter. In Ps 37, a late psalm, admonition and instruction are attached to avowal of confidence just as they are in Lam 3.

In the use of connections and transitions, the composer of Lam 3 has demonstrated admirable artistry. This follows from the fact that transitions had to be created which would tie together independent psalmic units having nothing—or very little—in common. Several times the composer relied upon catch-word association, as with the three lines beginning with "good" (vv 25-27) or the "you have" of vv 58-59. In each case the transitional devices were clearly thought out in advance—a fact which proves that the composer was fully aware of the necessity of such transitions. Above all, this is demonstrated in the way the composer attached the expansion to the avowal of confidence, thereby subtly transforming hope as a deliberate act into hope as an attitude or a stance (vv 25-27). With the transition to the communal lament in vv 39-42, the composer has the confession of sins (v 42—an element of the communal lament) follow directly upon the summons to confess and to acknowledge sins (vv 39-41—features of the parenetic interlude). With the transition from the communal lament to the psalm of praise, the composer has the retrospection upon earlier distress (vv 52-54) follow directly upon the description of misery in the immediately preceding communal lament (likewise told in the first-person singular). This makes the transition from one genre of psalm to another hardly noticeable. The transition from the final line of the psalm of praise (v 58) to the opening lines of the complaint about enemies (vv 59-61) is concealed by continuing to use the same verbal form ("you have...") in all four verses. Finally, vv 62-63 were constructed by the composer to serve as a transitional element between the preceding psalm of praise and the concluding petition directed against the enemies (vv 64-66).

The controlling intent of the composer of Lam 3 can be recognized, then, by starting out from the central position held by the avowal of confidence as a link between the outer framework and the core of the composition—the material that culminates in the praise of God. Addressing an era considerably after the catastrophe of 587 BCE, the composer calls for an attitude of humble perseverance in suffering, an acknowledgement of one's own sins, and a return to Yahweh. None of this is to be accomplished by continuing in lamentation. In taking this stance, the composer of Lam 3 links his teaching and his admonition to the piety of the Psalms, a piety in whose midst the composer also stands.

Lam 4

1   Ah, how lusterless[a] is the gold, how marred[b] the fine gold!
The jewels[c] lie scattered about[d] at every street corner!

2   The sons of Zion, precious, worth their weight[a] in gold, how

they are regarded as earthen pots, works of a potter's
    hands!

3 Even jackals[a] offer[b] the breast and suckle their young;
   but the daughters of my people became[c] cruel[d], like
       ostriches in the wilderness.

4 The tongue of the suckling stuck to its palate from thirst,
   children asked for bread, but no one brought them any.

5 Those accustomed to eating delicacies[a] languished in the streets,
   those accustomed to reclining on purple cushions now
       clasp the refuse pile.

6 The iniquity of the daughter of my people was greater than
       the transgression of Sodom,
   which was destroyed in an instant, without a hand being
       laid[a] upon it.

7 Purer than snow were her nobles[a], whiter than milk.
   Ruddier than corals were their bodies[b] like sapphire their
       limbs[c].

8 Their appearance became blacker than soot, they were no
       longer recognized in the streets.
   Their skin was shrivelled upon their bones, it became as
       dry as wood.

9 Those slain by the sword had it better than those who fell
       victim to hunger,
   who pined away, struck down by lack of fruit from the field.[a]

10 The hands of tender-hearted women cooked their own
       children—
   children served as their mothers' nourishment[a] at the
       collapse of my people.

11 Yahweh has carried out his wrath, poured out his anger,
   kindled a fire in Zion that destroyed it down to the ground.

12 The kings of the earth could not believe it, nor could all the inhabitants of the world,

that besiegers and foes would pass through the gates of Jerusalem.

13 It happened[a] because of the sins of her prophets, the iniquities of her priests,

who shed in her[b] midst the blood of the righteous.

14 They wandered blind[a] in the streets, defiled with blood, such that no one dared touch their garments.

15 Turn aside! Unclean! Turn aside! (...)[a] Turn aside, do not touch!

They became fugitives and wanderers, they were no longer permitted to remain here.

16 The countenance[a] of Yahweh has scattered[b] them, he regards[c] them no longer.

One no longer respects the priests, the elders find no favor.

17 Yet[a] our eyes looked longingly for our help—in vain!

From our watch-tower we reconnoitered for a people who did not assist.

18 They hunted our steps, we could not set foot in our squares.

Our end drew near, our days were fulfilled, indeed our end came upon us.

19 Our pursuers were swifter than the eagles in the sky, upon the mountains they pursued us, in the wilderness they lay in wait for us.

20 Our breath of life, Yahweh's anointed, was captured in their snares, he of whom we said, in his shadow we will live among the peoples.

21 Rejoice and be glad, O daughter Edom, you who dwell in the land of Uz[a],
the cup[b] will also come round to you, so that you expose yourself while in delirium!

22 Your punishment is complete, O daughter Zion, he will not again banish you;
but he will punish your iniquity, O daughter Edom, he will expose your sins!

Textual Notes

1a: The term *yū'am* is a *hapax legomenon*; according to the versions it means "to become darkened / lusterless." **b:** The terms *yišnā'* and *yišneh* can both mean "to be marred"; there is no reason to emend the text. **c:** The *'abnê qōdeš* are jewels (J. A. Emerton); cf. GKC § 128p. **d:** On the form cf. GKC § 54k.

2a: The plural participle of *sāla'* (a *hapax legomenon*) has the same meaning as the *sālāh* (likewise a *hapax legomenon*) of Job 28:16 and, following M. Löhr and others, is literally to be rendered "to be counterbalanced by / compensated for."

3a: The form is an Aramaizing plural. **b:** The literal translation of the verb would be "draw out." **c:** Following the Syriac, perhaps *hāyětāh* is to be added [cf. the textual apparatus *ad loci* in BHK[3]]. **d:** According to H. Gottlieb, the *lamed* here is emphatic.

5a: On the use of *lamed* as designating a direct object, cf. GKC § 117n.

6a: The meaning of the verb is questionable; it could also be 163 "turn against" (cf. the KBL lexicon at *hûl*).

7a: *Nězîrîm* here means "those of high rank," hence our "nobles" (cf. the KBL lexicon); no emendation of the text is necessary. **b:** Read *'eşmêhem* ("their bones," "their bodies") under the influence of the parallel *sappîr gizrātām* ("like sapphire their limbs") of the colon's second stichos; the meaning of the sentence remains unclear since the point of the comparison is not recognizable. **c:** Taken literally, *gizrātām* means "their cut"; Hillers suggests reading "their beards."

9a: The text is corrupt; H. J. Boecker translates "...those who died, as though pierced, by lack of nourishment" (similarly R. Gordis).

10a: Instead of MT's *lĕbārōt*, it is possible to read *lĕbārūt*, cf. G, S, V and also Ps 69:22 [21 Eng.]: "They gave me gall in my food".

13a: "It happened" is present in the text by implication. **b:** The referent is Jerusalem.

14a: They wandered as though blind.

15a: The clarifying expressions *qārĕ'ū lāmō* and *'āmĕrū baggōyîm* seem to be later additions to the text. **b:** In place of MT's *nāṣū* read *nādū*.

16a: Meant is "Yahweh himself..." (cf. Exod 33:14). **b:** Cf. Gen 49:7. **c:** Cf. 2 Kgs 3:14.

17a: Literally, *'ōdênnū* [sic] is to be translated "While we yet..." (cf. Gen 29:9: "While he yet spoke").

21a: Uz = Edom (cf. also Gen 36:28 & Jer 25:20). **b:** The reference is to the cup of wrath (cf. Jer 25:15ff.).

The Structure of Lam 4

1. As for the alphabetic form, two lines are assigned to each letter of the Hebrew alphabet, so in all this song of lamentation contains forty-four lines. Lam 4 differs in several regards from Lam 1 and Lam 2. The main difference lies in the nature of the contrasts employed in the description of misery. Also, in Lam 4 there are no petitionary elements. In their place we have the account in vv 17-20.

2. In vv 1-10 we encounter a community's direct complaint, transformed into a description of misery in the third person. With its sharp contrasts, this section is quite in the style of the dirge, with the only deviation from the pattern of the dirge being the intimation of guilt in v 6. The complaint is continued in vv 14-16, six lines that could be a direct continuation of v 10.

3. The description of misery is organized according to the groups of people affected. In vv 1-2 one finds lamentation over fallen heroes, a theme continued in vv 7-8. These two groups of four lines belong together; they have become separated under the force of the alphabetic arrangement. Interwoven with the description of the fate of the males is a corresponding depiction of the fate of the females and their children, first in vv 3-5 and then in vv 9-10. With regard to the females and the children, the emphasis lies on the ravages of famine. A third group appears in vv 14-16, namely the priests and the elders. Here the sequence of the verses is somewhat disrupted. The calamity which befalls this group is described throughout by means of contrasting comparisons.

4. In vv 11-13 one finds an accusation against God, cast in the third person. This is tied in with an attribution of guilt, focusing on priests and prophets. Recall that we had already encountered an intimation of guilt in v 6a, though there the focus was upon the people as a whole.

5. In vv 17-20, where we would expect to find a complaint about enemies, we instead encounter a report about the capture of the king. This motif falls completely outside the pattern of speech attested elsewhere in the Book of Lamentations; in Lam 4 it appears as an alien element. This motif starts out abruptly in v 17, without introduction or transition, as though a more extensive account of another sort had been taken up at its midpoint. These verses do not speak the language of lamentation. However, this motif does fit in with the rest of Lam 4 in the sense that it expands the boundaries of a group of human beings [viz., the fallen heroes] already mentioned.

6. Especially striking is the absence of any petitionary motifs, in particular an addressing of Yahweh and a plea for Yahweh to show favour. Since the conclusion (vv 21-22) follows just as abruptly upon vv 17-20 as do vv 17-20 upon v 16, it is possible that these missing elements have been displaced by the addition of vv 17-20.

7. Corresponding to the characteristic dual wish at the end of psalms of lamentation, the conclusion (vv 21-22) consists of the wish for retribution against Edom. Zion is mentioned along with Edom (v 22a), but only to affirm that the punishment of the former is now complete and that such a terrible fate will never again befall her. Vv 21-22 serve as the conclusion for vv 1-16, but not for vv 17-20, which bear no intrinsic relationship to the other verses of Lam 4.

Structural Outline of Lam 4

> 1-10, 14-16: community's direct complaint (description of
>   misery), developed by means of contrasts
> 1-2: males—destruction of the sons of Zion
> 7-8: the ruined beauty of the noble youths
> 3-5, 9-10: females and children
> 3: the cruel mothers
> 4: the children's torments of hunger
> 5: change from luxury to misery
> 6: the guilt of the people
> 9: better fallen than starving
> 10: mothers nourish themselves on their children
> 16b, 14-15: priests and elders
> 16a: the esteemed are despised
> 14-15: considered unclean, they must flee
> 11-13 (6): accusation against God and confession of sins
> 11: Yahweh has carried out his wrath
> 12: the astonishing fall of Jerusalem
> 13 and 6: guilt of the people, of the prophets and priests
> 17-20: flight and captivity of the king
> 21-22: punishment of Edom, end to Israel's distress

Exegesis of Lam 4

The smooth sequence of verses, or sentences, is somewhat disrupted in Lam 4. However, if one also includes a consideration of the relationship among the various motifs, one can start out from the concomitant establishing of three facts: (a) the section consisting of vv 1-10 & 14-16 is description of misery corresponding to that found in the community's direct complaint and shaped by the contrasting style of the dirge; (b) the section consisting of vv 11-13 is description of misery corresponding to that found in the accusation against God, tied in with an attribution of guilt; (c) vv 21-22 correspond to the concluding element of the communal lament.

The mournful cry [Ah!] introduces the first section, vv 1-10. Throughout, this section is shaped by the contrasting style of the dirge, in which the former state of affairs is juxtaposed to the present one.

1a: the gold is lusterless, the fine gold is marred
1b: jewels—scattered about at the street corners
2: worth gold—regarded as earthen pots
3: even jackals—but not the women of Jerusalem—like ostriches in the wilderness
5a: delicacies—languishing in the streets
5b: purple cushions—the refuse pile
7-8: purer than snow, whiter than milk, ruddier than coral—blacker than soot, disfigured, skin shrivelled and dry
10: tender-hearted women—cooked their children
14: prophets and priests—fugitives

While this pattern of contrasts determines the structure of vv 1-10, the unit is also divided according to the groups of persons whose suffering is being lamented (as also happens in the Lamentation over Ur).

1-2: the sons of Zion
3-5: the women and children, continued in 9-10
7-8: the nobles of Zion, continued in 14-15

The fact that Lam 4 more closely resembles the dirge than do

Lam 1 and 2, particularly through its heavy reliance on the contrast-motif, is clearly due to the way vv 1-10 lament the deceased, both those slain by the sword and those who have fallen victim to famine—as is expressly stated in v 9. Only gradually is mention of the survivors also worked into the lament. In this case, then, the interweaving of dirge and lament is fully justified.

Verses 1-2

The lament over the young men focuses on only one point, namely on the value of these young men for the community as a whole. They had been as precious as gold and jewels, but now their value is dissipated, gone, reduced to the equivalent of mere dirt. With their demise, there has also disappeared all that they meant for their community—in sum, the community's hope for the future.

In vv 7-8 special mention is made of the aristocrats. Here a different aspect is brought to the fore: "purer than snow were her nobles, whiter than milk." Set in contrast to this image is the clause "their appearance became blacker than soot...." Behind this contrast stands the tradition of praising heroes, a tradition which includes praising them for their physical beauty (cf., e.g., 1 Sam 10:23-24). The same practice is attested for other peoples as well.[1] The influence of the dirge is thus particularly evident in these verses.

Verses 3-5, 10

Women and children are hardly spared the horrors that befall the inhabitants of a city when it is overthrown. Vv 3-4 focus explicit attention on a single feature: mothers are unable to suckle their small children. Suckling their young is an activity common to human beings and animals alike ("even jackals offer the breast... "), but now the practice of this biological necessity is disrupted ("the tongue of the suckling stuck to its palate from thirst"). Again a contrast is employed in the

---

[1] For specifics, cf. Hedwig Jahnow, *Das hebräische Leichenlied im Rahmen der Völkerdichtung* and Enno Littmann, *Abessinische Klagelieder: alte Weisen in neuer Gewandung* (esp. pp. 14f.).

depiction of the situation ("those accustomed to eating delicacies languished in the streets"). The most gruesome feature is mentioned last ("the hands of tender-hearted women cooked their own children..."[v 10; cf. 2:20]). This unbearable horror obviously made such a strong impression on the eyewitnesses that they had to speak of it as something beyond comprehension (cf. 2 Kgs 6:28-30).

Verses 14-16

Vv 14-16 are a continuation of the description of misery which comprises vv 1-10. Along with the misery of the men, the women, and the children there is now mentioned the misery of another group, namely priests and elders. The conceptually meaningful sequence of the verses has been disrupted here under the constraint of the alphabetic arrangement. Consequently it is up to the interpreter to read as a unit the material that belongs together. V 16b speaks of the misery of the priests and the elders ("One no longer respects the priests, the elders find no favor"). When this material is recognized as a continuation of the contrasts which shape vv 1-10, then it is seen that vv 14-15 must once have followed v 16b ("They wandered blind in the streets, defiled with blood..."). The best explanation for vv 14-15 is that they refer to these priests and elders. The formerly esteemed are now despised—a poignant reversal. V 16a properly stands at the end of this description of misery ("The countenance of Yahweh has scattered them, he regards them no longer"). Regardless of how one might determine the sequence of these verses, in any case it is clear that vv 14-16 belong to a description of misery. As such these verses bear a correspondence to a community's direct complaint and properly follow a listing of the major groups within the populace. With its twenty-four lines, the description of misery constitutes the largest segment of Lam 4.

Verses 11-13

The accusation against God and the attributing of guilt to priests and prophets belong together. The description of misery thus follows a unified section. In this section the accusation against God (v 11) is bound up with the acknowledgement of guilt (v 13). Bridging these two motifs is reference to the unprecedented judgment which came over Jerusalem as the expression of divine wrath (v 12; cf. Isa 42:14-15, 51:17&20, 54:7-8). In v 11 the element of description of misery is summarized ("Yahweh has carried out his wrath, poured out his anger..."). At the same time, the ultimate cause of the misery is identified. It was Yahweh, acting on his anger, who brought about all this horror. The suffering which has had to be born came as part of Yahweh's judgment. It was Yahweh who "kindled a fire in Zion that destroyed it down to the ground." Echoing throughout v 12 is deep dismay at this display of divine wrath. Who would have believed that it could ever happen, that "besiegers and foes would pass through the gates of Jerusalem"? A similar reaction of shock is reflected in Ezek 28:11-19. However, this unprecedented event was brought upon the inhabitants by themselves. "It happened because of the sins of her prophets, the iniquities of her priests"—cf. Jer 6:13; 23:11. The rest of the people are also to blame, however. "The iniquity of the daughter of my people was greater than the transgression of Sodom..." (v 6). The guilt of the people is mentioned yet a third time in v 22. The expression "sins of the prophets" in all probability means the same here as it does in Lam 2:14—the prophets of weal have made deceitful pronouncements. It remains unclear just what is meant by the priests' shedding the blood of the righteous. The comparison between Jerusalem's fate and the judgment leveled against Sodom (v 6) merely confirms the direction of thought in vv 11-13, namely that in retrospect the guilt of Israel is accepted as an established fact. God's people brought the judgment of God upon themselves! Lam 1, 2, 3:42-51, and 5 all agree with Lam 4 in this assessment.

Verses 17-20

Next comes the account of the king's capture. This interspersed segment is a motif characteristic of neither the communal lament nor the dirge. It was probably transposed here from another context; its language is not in the style of the rest of Lamentations. Not only does this section begin abruptly, but the transition to the following section (vv 21-22) is just as abrupt. Vv 17-20 probably go back to some eyewitness, to some escort of the king who accompanied him on his flight and was present at his capture. This much, at least, is assumed by a number of interpreters. These eight lines give a lively and sympathetic account of an episode early on in the occupation of Jerusalem in 587 BCE. The drama of the event as captured in these lines clearly elevates vv 17-20 from their immediate context. The account focuses on the attempted flight of the king from the besieged Jerusalem, on the anxious expectation of help from without (a hope which was dashed), on the rapid and tenacious pursuit by the enemy, and finally on the capture of the king in an ambush. Much is merely suggested by the account; possibly it is condensed from some more elaborate report. This becomes all the more likely when it is recognized that nowhere else in Lamentations is there explicit description of any military engagement. One can see, however, a reason for the insertion of vv 17-20 at precisely this point. The bulk of Lam 4 is description of misery, with the description being structured according to the groups of people affected. Vv 17-20 set the king and his royal court alongside all these other groups (cf. Mic 4:9-10).

Following brief reference to a preliminary stage in the sequence of events, namely the vain anticipation of help from without, the account breaks down into three sections. (a) The king, with a small entourage, undertakes an attempt to flee (v 18); (b) the escape-attempt is discovered, the fleeing group is pursued over the mountains and through the wilderness (v 19); (c) the little group is overpowered in an ambush and the king is taken captive (v 20a; cf. Ezek 19:4).

The section which concludes the account is actually a lament over the loss of the king. In this little lament one can recognize the contrast-motif at work, and hence it resembles a dirge. The lament itself consists of only a single clause; the king "was captured in their snares" (v 20a). This clause corresponds to the theme of the announcement of the death in the dirge. Our basic clause is briefly expanded in two directions. Moving in one direction is the phrase which stands in apposition to "our breath of life" (viz., "Yahweh's anointed"). Pointing in the other is the clause expressing the impact of the king's capture on his people ("he of whom we said, in his shadow we will live among the peoples"). Both the appositional expression in v 20a and the expansionary clause in v 20b could be derived from some song in praise of the king. This would make the contrast all the more striking. Even the king, "our breath of life," was snatched away in the collapse.

What is reported in vv 17-20 corresponds to 2 Kgs 25:4-7. The "people who did not assist" refers to the Egyptians, for whose intervention people in Jerusalem had entertained hopes right up to the last moment (cf. Lam 5:6 and Jer 44:30). Those attempting to flee apparently headed in the direction of the Jordan; supposedly the king was captured south of Jericho. Here, in contrast to 2 Kgs 25:4-7, nothing further is said of the king's fate. This is another indication that vv 17-20 are derived from some fuller account.

Verses 21-22

The account which comprises vv 17-20 ends as abruptly as it had begun. The transition from v 20 to vv 21-22, the concluding petition directed against enemies, is all the more jarring for the fact that, in terms of their content, these final verses connect, not with vv 17-20, but all the way back with vv 1-16. As a petition directed against enemies, these concluding verses are consonant with the structure of the psalms of lamentation (cf. 3:64-66). For all that, however, it is also the case that the connection between v 16 and vv 21-22 is somewhat loose. The supposition lies readily at hand, then, that vv 17-20 are not only an insertion but also that they have displaced some section of the song of lamentation.

The conclusion amounts to a petition directed against enemies—in this case against Edom, the neighbor that became an enemy. An ironic summons introduces this final section ("Rejoice and be glad, O daughter Edom..." [v 21a]). The play here is upon the mockery voiced by the neighboring Edomites upon the occasion of Jerusalem's destruction. This becomes the grounds for the announcement against Edom ("the cup will also come round to you..." [v 21b]). The reference here can only be to Yahweh's cup of wrath; Yahweh will punish Edom for its lack of loyalty to its neighbor Judah. Of course, this statement

presupposes that Yahweh is the Lord also of other peoples in
the vicinity and of their destinies. The effect of Yahweh's
intervention will be "that you expose yourself while in delirium"
(cf. Gen 9:20-27). In other words, to the actual experience of
being conquered will be added the shame of defeat. What v 21b
states metaphorically is repeated explicitly in v 22b. In its
behavior toward Judah, Edom has burdened itself with guilt.
Therefore the announcement to Edom states "he [Yahweh]
will punish your iniquity, O daughter Edom, he will expose
your sins." This announcement directed against Edom is
expanded by the only clause in all of Lam 4 that speaks of
Judah's future ("Your punishment is complete, O daughter
Zion, he will not again banish you" [v 22a; cf. Nah 1:12-13]). To
be sure, this is not yet a proclamation of return from exile nor
a promise of any sort of restoration. However, Judah is clearly
told that she has by now suffered enough. In this the words
correspond to the very beginning of the proclamation of
Deutero-Isaiah ("...cry to her that she has served her term, that
her penalty is paid..." [Isa 40:2]).

*Excursus: The Petition Directed against Enemies as It Appears in
Lamentations*

> Let it yet come upon them as it has upon me; let all their
>   evil come before you!
> And do to them as you have done to me because of all my sins!
>   (Lam 1:22a-b)

> You will requite them, O Yahweh, according to the work of
>   their hands!
> Give them hardness of heart, let your curse come upon them!
> You will pursue them in anger and blot them out from
>   under "the heaven of Yahweh."
>   (Lam 3:64-66)

> Rejoice and be glad, O daughter Edom, you who dwell in
>   the land of Uz,
> the cup will also come round to you, so that you expose
>   yourself while in delirium!

Your punishment is complete, O daughter Zion, he will not
  again banish you;
but he will punish your iniquity, O daughter Edom, he will
  expose your sins!

(Lam 4:21-22)

The petition directed against enemies (1:22) or the dual
wish (4:21-22) is a fixed component in the psalms of lamentation
as they appear in the Psalter. This element always appears at the
end of the composition (in the alphabetic Ps 145 it occurs in the
last verse but one [v 20]). That this same pattern holds in the
corresponding places in the Book of Lamentations once again
shows how, in the latter, the structure of the Psalter's songs of
lamentation is presupposed. The petition directed against
enemies occurs in Lam 1 and Lam 4, as well as at the end of the
personal lament which constitutes the bulk of Lam 3. This
element does not appear in either Lam 2 or Lam 5.

It is noteworthy how, in the Book of Lamentations, it is only
in 3:64-66 that this element exhibits any trace of passionate
hatred ("...let your curse come upon them!"). In this case the
enemies are the transgressors, as in the so-called psalms of
vengeance [*Rachepsalmen*] in the Psalter. In the concluding
verses of both Lam 1 and Lam 4, it is expressly stated that
Yahweh is invoked against the enemies in his role as righteous
judge. The enemies have transgressed and must be punished
for their iniquity (intimated also in 3:64). Yahweh is to punish
these enemies just as he has punished Israel (1:22b). The issue
here is God's righteous governance over the affairs of all
peoples—which must then include also the enemies of Israel.
The language of these passages in Lamentations consists of
motifs and concepts taken over from other sources. However,
one must also note how it is nowhere said that God's punishment
of Israel's enemies will necessarily work to Israel's benefit. No
more is said than that the suffering which Israel has born up to
the present time constitutes a sufficient punishment for Israel
(4:22a). The songs in the Book of Lamentations are strongly
stamped by an awareness that the actions which the enemies
took against Israel were in essence God's punishment upon the
people of God.

In sum, the basic feature of Lam 4 is the emphasis it places on the community's direct complaint. By and large the chapter is arranged according to the groups affected by the calamity of Jerusalem's destruction, and therefore attention is primarily directed to the themes of loss, of suffering, and of death. It is only in keeping with this emphasis that the section comprising vv 4-10 bears a particularly close resemblance to a dirge.

The second feature characteristic of Lam 4 is its insertion, in vv 17-20, of the account dealing with the capture of the Judean king. Here the fate of the king and his entourage is presented as the fate of another of the groups of Jerusalem's inhabitants. In the way it treats its theme, Lam 4:17-20 is properly seen as one step in the development of a kind of historical writing, subsequent to the fall of Jerusalem, such as we also encounter in Jer 40-44, the so-called Baruch-account. The fact that this historical account occurs in Lam 4:17-20, which is to say totally within the context of a lament, simply tells us that this material was regarded by the composer of the lament as worthy of being preserved and passed on. It is a piece of the material worthy of being transmitted to the remnant of Israel. What is here related deserves to be remembered by Israel's descendants.

Lam 5

1   Remember, Yahweh, what happened to us!
    Look, and see our disgrace!

2   Our inheritance fell to the enemies,
    our houses were given[a] to foreigners.

3   We have become orphans, fatherless;
    our mothers became like widows.

4   We have to pay for the water we drink,
    only in exchange for money do we get wood.

5   The yoke[a] presses upon our necks; we are tired,
    no one lets us rest.

6   We stretched out the hand toward Egypt,
         toward Assyria, in order to get enough to eat.

7   Our fathers have sinned—they are no more;
         we, however[a]—we bear their guilt.

8   Servants are lords over us,
         no one sets us free from their power.

9   At danger to our lives[a] do we fetch our bread[b],
         threatened by the sword of the wilderness.

10   Our skin glows[a] like an oven
         from the ravages of hunger.

11   Women were raped on Zion,
         maidens in the towns of Judah;

12   princes were hanged by them,
         the countenance of the elders was not esteemed.

13   Youths were consigned to the hand-mill,
         lads stumbled under loads of wood.

14   The old men distanced themselves from the city gate,
         the young men from their stringed instruments.

15   The joy of our hearts is at an end,
         our dancing has been turned into mourning.

16   The crown has fallen from our head,
         woe to us that we have sinned!

17   Therefore[a] our heart has become ill,
         for these things our eyes have grown dim;

18   for the fact that Mount Zion lies desolate[a,]
         for the fact that jackals wander over it.

210   *Lamentations*

19 But[a] you, Yahweh, are enthroned forever,
　　your throne endures from generation to generation.

20 Why do you continually forget us,
　　abandon us for such a long time?[a]

21 Bring us, Yahweh, back[a] to yourself[b],
　　renew our days as before!

22 Or have you totally rejected us,
　　are you indeed so angry with us?[a]

Textual Notes
2a: The text is to be expanded by adding *nittĕnū* (cf. the text-critical apparatus of BHK[3] and Jer 6:12).

5a: Read ʿōl (with Budde, Nötscher, *et al.*)

7a: Read *waʾănaḥnū*.

9a: A more literal rendering would be "at the price of our lives."
b: A more literal rendering would be "do we bring in our nourishment."

10a: Read *nikmar* with G, L, V.

17a: Otto Plöger emphasizes that "...the ʿal at the beginning of each colon refers both to what is past and to what is yet to come."

18a: Here we have the adjective *šāmēm* preceded by the relative particle .

19a: Here read *wĕʾattāh* (with the text-critical apparatus of both BHK and BHS and, *inter alia*, H.-J. Kraus and O. Kaiser).

20a: This motif occurs frequently in the Psalms.

21a: Because it so obviously disrupts the rhythm, the *wĕnāšūbāh* at the end of the first colon is questionable (cf. Jer 31:18). **b:** Budde and Haller want to strike "to you/yourself," a solution to the colon's rhythmic problem which Rudolph *et al.* properly reject.

22a: The various translation possibilities for this colon are summarized by Hillers, who himself translates "But instead you have completely rejected us." Rudolph renders the colon "Lest it be that you had completely cast us off" (similarly O. Plöger). I join Löhr, Kraus, and others in taking it to say "Or have you totally rejected us…?" Even if this is not a strictly literal rendering, reading the colon as an interrogative best captures the sense it carries in its context.

The Structure of Lam 5
1. Lam 5 is not a true acrostic poem. However, it is constructed on the basis of the Hebrew alphabet in that the number of verses corresponds to the number of letters. One consequence of this variation from the pattern strictly followed in Lam 1-4 has is that the poem's structure is not constrained by the alphabetic sequence. The effects of this can be seen in the structural outline of Lam 5, below.

2. Of all five songs in the Book of Lamentations, the fifth most closely resembles a traditional communal lament. In fact, Gunkel and others assign it to this very category. The dirge has influenced this text, not through the addition of themes which stem from that genre (note the absence of a mournful cry at the beginning), but only in the development of the community's direct complaint—similar to a description of misery—in vv 2-18.

3. The song begins, in v 1, with an address of Yahweh and a plea for Yahweh to take heed. This is later followed, in v 21, by a plea for Yahweh to take direct action. In other words, the element of the communal lament is framed by the elements of petition in vv 1 and 21.

4. The lengthy direct complaint voiced by the community (vv

2-18) is essentially a development of the themes introduced in v 1: "...what happened to us...our disgrace." In this complaint, the survivors pour out their hearts before Yahweh. This complaint, a description of misery, is interrupted only by the acknowledgement of guilt—cast in the form of cry of woe—in v 16b, and by an attribution of guilt to the forebears in v 7. As happens in other communal psalms of lamentation as well, acknowledgement of guilt is thus brought into association with the community's direct complaint.

5. A sentence offering praise to God (v 19) follows the description of misery (vv 2-18). However, this sentence gives the effect of being a singularly isolated word of praise. It stands in the place customarily occupied by an avowal of confidence—an element noticeably absent here.

6. V 20 is accusation against God cast in the form of a question; it stands in full accord with corresponding sentences of the communal lament.

7. V 21, the second part of the element of petition (see paragraph 1), voices a plea for God to intervene in behalf of the people of God. That this petition is raised with some hesitation is evident in the way it is expanded in the last verse—an anxious, uncertain question.

Structural Outline of Lam 5

    1: opening address and plea for God to take heed
    2-18: community's direct complaint, assimilated to a
        description of misery
        bereavement and agony of the people (3,11,12)
        destruction of towns and houses—of property (2,18)
        servitude under the victors (5,8,13)
        hunger and thirst, physical suffering (4,6,9,10)
        festivities and joy have disappeared (14,15,16)
        a description of misery (17)
        interruption: acknowledgement of guilt (7,16)
    19: praise of God (in place of avowal of confidence)
    20: accusation directed against God, cast as interrogative

21: plea for God's saving intervention

22: uncertain question (continuation of question in v 20)

Exegesis of Lam 5

Verse 1

"Remember, Yahweh, what happened to us!" Only in Lam 5 do we find an address of God at the beginning of the song. In Lam 1, 2, and 4 such an element would not be possible, since those songs are introduced by the mournful cry. The feature of direct address of God comes later in chapters 1 and 2; it is totally lacking in chapter 4, where all traces of petition are missing. Framing a song of lamentation by elements of petition, as is being done here, means that the element of petition is being given determinative significance for the whole composition. Petition is not a feature of the dirge. It is, however, an important element of the communal lament—the genre which Lam 5 most closely resembles. The imperative *zĕkōr* (Remember!) at the beginning of the verse could be rendered as follows: Take to heart, O Yahweh, all that has befallen us! The second imperative, *habbêt ūrĕ'ēh* (Look, and see!), parallels the first and means essentially the same. The feature of repetition here adds emphasis. The sufferers are drawing attention to their suffering, just as in the New Testament sufferers draw the attention of the passing Jesus to their sufferings. It is part of the poetic artistry of the verse that a parallelism of direct objects corresponds to the parallelism of imperatives: in the wake of suffering as such comes the disgrace of suffering. Although the second part of the petition does not occur until v 21, both parts are to be taken as a unit and so understood.

Verses 2-18

The community's direct complaint (description of misery) develops the themes about which God is being encouraged to think, the realities toward which it is hoped God will direct merciful attentiveness. The lamenters pour out their hearts before God. Here, in the lengthiest description of misery in the entire Book of Lamentations, it is especially advisable to interpret the material, not line by line, but with an eye to the whole and on the basis of its central themes. The themes of this complaint stretch from what has happened in the past, namely the overthrow of Jerusalem, to the present effects of that past event, specifically the miserable condition in which the lamenters now find themselves. In the nature of the case, it is nearly impossible to draw a clear distinction between these two aspects. Both the collapse of Jerusalem itself and the particular circumstances which have ensued are included in the description of misery here.

The statement in v 18 that "...Mount Zion lies desolate" and that "...jackals wander over it" describes, to be sure, a later situation, but it also draws attention to the event which brought about that situation. It is not possible for one's gaze to rest upon the devastated Zion without also having one's attention drawn to the event—indeed, to the whole chain of events—that led up to this state of affairs.

Enumerated under the general rubric of the collapse of Jerusalem is an array of specific losses: loss of human beings ("We have become orphans, fatherless..."), loss of property ("Our inheritance fell to the enemies..."), loss of honor ("Women were raped...princes were hanged..." [cf. Lev 19:32]), loss of the very means of survival ("Our skin glows...from the ravages of hunger").

In statements such as these the miserable condition of the survivors is described. The sufferings they experience at the hands of the occupying forces reach into every domain of life. Most painful of all is the simple fact of oppression at the hands of foreigners ("Servants are lords over us, no one sets us free from their power" [v 8]). Forced labor is a part of this oppression ("The yoke presses upon our necks; we are tired, no one lets us rest" [v 5]; "Youths were consigned to the hand-mill, lads stumbled under loads of wood" [v 13; cf. Judg 16:21]). Daily life has become dreary and hard. This is evident above all in the struggle to find basic nourishment ("We have to pay for the water we drink, only in exchange for money do we get wood" [v 4]; "at danger to our lives do we fetch our bread, threatened by the sword of the wilderness" [v 9]—a reference to the danger posed by bands of robbers).

Under these miserable conditions such realities as joy, conviviality, and the spirit of festivity perish ("The old men distanced themselves from the city gate, the young men from their stringed instruments" [v 14]; "the joy of our hearts is at an end, our dancing has been turned into mourning" [v 15—cf. the same themes in the Lamentation over Ur]; "the crown has fallen from our head" [v 16a]). These lines (vv 14-16a), which are a part of the description of misery, show how a certain *joie de vivre* is normally taken for granted as an aspect of the community's life. The elders gather at the gate, the youth dance and play, festivals are celebrated, music resonates. Worthy of note is the way v 15b reverses the theme of Ps 30:12 [11 Eng.]. The section concludes with a summary description of the people's misery ("Therefore our heart has become ill, for these things our eyes have grown dim" [v 17]).

Inserted into the description of misery is a spontaneous confession of sins, cast in the form of a cry of woe ("woe to us that we have sinned!" [v 16b]). In this statement the present generation merges itself with its forebears. The speakers claim that it is they themselves who have sinned: we are the sinful folk! Just as the survivors have a share in the great deeds which God performed on behalf of the forebears, so also they participate in their sins—even though they also try to distance themselves somewhat from those sins. This attempted distancing takes place, in an almost rebellious tone, in v 7: "Our fathers have sinned—they are no more; we, however—we bear their guilt." This protest against the burden of the forebears' guilt seems to stand in tension with the acknowledgement of guilt in v 16b. In reality, however, both attitudes are appropriate for the lamenters. The guilt of the forebears is properly acknowledged as a component of the lamenters' own history. At the same time, they balk at the notion that they alone should bear the consequences of that guilt. Here we see a transformation of attitudes taking place. Those who have survived the catastrophe are no longer prepared to atone with their very existence for the sins of their forebears. We can see the same sort of move taking place in the rejection of the proverb cited in Ezek 18:2 ("The parents have eaten sour grapes, and [yet] the children's teeth are set on edge"). In the situation in which this song of lamentation was raised, both attitudes (i.e., the one voiced in v 7 and also the one expressed in v 16b) have a certain cogency (cf. Jer 16:10-13).

Verse 19

Now we come to some rather reserved praise of God ("But you, Yahweh, are enthroned forever, your throne endures from generation to generation"). This is a citation from some psalm extolling the majesty of God—i.e., the line comes from some hymn or descriptive psalm of praise. In its present context the verse takes the place of an avowal of confidence such as one would find in other communal laments. However, it is important to note that this verse is not spoken with straightforward jubilation.[1] One must hear this verse in conjunction with the accusation against God that follows in v 20. The perpetual enthronement of God in the heavens locates God so far away that God's view from above apparently does not reach all the way down to the level of the human misery which has just been described. The exalted glory in which God sits enthroned, in other words, also places God at an unfathomable distance from the human scene. The survivors have not forgotten to praise God. When they do offer praise, however, a note of bitterness intrudes (cf. Ps 22:4 [3 Eng.]).

Verses 20 & 22

This bitterness comes to the surface in the accusation against God which now follows. Such a motif is a steady feature of the communal psalms of lamentation. It especially appears in the voicing of the questions "Why?" and "How long?"—the second of which echoes especially in v 20b ("Why do you...abandon us for such a long time?"). Although the question reproaches God for having forgotten the speakers, at the same time the speakers are clinging to that God whom they have reproached, that God whose ways they no longer comprehend. Even though the people who are raising the lament fear that God might have abandoned them (v 22), they are not prepared to give up their God. Expressions such as these terse, uncertain questions could only have been voiced by people who can by no means separate themselves from God (cf. P.R. Ackroyd).

---

[1] *Contra* S. P. Re'emi, who here claims that "Israel's faith bursts forth with a victorious cry."

Verse 21

V 21 is a petition for restoration ("Bring us, Yahweh, back to yourself, renew our days as before!"). This petition follows up on the plea in v 1; together the two set a framework around the whole psalm of lamentation. Such petition is an element completely lacking in Lam 1, 2, and 4. It is ventured only here, in the context of the communal lament which is Lam 5. The element of petition looks toward the future; it moves forward. The force of the parallelism is such that the first colon is to be understood in the light of the second. In effect, the petitioner is saying, "Bring us once again, O Yahweh, into the domain of your loving-kindness!" Where God can be addressed in this fashion, it is no longer necessary for the speaker to remain trapped and unconsoled in a desperate situation. Still, in v 22 there follows an anxious question, one that runs contrary to the whole tradition of the concluding verses of the communal lament. Tersely put, "have you totally rejected us?" Nothing could more forcefully depict the situation in which this particular song of lamentation arose. Nothing could more poignantly express the solemnity with which the survivors voiced this lament. Viewed from a form-critical perspective, this hauntingly brief question[2] finds a parallel in the melding of dirge and plaintive lament in other songs of lamentation.

Excursus on Lam 5:22

R. Gordis has assembled previous translations of Lam 5:22 and also offered one of his own.[3] Among the possibilities are the following (already noted on p. 313):

1. "You can not have completely rejected us." (The similar "It could be, then, that..." of M. Haller is not a possibility.)
2. "For if you have completely rejected us, then you must indeed be very angry with us" (O. Kaiser—but shown to be inadequate by H. J. Boecker).

---

[2] As noted, some interpreters do not read this verse as a question.

[3] Robert Gordis, "The Conclusion of the Book of Lamentations [5:22]," *JBL* 93 (1974) 289-93.

3. If one follows the Septuagint and simply strikes the *'im*, one could render the colon "For you have indeed rejected us."
4. With Gen 32:27 [26 Eng.] as a parallel, one could read *kî 'im* as "unless."
5. D. Hillers translates as an adversative: "But instead you have completely rejected us."
6. The traditional rendering is the one reflected in RSV [but not NRSV—*Trans.*]: "Or have you utterly rejected us?" Many interpreters, from the time of Max Löhr to the present, essentially adopt this translation.

Gordis then suggests that we read Lam 5:21-22 in the light of Ps 89:51-52. On the basis of this analogy, Gordis sees in v 21 a main clause voicing a petition, which then leads him to see v 22 as a subordinate clause stating attendant circumstances. For Gordis, then, the *kî 'im* carries the meaning "even if, although"; he cites Isa 10:22, Jer 51:14, and Amos 5:22 as parallels for this reading of *kî 'im*. All of this leads to the following translation of Lam 5:22: "even though you had despised us greatly and were very angry with us." This reading requires taking the verbs as pluperfects.

However, it is precisely taking the verbs as pluperfects that is objectionable. From the standpoint of those engaging in the lament, the display of Yahweh's wrath is hardly something in the past; it is still working itself out in their midst. Moreover, the syntactic arrangement suggested by Gordis—main clause consisting of a petition directed to God, subordinate clause stating attendant circumstances, "even though" as the connective—is without parallel in the psalms of lamentation and is questionable on stylistic grounds.

The scholarly lexicons identify as one cluster of meanings for *kî 'im* expressions such as "unless" or "except that." Examples of such usage include Gen 32:27 [26 Eng.], Ruth 3:18, 1 Sam 27:1, Lev 22:6, and Isa 55:10. This is the meaning which best corresponds to the context of Lam 5:21-22 (so also, *inter alia*, W. Rudolph). Strictly speaking, the verse in question should be read "unless you have totally rejected us...." The same thrust is captured in the traditional, interrogative rendering "or have you totally rejected us...?" Moreover, taking the colon as an interrogative makes it fit better with its poetic context.

Summarizing Conclusion

In conclusion, I offer a suggestion regarding the origin of Lam 5. It is generally recognized that Lam 5 is a communal psalm of lamentation, or at least that it closely resembles one. Yet there is a sound reason why this particular text is to be found, not in the Psalter, but in the Book of Lamentations. It is only too obvious that the catastrophe of 587 BCE is reflected in the lengthy direct complaint of the community in vv 2-18. Apart from vv 2-18, Lam 5 contains only one verse that does not, and could not, stand in any communal psalm of lamentation: the uncertain question of v 22. This state of affairs readily leads to a supposition regarding the origin of Lam 5. Specifically, one of the communal psalms of lamentation that had been carried over from pre-exilic times was simply expanded, after 587 BCE, for use in the new situation of lamenting the destruction of Jerusalem. By means of the expansion which now appears in vv 2-18 and v 22, the traditional psalm of lamentation was rendered compatible with the other songs now found in the Book of Lamentations. It is quite possible that, in the process of adapting the traditional psalm for its new function, parts of the original were lost. Arguing for our supposition that a traditional communal-lament psalm was adapted to become a psalm specifically designed for lamenting the destruction of Jerusalem is the way the situation depicted in vv 2-8 seems to stand at a certain distance from the actual downfall of the city. The language does not speak directly of the destruction of Jerusalem. Rather, it speaks of the desperate straits of those who must still live in the occupied city. Another argument is the fact that only in Lam 5 do both components of the petitionary prayer appear: the plea for God to take heed and the plea for restoration.

The distinctive feature of this fifth song in the Book of Lamentations, then, resides in its resemblance to the pre-exilic communal psalms of lamentation. In fact, it might well be an actual communal lament, adjusted to fit the situation of 587 BCE. The singularity of this psalm thus inheres in the way the traditional elements of avowal of confidence and retrospection upon earlier felicitous times are both lacking. In place of these, there stands a sentence offering praise to God—rather hesitant praise, to be sure. When viewed in contrast with the uncertain query at the end, however, this modest bit of praise is enough to bring to remembrance the earlier praises of God. Consonant with such remembrance is the fact that only here, in Lam 5, do the speakers finally dare, once again, to voice a plea for God's gracious intervention in their behalf.

With Lam 5 the little collection of laments over the destruction of Jerusalem comes to its end. The original collection comprised only Lam 1, 2, 4, and 5. The third song / chapter of the present collection was inserted later. It is not contemporaneous with the other songs of the collection; it arose only later. In short, Lam 3 presupposes the existence of the rest of the collection.

Chapter Five

The Theological Significance of Lamentations

First it is necessary to clarify a preliminary matter. The theological significance of Lamentations will necessarily be judged differently depending on whether one treats all five chapters as a whole or whether one selects chapter three as decisive for the determination of the collection's theological message. Most interpreters choose the latter course; most exegetes regard chapter three as the pivotal chapter of the collection, as the key to the understanding of the whole. However, this is a problematic stance—for two basic reasons. The first is the composite nature of chapter three. The second is the enigmatic relationship of chapter three to the other chapters. The third chapter has been constructed out of different sorts of material, and the relationship of these parts to each other is anything but clear. Controversy also reigns over the question of the relationship of the third song to the other four songs. The controversy resides in the fact that, in the opinion of almost all interpreters, Lam 1, 2, 4, and 5 arose as reaction to the collapse of Judah and Jerusalem in the year 587 BCE. However, the relationship of chapter three to this calamitous event is uncertain. Apart from the fragment comprising vv 42-51, not a single verse of Lam 3 clearly and unambiguously refers to the collapse of 587 BCE. An additional consideration is the fact that, in Lam 1, 2, and 4, the communal lament incorporates motifs from the dirge. No attention would be accorded to this distinctive feature if the theological significance of Lamentations were to be determined solely, or even primarily, on the basis of Lam 3. For all of these reasons, the question of the theological significance of

221

Lamentations is better answered on the basis of the complete text, the text consisting of all five chapters.

It is equally important not to restrict the question of the theological significance of Lamentations to a single issue, or to try to discern one particular tension underlying the whole collection. Essentially, we are here repeating what was demonstrated in our second chapter of this book, the chapter on the history of the interpretation of Lamentations.

So it is best to start from the perspective of what the text of Lamentations as a whole says about God—about God's words and deeds. The first feature to be established is the fact that the overwhelming majority of the verses which speak of God are laments. More precisely, from a form-critical perspective they are seen to be one distinct component of the lament: accusations against God, or complaints addressed directly to God. All these verses voice the complaint that God has inflicted severe hardship upon the people of God. Altogether some fifty clauses speak in this way. This particular mode of speech about God is the theological mode most often encountered in Lamentations; it dominates throughout. Moreover, this theme of accusation against God occurs in all five songs. Thus we appear to be on firm ground in starting out from the fact that, in the lament directed toward God, we are dealing with the most important type of theological statement which Lamentations has to offer.

This particular type of statement deals with the actions of God in history. The claim is being made that God has brought about the political collapse of the people of God. God is accused of having been the one fundamentally at work in the people's defeat, destruction, and humiliation. Being presupposed, of course, is God's power to do all this. As with the prophets of judgment, then, so also here God is being viewed as the Lord of history.

Excursus: Yahweh as "Lord of History" in Lamentations

In Lamentations, as also in the writings of the prophets of judgment and in the Psalms, the theme "praise of the majesty of Yahweh" presupposes that God is directing history. God directs not just the history of Israel; God directs the history of all peoples. It is God who effects wars, determining who will be the victors and who the vanquished. In Lamentations, however, there is indirect recognition that talk about Yahweh as Lord of history has its limits. Specifically, in Lamentations speech about the "Lord of history" encompasses other peoples only insofar as the activities of those other peoples—such as the Assyrians, Babylonians, or Edomites—affect Israel. Elsewhere in the Old Testament as well, Yahweh is described in a general way as the Lord of history. However, Yahweh's deeds in the realm of human history are spoken of explicitly only where those deeds in some fashion directly affect Israel. The upshot is that one can draw no general conclusions from the Biblical language addressed to the theme of the acts of Yahweh in human history—conclusions such as that victory is always owed to Yahweh or that defeats are meant to be punishments. In sum, the Old Testament knows of nothing like a general revelation of God that can be read out of the events of human history. One consequence of this state of affairs is the fact that, when Israel ceased to exist as an independent state and was transformed instead into a province of various imperial powers, this particular sort of language about the acts of God in history disappears. Instead, a totally different sort of language appears, in apocalyptic writings. The acts of God **in** history, then, do not amount to a revelation of God **through** history.

The "wrath of God" is identified as the force behind the destructive acts directed against the people of God. The divine wrath serves as a *leitmotif* in Lam 2 ("Ah, how Yahweh in his wrath overclouds daughter Zion!"). The same theme occurs seven more times, including in 4:11 & 4:21b. In fact, in Lamentations the wrath of God is the theme most frequently mentioned in conjunction with reference to actions on the part of God. In this context it is important to note that, in the Old Testament, reference to the anger or the wrath of God carries more of a positive than a negative overtone. This is because, in certain situations at least, an angry reaction by God is precisely what is needed, even when the reason for the divine wrath which falls upon human beings is not fully clear. The wrath of God can have a purifying and renewing effect. For ancient Israel, a God who could not become angry even when such anger was called for could not truly be God. It is important to add, however, that this is not the whole picture. Wrath and anger are moods. They tend to flare up in the course of an interpersonal relationship; they are also extinguished within the ongoing course of such a relationship. Wrath is not a permanent trait of the personality. Wrath wells up, and it goes away again. Thus the lamenter is able to say such things as "How much longer will you be angry?" and "How long will your wrath burn?" Wrath is not equivalent to rejection. It is with these considerations in mind that one should listen to the language about the wrath of God in Lam 2. As frightful as it is, the wrath of God does not persist.

In the way it talks about the wrath of God, Lamentations agrees with the prophets of judgment. This agreement is particularly clear in the way Lamentations recognizes and confirms the prophets' earlier announcement of a wrathful judgment that would come upon Israel.[1]

In the case at hand, there is clear cause for the wrath which prompts Yahweh to inflict heavy punishment upon Israel. As all five chapters emphasize, the people of God have incurred guilt over against God. Thus the references to the wrathful acts of God are set in conjunction with language about guilt and punishment. The heavy blows that have fallen on the people of God are recognized by them as a form of divine punishment. This amounts to a concurrent admission of the people's guilt. The intrinsic connection between guilt and punishment, as a feature of God's activity in the realm of human history, was already recognized by the prophets of judgment long before the great catastrophe fell, for example by Amos and Hosea. At issue here is not primarily the specific sins of particular individuals in the realm of their personal dealings. Rather, the focus is on a guilt which all the people bear, in the very nature of their being. Here Lamentations also stands in agreement with the prophets. Attention is being directed to a guilt which has corrupted the whole people. As in the prophets so also here in Lamentations, those most responsible for leading the people into such comprehensive guilt are singled out and castigated.

---

[1] Cf. Claus Westermann, "Boten des Zorns," in *Ibid., Forschung am Alten Testament: Gesammelte Studien III* (ThB 73; 1984) 96-109.

However, the agreement between Lamentations and the prophets of judgment does not consist solely in drawing attention to the two features of Israel's guilt and Israel's punishment by Yahweh. Finding Israel guilty presupposes the existence of a prior relationship between Yahweh and Israel, a relationship which Israel was able to violate. All along God has been accompanying these people on their way. This is a reality made abundantly clear in the wording of the prophetic announcements.

If Lamentations confirms as fitting the prophetic announcements of judgment, nonetheless Lamentations is speaking in a situation dramatically different from that in which the prophets first proclaimed their judgments. The prophets were isolated voices. Their pronouncements were rejected by the people at large, and also by the people's leaders. According to the testimony of Lamentations, however, the community as a whole—the surviving remnant which now comprises the people of God—is confirming those same prophetic pronouncements in cultic ceremonies of lamentation. In other words, the announcements of judgment that were spoken by the pre-exilic prophets are finally being acknowledged. This acknowledgement of the message of judgment is also making it possible for the people, despite all that has happened, to plead for God once again to turn toward them in favor.

In order to recognize what is distinctive in the way Lamentations speaks about God, one must set these chapters, not only in the context of prophecy, but also within the history of the lament. One of the characteristic features of the pre-exilic communal lament is a retrospection upon earlier saving deeds of God. It is this feature that constitutes the contrast motif in communal laments such as Ps 80. In the communal lament after 587 BCE, however, the impact of destruction has been so strong that the speakers no longer dare to include this same sort of retrospection. To them the continuity in the history of God's saving deeds seems to have been broken. In the place formerly accorded to such retrospection, one finds instead the insertion of themes from the dirge: the mournful cry, the contrasting of the state of affairs before and after the "death," the description of misery. The particular significance of Lamentations now surfaces with the recognition that, in these songs, the dirge is transformed into a plaintive lament. Out of the description of misery there grows the address of God; the God who has become enveloped in anger is nonetheless directly beseeched. Despite the people's anxiety that they might have been rejected by God (5:22), God is nonetheless implored to turn once again in favor toward the people of God. In the final analysis, those who have been smitten still hold fast in their lament—in their language of suffering—to the one who smote them. To be sure, an explicit avowal of trust is lacking. However, the *wāw adversativum* ("and yet you...") that so often introduces this element in the Psalms is discernible here as well (see below, p. *232*). A singular logic of faith is at work in all of this, a logic which lies behind the joining of the plaintive lament with themes from the dirge. It is this logic which prompts the lamenters, on the one hand, to confess "Righteous is he, is Yahweh, for I have rebelled against his word" (1:18) while not forcing them, on the other hand, to conclude that they no longer dare lament. Even though they have deserved their fate, they proceed to pour out their hearts to the very one who struck them down! It is this logic which leads them to cry "Woe to us, for we have sinned" while at the same time pleading for mercy from the one against whom they have sinned! Here comes to the fore the other aspect of the divine action with regard to the people of God, namely the divine mercy upon those who beseech God in their suffering. To be sure, Lamentations attests to God's mercy upon the suffering in a cautious and reserved fashion. However, it is precisely because of this muted tone that Lamentations is able to speak with a power and a profundity unparalleled elsewhere in the Old Testament. The power of the affirmation comes precisely from the fact that it is a cry from the depths of the people's experience: an experience that brought the people as a whole to the brink of extinction, an experience that entailed the death of a major portion of the populace and included the destruction of almost everything that had made life worth living.

The unique situation of trying to refer to the mercy of God despite having been led to the brink of extinction makes it impossible for the survivors openly to hymn a compassionate deity. On this score they must be silent. In not one of the songs is there direct reference to God's mercy. The same constraint holds with regard to the retrospection upon God's earlier saving deeds, and also when it comes to a consideration of the prospects for restoration. Nowhere is there ventured a direct plea for God to intervene, to rescue, or to restore. (The only apparent exception, 5:22, is discussed above.) And yet, despite everything, there is still the urge to beseech God to look with compassion upon the sufferers.

To be sure, Lam 3 comes from a later time and is addressed to a situation of personal, not communal, suffering. Nonetheless, what is openly said there ("The mercies of Yahweh are not at an end" [3:22]) indirectly comes to expression also in the earlier situation of utmost extremity, when the people as a whole stand on the edge of annihilation. Those who can see no way into the future nonetheless persist in turning toward a compassionate God; despite all that has happened they hold fast to a merciful God. In effect, all of this amounts to a silent praising of the compassionate God. Only in this part of the Old Testament, in Lamentations, does such a phenomenon occur.

The theological situation in which lamentation directed toward God has its proper place is hereby significantly expanded. Lamentation that has been directed toward God out of the depths of despair is also being passed on to the following generations, that they might do likewise when in similar situations. The sense of dismay that comes to expression in these laments is so deep that the words which grow out of that dismay have to be very carefully crafted. It is through the actual carrying out of lamentation amidst the ruins of Jerusalem that the act of remembrance arises ("Jerusalem remembers the days of her misery and anguish" [1:7]). The lament comes to be taken up as a component of divine worship, worship within which the terrible event is memorialized. The remnant is thus told of the pathos of the city and its inhabitants. Out of its deepest passion, in other words, the city of God seeks to address the coming generations, testifying that it did not stop at the voicing of dirges but went on, finally, to call upon the very one who had struck the city down. The city called upon God to pay attention to its suffering. In the broader context of Old Testament tradition, Deutero-Isaiah's announcement of restoration thus finds a point of attachment in Lamentations and its recollection of "the days of her misery and anguish."

The opinion has been voiced, by several interpreters, that the act of lamentation as such has no theological significance when it comes to hearing the message of the Book of Lamentations. Such an assertion is already contradicted by the mere fact that these songs have been passed down through the course of the generations. It was precisely the extensive and explicit descriptions in these laments that guaranteed their transmission to future generations; it was the narrative quality of these laments, replete with details, that awakened a sense of participation on the part of those who heard them. Had the elements of petition in these laments been severed from their original contexts, or had the thrust of the laments been reduced to some abstract summary such as "In those days the inhabitants of Jerusalem suffered much hardship," the truncated tradition that would have been left would never have been passed on.

The same considerations hold with regard to the original situation in which these laments were voiced. They were directed to God; they were brought before the divine throne. In these laments the sufferers genuinely poured out their hearts before God. Moreover, these laments were brought before God in the form of narratives (direct complaints), as descriptions of all the terrible things that had happened. Only in such a way did the lamenters feel they could awaken the sympathy of God; only thus could they stir the divine compassion. Here it is perhaps worthwhile to recall that in primitive religions prayer closely resembles narrative. In such contexts the divine-human relationship is so understood as to allow one simply to relate to the deity what has happened to one. Such a simple—indeed, one could just as well say child-like—understanding of the divine-human relationship is not unlike the one that stands behind the lament that turns to a description of what has been suffered.

The Theological Significance of Lam 3: Admonition and Instruction

In the middle section of Lam 3 (vv 26-41), the author moves outside the domain of psalmic language—which of course also entails leaving behind the language of lamentation. In these verses the author instead speaks the language of admonition and instruction. What is counseled is to bear suffering with patience, to engage in introspection, and to return to Yahweh. In vv 33-38 we are instructed that human suffering is compatible with divine activity. This bit of admonition and instruction is spoken in a situation quite different from that presupposed by Lam 1, 2, 4, and 5. In Lam 3 "sin" does not mean the historical guilt of the people as a whole, but rather personal transgressions in the course of an individual's daily conduct. Likewise in Lam 3 the suffering that is envisioned is mistreatment of the pious at the hands of the wicked, as is shown by the incorporation of motifs from the complaint about enemies within the context of the personal lament (vv 34-36).

Standing at a considerable remove from the catastrophe of 587 BCE, the author of Lam 3 tries to say what is necessary for his own contemporaries to hear. His admonition is rooted in post-exilic, deuteronomic paranesis—right up to the incorporation of the "perhaps" in the motif of hope. This material stems from a time of continual oppression and danger, a time in which admonition to silent perseverance is totally appropriate. In such a time one could easily come to regard persistent and passionate lamentation as not only inappropriate but actually dangerous; one could easily be led to insert into the collection of laments some material that represented a deliberate attempt at "correction." So our author set his admonition and his instruction into the midst of what to him was a small, already extant collection of psalms. In the process he simply let drop out the explicitly liturgical sections of those psalms. He unified his whole composition by casting it in acrostic form. His point of entry into the extant material was an avowal of confidence, set into a personal psalm of lamentation— viz., 3:20-25. With this move he bequeathed to subsequent generations one of the most beautiful of all expressions of this theme. The author hopes to persuade his own generation to share in the sense of trust which finds expression in these words. He describes this sense of trust as a pious attitude, urges that this attitude be emulated, and grounds it all with a bit of midrashic instruction resting upon various passages of scripture.

So when our author takes his own didactic poem, constructed in acrostic form, and sets it in the middle of Lam 1-5, he aims at transforming the earlier material. On the one hand, he does want to preserve these laments that refer to the catastrophe of 587 BCE. On the other hand, however, he also wants to recommend for his own time a kind of piety that emphasizes, more strongly than do those laments, a deuteronomic spirit of repentance and public confession. In this our author takes his stand closer to an Ezra or a Nehemiah than to the original Lamentations.

The Significance of Lamentations within the Old Testament

In order to evaluate the significance of Lamentations within the Old Testament as a whole, one must determine the place of Lamentations within the history of the communal lament as a genre. This has already been investigated (see above, pp. *94-95*). The connection with elements of the dirge, a connection found only in the Book of Lamentations, suggests that here the communal lament has come up against its limits. We do not know of any further development of the lament in the difficult times following the exile. Quite likely there was no further development. Rather, pre-exilic laments were taken over and passed on, altered to some degree. The more important development was the fact that penitential ceremonies largely replaced occasions of public lamentation. This is indicated already by Lam 3, a didactic poem in which the penitential summons plays a more important role than does the community's lamentation as such.

At the same time, however, Lamentations prepares the way for Deutero-Isaiah's proclamation of salvation as well as for words of assurance stemming from other sources. This happens, in the first place, through the fact that, in Lamentations, the message of the prophets of judgment is accepted and confirmed by the whole remnant of the people. This unqualified assent to the prophets of judgment on the part of the survivors is necessary in order for forgiveness to be mediated to the full remnant of the people. It was this move that made it possible for Deutero-Isaiah's proclamation of salvation, as well as for anonymous words of assurance, to follow upon the lamentation of a people smitten by God. That there is a close connection here follows from the very nature of Deutero-Isaiah's proclamation. The promise that Israel is to be restored presupposes the lamentation of an Israel that recognizes in its defeat the wrath of God. The divine promise of restoration enters where the divine wrath has been acknowledged. For reasons such as these Deutero-Isaiah more than once actually cites lines of lamentation ("Why do you say, O Jacob, and speak, O Israel, 'My way is hidden from the Lord, and my right is disregarded by my God?'" [40:27], or "But Zion said, 'The Lord has forsaken me, my Lord has forgotten me'" [49:14]). These citations from actual communal laments on the part of Deutero-Isaiah indicate, first of all, that such laments were indeed being transmitted during the period of the exile, above all in public ceremonies of lamentation not only in Jerusalem but also among the exiles. Secondly, such citations establish the fact that the message of salvation which Deutero-Isaiah proclaimed was meant to be taken as a response to the remnant's lamentation and supplication. In this way the covenantal history between God and people manages to move beyond the abyss.

If one takes care to note the singular features of Lamentations, the features which occur only here and nowhere else in the Old Testament, then the Book of Lamentations becomes a central witness to the history of lamentation—and beyond that, of prayer itself—throughout the time of ancient Israel. As such, Lamentations is an indispensable part not only of the history of God's dealings with the people of God but also of the history of God's self-revelation in the Old Testament. Only in this one book of the Bible is the wrath of God spoken of with such intensity and the mercy of God with such reticence.

The Importance of Lamentations for a Biblical Theology
1. The question of Lamentations' importance for a Biblical theology can best be approached, at the outset, by noting the similarity between Lamentations and a text in the New

Testament, namely the text where Jesus laments over Jerusalem
(Matt 23:37-39 and parallels). When Jesus addresses the city by
saying "If you...had only recognized...the things that make for
peace!" (Luke 19:42), his words in effect announce an
impending conquest and destruction of Jerusalem. However,
Jesus is here not so much confirming that Jerusalem's fate will
be a righteous punishment of God upon a sinful city as he is
raising a lament over the suffering that the destruction will
bring upon the city's inhabitants. In the tears that Jesus sheds
over this city [Luke 19:41], the divine compassion toward those
who must suffer is more pronounced than is the divine wrath
that makes such a punishment necessary. In this way Jesus'
lamentation over Jerusalem is comparable to psalms of
lamentation voiced by the survivors after the destruction of 587
BCE. In both cases the downfall of Jerusalem is due to divine
punishment. However, the travail of a conquered city, such as
is described in the songs in Lamentations, is both something
more and something other than the discomfort of an imposed
punishment. The destruction of a city yields a surfeit of suffering,
a surfeit which spills over onto those who were not directly
involved in the battle for the city: mothers and their children,
the ill and the infirm, even animals (Jon 3:7-9; 4:11). It is to such
a surfeit of suffering, especially the suffering of the innocent on
the occasion of a catastrophe like this, that Jesus directs his
compassion. Those who must bear this excess of suffering
speak out in lamentation. They need to do so, and they have
every right to do so. Furthermore, this sort of suffering is not
merely noticed but acquires a dignity in the way it is given a
voice in lamentation. When Jesus weeps over Jerusalem, he
anticipates the lamentation of those who will have to face the
horrors of the conquest of Jerusalem in the year 70 CE. Not only
that, but he shares in their suffering! By proleptically sharing
in the impending lamentation over Jerusalem, Jesus also
retroactively gives to the laments which were raised on the
occasion of the city's earlier destruction their dignity as a
proper response to suffering.

2. These laments were preserved in the memories of the
survivors, and they were written down. They were recited on

occasions for memorializing the destruction of Jerusalem. Such memorializing has continued within the Jewish community right up to the present. The lamentation of Jesus over Jerusalem, on the contrary, established no living tradition within the Christian community. To be sure, the relevant pericope has found a place in the cycle of scripture readings. Nowhere in the history of actual Christian practice, however, has there been established a remembrance of the suffering of a conquered city—despite the fact that both testaments of the Bible speak of such. Since the Old Testament stands with the New as together comprising the Bible of Christianity, one would expect that the pericope about Jesus weeping over Jerusalem would be read in conjunction with the lamentation over the destruction of Jerusalem in 587 BCE. Moreover, this ought to lead to some rethinking about what the Bible here has to say. This much has already been suggested by one of the modern interpreters of Lamentations, Norman K. Gottwald, in the following words:

> The message of Lamentations is one that the modern church needs desperately to hear if Christendom is to understand its own mission as something more inclusive than the cultivation of personal piety while the common life of man perishes in the inferno.[2]

Were it possible for the Christian church to hear anew the lament of Jesus over Jerusalem by setting it against the background of the lamentation over the destruction of Jerusalem in 587 BCE, one could anticipate some rethinking in two directions First of all, it is undeniable that the various denominations of the Christian church have, as national churches, actively—sometimes passively—participated in the various wars of the states with which they have been associated. This is a pattern which saw little change right up through the Second World War. As national churches, they have recognized as necessary—or at least as unavoidable—precisely that over which Jesus wept and over which the survivors of 587 BCE lamented, namely the fact that horrible suffering befalls

---

[2] *Studies in the Book of Lamentations* (SBT I/14; 1954, ²1962), 113-14.

noncombatants when military action swirls around a city: children, mothers, the aged, the ill, the infirm. As the scope of warfare has widened, the suffering of noncombatants has grown to horrific dimensions. Would that a renewed hearing of the Bible, and precisely of those passages which speak of the suffering imposed on conquered cities, might lead to a new attitude— indeed, to a repentance—on the part of the national churches.

At the same time, some rethinking in another direction would be unavoidable. If one were actually to hear how Jesus laments over Jerusalem, which is to say if one were to take seriously the lamentation of those who suffer in the destruction of a city, then one could no longer rest content with a type of historical writing which basically ignores all that which finds expression in lamentation. The destruction of a city through warfare is such a familiar phenomenon in human history that we have become rather too accustomed to it. Hardly anyone gets all that troubled by such reports anymore. This is reflected in the way history tends to get recorded. Only rarely in historical documents do we find the actual laments of those who were forced to endure the destruction of their city. This makes all the more significant those few documents where such does happen, as in the Lamentation over the Destruction of Ur or the lamentation over the destruction of Jerusalem. These latter were passed on from generation to generation in remembrance of the unspeakable suffering that such destruction brought upon the innocent. Since the dawn of historical writing, the customary practice has been to report the destruction of a city only from a military standpoint. This has meant focusing on the victory of the conquerors, with the losses of the defeated being coldly summarized in numerical terms. At best one finds a terse comment about the devastation wrought among the civilian population. The laments of the sufferers, however, fade away and are soon forgotten. In the thinking of most historians, in the final analysis, such laments have little significance. With regard to this tendency, there is precious little to distinguish between historical writing done before the time of Christ and historical writing done since. One must seriously ask, however, whether one can honestly deem "objective" a type of historical writing which fails to reflect any sympathy for the suffering of those who innocently had to bear the brunt of warfare and its barbarities. Certainly no historical writing as insensitive as this can claim to be reporting "how it really was." Whenever a people exults in a victory that brought horrific suffering upon the innocent and upon noncombatants, it is imperative to respond with a reminder of the realities of such warfare. The "revisionist" kind of historical writing here being urged is vitally important in a time such as the present, when the potential for destruction has grown to monstrous proportions.

3. The history of the interpretation of Lamentations sets up in exemplary fashion the question of whether, or to what extent, lamentation is or can be an aspect of prayer. Succinctly, is lamentation an aspect of calling upon God? It is indeed striking how many Bible interpreters ascribe little significance to the lament, sometimes even going so far as to reject it entirely as unsuitable to the life of prayer. This is certainly in keeping with the fact that lamentation has found no firm place in the context of Christian prayer. Yet it must be asked if this reluctance to accept lamentation as an aspect of prayer can really find a basis in the New Testament. Does the confession of Jesus as the Christ necessarily constrain Christians to exclude lamentation from their prayers? If it could be shown that this is indeed the case, then it would also mean that there is a contradiction between what the Old and New Testaments respectively say of God. This, in turn, would be a development of overwhelming significance. Carrying this thought a step further, one would then have to ask why such an essential difference between the Testaments was not earlier recognized. Why has the issue of such a difference not yet entered into the discourse of the theologians?

Jesus acknowledged that sufferers have the right to lament their suffering. He accepted lamentation as the language of suffering and thereby granted it both validity and dignity. The history of the people of God is grounded in the fact that God heard the lamentation of those who did not understand God but nonetheless cried out to God. To such God came as Deliverer. It is with a cry out of the depths that each story of deliverance, each account of rescue, begins. The Bible speaks of God as One who is moved to compassion by the laments of those who suffer.

Index of Modern Authors

Index of Biblical References

DATE DUE
